Heritage Hunting

Donna Potter Phillips

Heritage Books, Inc.

Published 1998 by

HERITAGE BOOKS, INC.
1540E Pointer Ridge Place
Bowie, Maryland 20716
1-800-398-7709
www.heritagebooks.com

ISBN 0-7884-0880-1

PREFACE

At the request of both my local genealogical society and my local newspaper, I began writing a weekly genealogy column back in 1986. I worked very hard to inform, educate and enliven the genealogy lives of my readers, and think now, some 500 columns later, that I did achieve that goal. Membership in several area genealogical societies rose, members became more active in their societies, classes in genealogy were swamped with students, genealogy success stories flowed like rivers, and letters poured in to me by the hundreds. I heard from readers all over the Pacific Northwest, all points of America, many times from across both oceans and several times from folks in jail. I did my best to help each one, and can honestly say that I never submitted the same column twice to my paper.

As you enjoy and learn from reading through these past columns, please remember that they were written between 1986 and 1996. That means that some addresses might not be valid any longer and some resources might be unavailable. But I promise you that a careful study of the thoughts and ideas contained in these columns will most assuredly help you with your family questing some things never get outdated.

1992

ANYONE CAN ENJOY THE FUN OF GENEALOGY

It has been said that everyone has ancestors and anyone can do genealogy. Since we all do have ancestors, and all it takes to begin your family history is a love of family and an interest in your own forebears, it is true that anyone can do genealogy.

It helps to have an interest in history and a sense of humor, just in case you find out that your ancestor died "of a neck wound" (i.e., he was hanged!).

You begin your family history by talking and writing. You talk to your parents, your Aunt Sadie and Cousin Leroy, and ask them what they remember about your family. You interview your father about his experiences in the Battle of the Bulge, the Berlin airlift or Vietnam.

You ask your mom what her favorite childhood activity was. The grandfather that my cousin Karen remembers, and wrote me about, doesn't seem like the same man I remember because we had such different perspectives.

As you talk to relatives, it's best to record the information on special genealogy charts. The ancestor chart, or pedigree chart, is the "road map" for your family. The chart begins with a line on the middle left edge for No. 1 — you. The chart spreads across the page to the right in pairs of brackets, each representing a marriage. Thus, person No. 2 is your father, and No. 3 is your mother. Person No. 4 is your paternal grandfather, and No. 5 is your paternal grandmother. Numbers 6 and 7 are for your maternal grandparents. A typical chart has room to list 16 ancestors.

Since the chart represents your personal pedigree, you list only your ancestors. By that I mean if there were multiple marriages by one grandfather, you list only the wife that was your grandmother on this chart.

The family group chart is the companion form to the pedigree chart. There is room on the family group chart to list husband and wife for any marriage and all their children. You should fill out a family group chart for each and every marriage. Begin with you and your spouse and children; then complete a chart for your parents showing you as a child, and one for each set of grandparents showing your parents as children.

There are spaces on both charts for the six identifiers needed for each ancestor: Born When, Born Where, Married When, Married Where, Died When and Died Where. There are also spaces for personal information like church affiliation, military service and occupation.

To obtain copies of these charts so that you can begin your family history, contact any LDS Family History Center.

Everton Publishers offers all sorts of charts. Call them at 800-443-6325 and request a catalog.

The Skeleton Closet, P.O. Box 91392, Louisville, KY 40291, offers a complete organizational system for the beginning genealogist. I have seen this system, and I recommend it. Send a check for $2.50 for a catalog and sample forms.

BOOKS ARE A BIG HELP IN GETTING STARTED

The beginning genealogist frequently asks, "How do I do this?" or "Where do I write for that record?" And today's genealogist also asks, "What about computers?"

Novice family historians need to know that there is a book to answer almost any genealogical question.

Following the advice in the last column to talk to your relatives, are you planning a family reunion this summer? *Celebrating the Family: Steps to Planning a Family Reunion,* by Vandella Brown is a 64-page guide that will lead you step by step through the planning process. Order the book for $8.95 from Ancestry by calling 800-531-1790.

Many folks get interested in family history because they have a box of old family photos. If you are one of these lucky folks and want to glean all the information you can from these photos (from the dress style, furniture, etc.), then *Unlocking the Secrets in Old Photographs,* by Karen Frisch-Ripley might be a good way to spend your birthday money. Order this 202-page book for $12.95 from Ancestry.

Would a book that discusses virtually every aspect of computers and their usefulness to genealogists in simple and non-technical language interest you? *Computer Genealogy: A Guide to Research Through High Technology,* by Richard Pence might be just what you need. This 280-page book costs $12.95 from

Ancestry. Whether you're a seasoned computer genealogist or just beginning to use a computer to manage your genealogical research and records, you'll find that this is essential reading. The Census Bureau says that as a group, Americans are one-quarter German. This means that nearly every beginning family researcher will have to learn how to use German records. *Finding Your German Ancestors,* by Ronald Smelser is a dandy little 40-page book offering a brief, but thorough, introduction to researching your German ancestors. The book gives a peek into history, records and methodology and costs $2.95 from Ancestry.

Another German research help book is "Address Book for Germanic Genealogy" by Ernest Thode. This 218-page book has an impressive table of contents, 196 genealogical, historical and German-related societies outside Europe, 56 American archives, 175 German-American religious organizations, 24 German language newspapers in America, 32 German archives, 250 other European archives, 777 municipal archives, 383 religious archives in Germany, and 253 genealogists specializing in German research.

Anybody working on ancestral problems in any of the Germanic areas of Europe will need this book. Order it for $24.95 from Genealogical Publishing Co. at 800-727-6687 (ask for a free copy of their catalog while you're talking with them).

TODAY'S TIP: You can place a query about your southern Michigan or northern Indiana ancestor in the "Family Heirloom" newspaper column in *The Tri-City Record.* Send your query to Carole Kiernan, P.O. Box 81, Watervliet, MI 49098.

FIND YOUR FAMILY IN FAMILYSEARCH COMPUTER FILE

Imagine that you have located a giant gathering of amateur and professional genealogists. On the auditorium wall is a massive pedigree chart on which everyone in attendance has added what they know about their families.

There are some extensive links of many generations, and some links with just two or three generations. Suddenly, you find a part of your family on the chart and it has more information than you knew about. You check the note, copy the name and address of the person who added it and copy down the new information to check out yourself. Later, you will write to the person who posted it on the wall chart.

You also notice that many members of your family whom you have researched are not on the chart. You take out a pencil and add them. As you step back, someone else notices the information you just added; they are as excited as you were when you found it yourself! You finish checking the chart and go home to write the person who submitted the information you found, hoping you can exchange information which could help both of you in your research.

Wouldn't it be great if you really could find just such a gathering of genealogists? Well you can, at your nearest Family History Center. The "wall chart" is on computer, and it's called the Ancestral File. You might find your family in this file, and you can submit your own family information to the file. You can even correct errors you might find. And it is all free.

The Family History Centers are branch libraries of the world's largest genealogical library, the Family History Library in Salt Lake City, UT. They welcome beginners as well as seasoned genealogists. The FamilySearch computer program will furnish information to any genealogist; Ancestral File is one part of this program.

They also have pedigree charts and family group sheets — forms that all genealogists use in great numbers. All Family History Centers also have the 100 most-used genealogical reference books on microfiche.

GROUP CHERISHES NORWEGIAN ROOTS

Last October, I rode Amtrak to Minot, ND, to visit my brother and his family. My sister-in-law, Kirsten, is of Norwegian descent, and she and I went to the annual Hostfest (pronounced HOOST-fest) in Minot. For me, it was an exciting crash course in Norwegian culture.

Many people in the crowd wore traditional costumes. There was food like lefse and pickled herring (and Uff-Da tacos, thank goodness) and folk dancing demonstrations.

Craft vendors were there in full force, but every booth had something Norwegian: dolls in regional costumes, jewelry, food, sweaters, weaving and hardanger embroidery.

One booth was set up for genealogy and offered information on the Norwegian-American "bygdelags" (pronounced BIG-de-laag). I spent a long time at this booth, talking to the folks and learning about a new facet of genealogy. (I'm not one bit Norwegian.)

The Norwegian-American bygdelag is an organization of emigrant descendants from a particular area of Norway who live in North America. Every "lag" seeks to preserve and strengthen bonds with its community of origin in Norway. Annual bygdelag gatherings usually are held in summer. Publications or newsletters help people keep in touch during the rest of the year.

Demonstrations or displays of Norwegian arts and crafts — along with a selection of banquet foods, books and readings, choral and instrumental music, fiddlers and folk dancing, films, genealogy workshops and noted speakers — are likely to be included in the program for these gatherings.

"Bygdelagenes Fellesraad," the national bygdelag council, is the umbrella organization for all the "lag" clubs.

CENSUS RECORDS:
A VALUABLE SOURCE OF GENEALOGICAL INFORMATION

Today's column is part of a series designed to help the beginning genealogist. The lesson is from a new book distributed by American Genealogical Lending Library (AGLL) called *Beginner's Guide to Family History Research,* by D. Allen and C. Billingsley ($5.00, P.O. Box 244, Bountiful, UT 84011).

Census records are one of the most valuable primary sources created by the federal government. Census enumerators counted America's population every ten years beginning in 1790. As with all primary sources, you must learn how and why these records were created and where copies may be obtained for your use. All federal censuses have been microfilmed; after a certain period of time, all their details are open to public access.

The best method for using census records is to start with the most recently released census and work backward in time. The 1920 census is the latest to be released, and can be accessed through AGLL or any Family History Center. It's a good rule to try and find your ancestor on every census year of his or her life, working from present to past.

With each census year, more questions were asked. Twice as many questions were asked in 1900 as were in 1800, giving you twice the amount of information on your ancestors. Prior to 1850, only the name of the head of the household was listed. Small marks indicated the numbers of males and females in each household.

There are several ways for any genealogist to access the U.S. censuses. Look first in your nearest genealogy library, and next at your nearest Family History Center. Films may also be borrowed from AGLL.

It is best to use a printed census index before trying to find your family on the actual census. Census indexes exist for all censuses between 1790 and 1850, and many for the years 1860 1880. A special kind of index, called Soundex or Miracode, was created for the 1880, 1900, 1910 (most states) and 1920 censuses. (The 1890 census was accidentally destroyed by fire.) Look for these indexes in any genealogical library.

I could fill this entire newspaper teaching you what you need to know about the U.S. Census and how to use it to find your ancestors! But I recommend that you visit your nearest genealogical library or a Family History Center, and take some time to browse through all the "how-to" books you'll find there, especially the chapters on using the census. *The Source*, by Arlene Eakle, would be especially helpful to learn more about using the U.S. censuses.

PERSONAL ARCHIVES START IN THE HOME

Do you realize you have "Your Family Archives" right in your own home? All those family papers document the story of your family and the family's activities. These papers should be treated with interest and respect, and retrieved from basement trunks and top-of-the-closet boxes. Family materials should be collected into one central, safe spot in the home.

There are two good reasons why you should do this. First, with all your family archives in one place, it would be easier to get them out of the house in case of emergency. In my classes I recommend that folks keep an oversized "pillowcase" made from an old bedsheet folded and near the collection of family treasures. Such a bag is easy to stuff and drag away. The other reason would be that with all your family papers and documents in one place, you can glean information from them to fill in those blank spaces on your pedigree charts.

So what do I mean by "Your Family Archives?" Here's a list:

♦ School records — yearbooks, report cards, diplomas, special awards.
♦ Employment records — citations and proof of employment.
♦ Military records — service, discharge and pension papers.
♦ Newspaper clippings — birth, marriage and death announcements, obituaries, engagement and military enlistment announcements.
♦ Certificates — birth, marriage and death certificates.
♦ Court documents — deeds, tax records, court actions, marriage/divorce papers.
♦ Church records — baptism, confirmation, birth, death or burial records, membership records.
♦ Family Bible — prayer books or hymnals.
♦ Family letters — diaries, memoirs, autobiographies, sketches, etc.
♦ Family photography — photo albums, master copies of framed photos kept elsewhere in the home.
♦ Artifacts — Grandma's old cherry bowl, baby slippers, Grandpa's metal box or eyeglasses, jewelry, etc.

To carry this concept of "Your Family Archives" a bit further, I recommend that you make an inventory of all these things. Take sheets of paper, and list the items with a description of who they belonged to and how you came to have them.

You may not have museum-quality things in "Your Family Archives," but they are things that belonged to your family. That makes them priceless to you, and worthy of special consideration in storage.

YES, PUBLIC OFFICIALS ARE WILLING TO HELP

Today's column continues the series designed to give the fledgling genealogist some extra help. Here are "Ten Ways to Get More Genealogy from Public Officials."

Correspondence with public officials requires a special approach. Clerks are besieged with genealogy requests, and often it takes them weeks to get to the bottom of the mail pile — where your letter waits. Clerks will often pick letters from the pile that can be quickly answered within the time they have to spend on correspondence. (Strange to imagine, but these public officials are not hired to help genealogists, but to keep public records orderly!) Here are some sure-fire tips to get answers to your letters:

- ♦ Keep your letters brief and to the point. Clerks are NOT interested in your family stories.
- ♦ Use correct addresses. (Consult *The Handy Book* or *The Red Book* or *Where to Write for Vital Records*, all available in any genealogical library.)
- ♦ Address officials by their correct titles. (See above references for this.)
- ♦ Use white, 8 1/2 x 11 paper, and double space your letter. Typing is preferred for legibility. Leave plenty of "white space" on your letter for clerks to write you a quick answer. This saves them time. Include your return address on your letter; use proper letter-writing form.
- ♦ Always include a self-addressed, stamped envelope (SASE) with your request. This gives you a better chance of an early reply even when there is no information on file.
- ♦ If your first letter does not bring a reply, send a courteous reminder. Refer to the letter you sent, give the check number and date (if you enclosed money), briefly restate your request, and send another SASE in case your first letter went astray.
- ♦ If the clerk says there is no record, wait a couple of months and try again. Sometimes a different clerk knows where certain little-used records have been shelved.
- ♦ Request a photocopy of the original record, not a certified extract. The cost is usually the same, but you'll get all the information the record contains, not just what will fit on the abstract form.
- ♦ Calculate search dates carefully. Clerks vary in their search policy; some will check the records for a wide range of dates and some will check only a small bracket of years. Also, when requesting information on a very common surname, you must be as specific as possible.
- ♦ Be considerate of a clerk's time and express appreciation for the help. When a clerk goes out of the way to help you, send a thank you note. This will help the genealogist who writes the next letter.

BOOKS AID YOUR SEARCH FOR LOYALIST KIN

They were called "Tories" in colonial New England and "Loyalists" by Mother England. Both terms meant the same thing; they were people who did not espouse the cause of American separation from England and did not fight in the Revolutionary War. They remained loyal to England, sometimes at great personal risk and loss of property.

Most books about the American Revolution do an admirable job of portraying the patriot side, but they generally do a very poor job of presenting the history of the Loyalists.

These men, some 100,000 strong, were driven into exile in Canada and elsewhere by their former neighbors. Peter Wilson Coldham, in his book, *American Loyalist Claims,* says that "next after the dead and permanently wounded, the Loyalists were the real victims of that war."

Space limitations here don't permit a long history about the Loyalists, but if your ancestor was one, here are some references that will give you the desired history.

The Loyalists of the American Revolution, by Claude Van Tyne gives the history of these Americans, with references drawn primarily from the files of the Loyalist newspaper of the times. This 360-page book was written in 1902, and has been republished by Heritage Books, 1540-E Pointer Ridge Pl., Bowie MD 20716. It costs $22.50 (plus postage).

The Loyalists of Massachusetts, and *The Other Side of the Revolution,* by James Stark, written in 1907, has also been republished by Heritage Books. While this book also gives Loyalist history, the bulk of the book contains biographies of Loyalists. (This is where your ancestor may be hiding!) You may order this book for $37.50 (plus postage) from the address above.

Many genealogical libraries will have these books, and there are many other good reference books for those searching their Loyalist ancestors. One is *American Loyalist Claims,* by Peter Wilson Coldham. The data in this book was extracted from English courts; recorded there were the claims by loyal British citizens to their government for their losses to the enemy.

There is also a Society of Loyalist Descendants. For information, write to Joe McLaurin, Desk 120, P.O. Box 848, Rockinham, NC 28379. Please include an envelope with 45 cents postage with your request.

ARCHIVIST PRESERVES LINKS TO STATE'S PAST

(Author's note: This article pertained specifically to the Eastern Washington branch of the Washington State Archives; a good genealogist will realize there are similar archives in their state.)

The Eastern Regional Branch of the Washington State Archives is currently housed in the Kennedy Library on the campus of Eastern Washington University at Cheney. The archives have the responsibility to collect, appraise, preserve and make available for research the historical records of Washington state. These records document Washington's territorial, state and local governments and their dealings with the citizens. Genealogists are interested in these archives because they contain information on our pioneer ancestor families.

The Eastern Regional Archives contain the Territorial Census records, 1857-1892. These early censuses were taken to help determine when the population reached the magic number to qualify for statehood. The archives also contain early local school census records, assessment rolls, court dockets and case files, photographs, and maps.

JoAnn Gemmrig and Doris Woodward, members of the Eastern Washington Genealogical Society, "discovered" several big old books containing the indexes for immigration and naturalization papers for Washington Territory, spanning the years 1871 to 1910. This is great news for those seeking to document an ancestor's early arrival into Washington Territory or that the ancestor applied for citizenship.

Dr. Richard Hobbs, regional state archivist, is dedicated to helping the people of Washington use their archival records. He will help researchers to use these archives effectively, but would like to remind us of some basic rules for researching in archives, in Washington or elsewhere.

♦ Make an appointment. Archivists are busy, and while they are glad to help, they can best give help when time has been scheduled. You can call Hobbs for an appointment at (509) 623-4200.

♦ Bring only a pencil and small notebook when using archival records. No pens are allowed. Briefcases, purses, bags, boxes, backpacks and other containers must be checked with the staff — or better left at home. Eating, drinking and smoking are prohibited.

♦ All possible care must be taken by researchers to prevent damage to the records, which also must be kept in the order in which they are received. Photocopies, if allowed, will be made by staff members. Plan to sit at a special table and have the records brought to you.

PUBLICATIONS ABOUT SURNAMES ABOUND

Fledgling genealogists want to find a big batch of information on their family, or at least on their family surname. ("Old timers" do, too, for that matter!) One way to do this is to locate a surname publication that contains information on families bearing the surname you are researching.

There are dozens of these kinds of publications, and they range from small newsletters to large booklets. They usually contain pedigrees and lineages for the surname, and all kinds of other information gleaned from vital records, census records, military records, biographies, etc.

The information in these publications comes from the editor's own research, from the editor's travels to various libraries, and from folks bearing that surname sharing information with the editor. Surname publications can be a real gold mine of information!

The annual May-June issue of *The Genealogical Helper* always carries a listing of family periodicals. One can subscribe to *The Helper*, but current issues can be seen in most genealogy libraries.

Another source helpful in locating a family periodical is *Directory of Family Associations,* by Elizabeth Petty Bentley. The latest edition of this book lists nearly 5,000 family associations, and many of these will have some sort of publication available. This book is marketed by Genealogical Publishing Co. and costs $29.95. To order, call 800-727-6687.

I would hope, as beginners, that you get the idea of sharing information. By putting queries every possible place, by contacting every researcher of your surname that you can find and by sharing your family information freely, you'll vastly improve the likelihood of obtaining answers to your genealogical questions.

Think of it as advertising: The more you advertise that you're working on XXX family in XXX state and XXX time period, the more likely it is that somebody will see your "ad" and share with you. Family surname publications are a great place to begin that sharing.

CIVIL WAR SOLDIERS ARE BEING INDEXED

Have you heard about the Civil War soldiers project?

When completed, information about every Civil War soldier will be available at computer terminals at all Civil War battlefield sites in the National Parks system.

The project's thrust is to computerize the soldiers' basic information now found in their files housed in the National Archives.

These 5.5 million hand-written pages have not been microfilmed, and until now have been available to researchers in only three ways: by personally searching the archives, by hiring an agent to do the searching for you or by having archives officials do the search by filling out form NATF-80.

Called the Civil War Soldiers Index, the new data bank will contain the name of every soldier who fought in the Civil War, along with such information as whether he was Confederate or Union, his regiment and his rank.

The system will work this way: Each Civil War park will have one or more microcomputers available for use. At some sites, a park interpreter may operate the system; at others, the visitor may do it. The system will be easy to operate and will require no special computer knowledge. All the visitor has to know is the name of the soldier.

The system will display all the types of records available for that soldier and will direct the visitor to additional information.

Many groups are involved in the creation of this index. In addition to the National Parks Service and the National Archives, also involved are the Federation of Genealogical Societies and the Genealogical Society of Utah (meaning the Family History Library).

The Federation of Genealogical Societies is recruiting an army of volunteers for the necessary data entry work. Some work will be done in the National Archives Regional Branches, and some in private homes.

If you wish to volunteer, send your name, address, phone number, information regarding computer experience and what kind of computer owned, to: Civil War Soldiers Index, P.O. Box 3385, Salt Lake City, UT 84110-3385.

Don Wilson, former Archivist of the United States, said, "The National Archives is constantly seeking new avenues and employing new technologies to bring the history of this nation to all Americans. The National Archives receives nearly 1,500 inquiries each week relating to pension files of Civil War veterans."

"This project could have an enormous impact on students, scholars and genealogists interested in the Civil War."

MANY SCOTS TRACE ROOTS TO OLD BATTLEFIELD

Dumfries and Galloway are in a beautiful part of southwest Scotland. Today, this borderland area is dotted with bustling market towns and picturesque villages. Centuries ago, it was a battleground for the Scots and English.

The history of the area stretches back into the mists of time; it is suggested that the Camelot of King Arthur was here.

Many people today living all over the world can trace their origins back to Dumfries or Galloway, and because of that, the International Family Association for Dumfries and Galloway holds gatherings periodically.

At these gatherings, there are exciting "programmes" of pageant, historical reenactment, Scottish music, dancing and drama, and lectures, exhibitions and heritage information. The address for more information is Magdalene House, Bruce Street, Lachmaben, Dumfries, DG11 1PD Scotland. If you are interested in a "gathering" in this historic place, do write.

"Tracing Your Scottish Ancestry" by Kathleen B. Cory is a new book published by Genealogical Publishing Co., and is a cheaper alternative to going to Scotland. (But certainly not as much fun!) Cory's book is a practical, up-to-date guide to Scottish genealogy and one any genealogist needing help with Scottish research can use.

Packed with information, the book focuses on the holdings of the two principal Scottish record repositories, the General Register Office and the Scottish Record Office, both in Edinburgh. The author guides you, record by record, to a successful search for your Scottish ancestry.

Additional records and repositories are covered in the book, as are such subjects as Scottish surnames, heraldry, clans and tartans. Among the many appendices is a 43-page list of Scottish parishes, counties and commissariats. The date of the earliest birth or marriage record in each parish is also given.

A county map of Scotland and a street map of Edinburgh are also in this book. *The Manchester (England) Genealogist* says that "everyone with an interest in Scottish genealogy will welcome this publication, which is probably the most comprehensive guide to the subject ever produced."

Tracing Your Scottish Ancestry is 195 pages, paperback and costs $16.95. Call GPC at 800-727-6687 for a brochure on this book or to place an order.

Marshall Shore of Spokane called to tell me that the long-awaited microfiche collection of the Old Parochial Registers of Scotland are now at the Family History Centers. These indexes cover the 6 million births and 2.2 million marriages in Scotland for the Established Church of Scotland (Presbyterian) for the 300 years prior to 1855 (when civil registration law took over).

These records are only available in two places: Scotland and through the Family History Library in Salt Lake City.

Shore says that when you visit the Family History Center, take some time to learn how to use this collection.

"Each county has four indexes — alphabetically by first name, and then chronologically by date and also alphabetically by surname and date," he says. "There are several pages of instructions included, so don't be scared off. But if your Scottish ancestor was Presbyterian, or Church of Scotland, do look to document him in this file."

EXPLORE YOUR ANCESTRY FOR VACATION FUN

August is almost upon us, and I'd like to suggest some genealogical summer fun to liven up your final month of summer vacation.

Genealogy isn't always "collecting dead relatives." In my opinion, getting your kids and family interested in their forebears and background give them a richer understanding of who they are.

If possible, take the family to places where your parents and grandparents lived, and maybe where you grew up. Or visit there on your own and relive some memories as you look at the old hill, home or trees.

Visit the cemeteries where your family is buried and wander among the tombstones of other folks who knew your ancestors. Visit historic places, homes, battlegrounds or monuments near where your forebears lived. Just as you don't live isolated in your own four walls, neither did your ancestors, and they may have participated in the history-making events that went on in their own backyard.

If you cannot travel the distance to visit where your ancestors lived or are buried, then visit cemeteries and historic places near your home. Cemeteries are beautiful, cool and safe places for an afternoon walk.

The tears, chuckles and history learned as you wander will send you home with a comfortable feeling. Many books have been written about the historic homes and locations in your area, and they are worth your time to visit and support. Ask your librarian for books on walking tours, biking tours and car tours to these places.

For adults, a visit to any library can be rewarding. As I've said so often in this column, the very book that you're seeking might be in any possible library. Have you investigated every library in every town within a 300-mile driving distance? Make it a picnic day, or an overnight trip, and see what your area's libraries really have to offer.

Some rewarding things you might do with your family would be to make a picture album. Sort that box of old pictures into piles and get those albums done, either a big one for the family or let the children do their own. Or get Grandma to do one, complete with her written memories.

Another suggestion would be to get a notebook (for kids) or plan an afternoon at your computer (for older kids and us!) and put something of your personal history into words. Kids can draw pictures of what they remember of Grandpa's boat or that trip to Mount St. Helens in Washington state.

We parents are always wanting our kids to do more reading, so take your family to the library and get books about where your family lived and what they might have seen and experienced. My roots come from Maine and Missouri, very different places from Spokane and Pullman, here in Washington, where my grandchildren live.

Books about those places together with my stories could expand their understanding of their background. One of my early ancestors came over on the *Mayflower*, and I'm always pushing "Pilgrim books" onto my kids. A good friend's forebear was on the Lewis and Clark expedition, and so western history figures in their reading program.

A last suggestion would be to investigate your rich cultural and ethnic heritage. What foods, games and crafts did your Irish, Norwegian, Hispanic, African or Native American ancestors enjoy? The library can suggest books on all these topics, and perhaps places to go where you can learn more about your heritage.

ALL GENEALOGISTS ARE SEEKING SOURCES

Genealogists, beginning ones or old-timers, are continually looking for new and effective sources. They seek a source for the information they need to fill in the blank areas on their charts and forms. Webster's dictionary defines a source as "a person, book, etc., that provides information." May I suggest a few sources for you?

In every genealogical society there are those whose personal research has made them specialists in different areas. In order to catch up with these folks, you need only go to a meeting and speak up. Ask for help with Maryland research or Native American research, or for someone who knows how to read German script, and somebody will jump to your aid.

Your public librarian is a wonderful source person for general knowledge. Do you need the address for a library in Bath, ME? Or for the Methodist Church in Newton, TN? Or do you need to know more about the Trail of Tears through the Southern states? Perhaps your ancestor experienced the New Madrid earthquake in Missouri in the early 1800s, or perhaps a great-uncle was a cowboy in Montana. Your librarian can recommend books on these and any other subject.

The Family History Centers are staffed with very helpful source-persons. They will cheerfully answer your questions, and are always happy to introduce you to the wealth of research material available through the big library in Salt Lake City. Contact any area center with your questions. You may call Family History Support at 800-346-6044 to obtain the address of the Family History Center nearest you.

The Family History Library in Salt Lake City offers inexpensive published guides to all the American states and Canadian provinces, and for many other countries. Called "Research Outlines," these guides tell in a few pages all about the area in which you are researching. They are usually about 50 cents each; write to the Library at 35 N. West Temple St., Salt Lake City, UT 84150, for more information. Or inquire about these guides at the Family History Center.

The National Genealogical Society exists to help genealogists. Their publications are all designed to be source material. Recently they have begun publishing a "Research in the States" series. Costing only $6.00 each, booklets for six states are available so far: District of Columbia, Indiana, Minnesota, Oregon, South Carolina and Texas. Contact NGS at 4527 17th Street North, Arlington, VA 22207-2399.

Genealogical Publishing Co. Inc. has long been a leader in making source books available to genealogists. To detail the list of such books would take the rest of this entire page! Call them at 800-727-6687 to request a free catalog.

Heritage Books, Inc. has over 1000 genealogical and historical titles in print, and offers approximately twenty new titles every month. To receive their free catalog, call 800-398-7709, or browse their web page at www.heritagebooks.com.

Webster's also defines a source as a place of origin. Your best genealogical sources are your own ancestors. If they're alive, talk with them. If they're gone, look for records that they created when alive.

GENEALOGISTS SHOULD TRY TO BE BETTER CONSUMERS

As a genealogical consumer, you have certain responsibilities. Fran Carter, in an article for *Heritage Quest* magazine, outlines some of these responsibilities. She wrote, "The consumer is someone who buys or uses the products or services of a genealogical business. Failure to be a good consumer may cause difficulties and aggravation not necessarily the responsibility of the business."

Fran's article suggests that as genealogical consumers we should follow these guidelines:

♦ Read advertising carefully — know exactly what you are ordering. If something is unclear, contact the company and ask for clarification before you order.

♦ Do not expect any supplier to check its books or files for your surname prior to placement of your order.

♦ Make sure your complete name and address are on both the order and the check, not just on the envelope.

♦ Never send cash!

♦ Keep a copy of your order, complete with date and check number. This information makes a reference easier if it is ever needed.

Following Fran's guidelines will make happier consumers out of all of us.

TODAY'S TIP: It is impossible to do effective genealogical research without knowing how the county boundaries within the states have changed over the years. *The Map Guide to the U.S. Federal Censuses, 1790-1920,* by Thorndale and Dollarhide, fills this need and has been issued in a paperback form. Order your copy for $39.95 from Genealogical Publishing Co. at 800-727-6687.

TODAY'S TRIVIA: The Cuban Genealogical Society, formed in 1988, has entered 15,000 names into a computer file maintained by the society. If you have Cuban ancestors, contact the society at P.O. Box 2650, Salt Lake City, UT 84110. Also, the *Guide to Cuban Genealogical Research,* by Peter Carr can be obtained from The Cuban Index, P.O. Box 11251, San Bernardino, CA 92423-1251.

CHURCH RECORDS ARE A GOOD FAMILY HISTORY SOURCE

At the Washington State Genealogical Conference, held in May, 1992, in Everett, Janet Armbrust presented a wonderful lecture on using church records in genealogical research. Janet said that researchers under-utilize church records as a source of family history information, but these records are primary (which means "created at the time of the event") and should not be overlooked. The efforts to find and use church records will be rewarded with answers to puzzles that cannot be gleaned from other sources.

What records were typically kept by churches? Consider the following:

♦ Baptism or christening records.
♦ Confirmation records.
♦ Marriage records and/or banns.
♦ Burial records and/or funeral records.
♦ Communion records.
♦ Membership records, transfers, disciplinary actions.
♦ Pew rental records.
♦ Vestry or church council minutes.
♦ Financial contribution records.
♦ Cemetery plat books.

Not all churches kept all those types of records. Policy varied from denomination to denomination and differed through the ages. Some churches, especially the established churches like Episcopal and Congregational consistently kept good records. Evangelistic churches–Methodist and Baptist for instance–kept fewer records.

How can we determine our ancestor's religious affiliation? Some families went to the same church for generations, and others attended whatever church there was (as on the frontier). To help you discern what church your ancestor might have attended, consider the following:

♦ Obituary information.
♦ Cemetery location and affiliation.
♦ Family tradition and naming patterns.
♦ Family Bibles.
♦ Newspaper articles.
♦ County histories and biographies.
♦ Predominant denomination in the area where your family lived.

Once you've determined the church to which your ancestor might have belonged, I suggest that you check with the Family History Centers to see what records from that church in that area might have been microfilmed and would thus be available through the Family History Library in Salt Lake. Check an out-of-town phone book or contact the secretary in the same church locally for the address, and write to the church where your ancestor might have attended. (I suggest that you always include at least a $5.00 check when writing to a church; their time is valuable and they are doing you a favor.)

CHOOSING A COMPUTER PROGRAM ISN'T EASY

What genealogy computer program should I buy? That's a question that I'm often asked in my genealogy classes. The answer is that, in my opinion, computer programs are about 75 percent alike (in that they allow you to enter family data onto different charts and forms), and you must choose the program that's best for you by evaluating the other 25 percent of the features. Also remember that only your personal evaluation tells how easy or difficult any given program is for you to use.

There are several ways to find out the differences in the genealogy computer programs now available. One way is to attend any genealogy meeting and talk to the folks — see what they use, and why they like their particular choice. Another way is to read the computer section of Everton's *Genealogical Helper*. This periodical is available in most genealogy libraries, or by subscription at $21.00 annually from Everton Publishers (800-443-6325). This magazine carries ads for many different genealogical computer programs, and you can learn a lot about a program from scanning the ads. Computer stores carry only the most popular genealogy programs.

Genealogical Computing is a bi-monthly publication of Ancestry and is loaded with valuable articles about different genealogy programs. A one-year subscription is $25.00 and a three-year subscription is $60.00. Call Ancestry at 800-262-3787 to subscribe. Reading this periodical will definitely help you choose a genealogy program.

I usually recommend PAF, Personal Ancestral File, developed by the staff at the Family History Library. This program costs the least of any, only $35.00, and comes with a detailed manual, making it an easy program to use. I tested this with my daughter-in-law: I hired Treena to input all my names into this program as a summer job – as she stayed home with granddaughter Aleena!

Treena loaded the program and got right to work with no trouble, and she knows nothing about genealogy. "Just push the buttons," she says. Because this program was developed by the folks who are the leaders in genealogical research, it will be the standard of the industry, in my opinion.

It will interface with the computers in the Family History Library, making it easy to share with them and get help from them. PAF can be purchased through your local Family History Center, or by credit card from the LDS Church Distribution Center at 800-537-5950.

NEXUS, the newsletter of the New England Historic Genealogical Society, in the summer 1992 issue, carried a three-page article titled "What Program Should I Buy?"

The article suggests that you ask yourself these questions: What type of computer do I have? Is space limited on my computer? What do I want a genealogy program to do? How good am I with technology? What can I afford? What do my friends and relatives have?

Whatever genealogy computer program you decide upon, remember that no computer will do your genealogy for you. Genealogy computer programs allow you to sort and rearrange your data, and to more effectively keep track of your family information. But no program is going to do research for you — you still must write letters, request certificates, read books and use libraries.

And you certainly can do genealogy without a computer! Computers just make doing the necessary paperwork easier and more fun.

TODAY'S LAUGH: Why is it that your grandmother's maiden name, for which you've searched for years, was on an old letter in a box in the attic all the time?

YOUR ROOTS MAY RUN TO NEW HAMPSHIRE

Out here in the Pacific Northwest we don't often hear much about the tiny state of New Hampshire, but chances are good that many area genealogists have ancestral roots extending to there.

Sandwiched as the state is next to Vermont and in between the bigger neighbors of Maine and Massachusetts, New Hampshire had a population of nearly 150,000 in 1790. The bulk of the settlers were from Massachusetts and Connecticut, but a goodly number of Ulster Scots settled in what was to become

New Hampshire in the early 1700s. Were any of these folks your ancestors?

While the records were originally kept at the town or city level, all existing records have been gathered into the state office. Any existing birth, marriage or death records since 1640 for the area known as New Hampshire can be accessed by writing to the Bureau of Vital Records, Health Services Building, 6 Hazen Dr., Concord, NH 03301. I suggest that you call this office at 603-271-4654 for a recorded message verifying current fees.

Town histories are abundant, particularly for southwestern towns in New Hampshire. The largest collections are held by the New Hampshire State Library (20 Park St., Concord, NH 03301) and by the New Hampshire Historical Society (next door at 30 Park St.). Both of these places will answer your letter of inquiry, so do write to them asking about their family history collections. (And do remember your stamped, self-addressed envelope for their reply.)

The New Hampshire Historical Society also has an excellent manuscript collection of original church records, and a typescript collection of church records that lists all sorts of information on church members. I understand that a project to inventory and index these church records has been underway for quite some time, and so I'd suggest that you ask about these files when you write.

The probate records for New Hampshire are kept at the county level, and the records begin in 1640 when the area was a Royal Province and continue through the time when the area was part of Massachusetts right up until modern times. The probate files of New Hampshire are especially rich in genealogical material, and should top the list of potential resources. The county address can be obtained from Ancestry's *Red Book* or the Everton *Handy Book*, both available at most genealogy libraries and Family History Centers.

Luckily for genealogists, especially descendants living 3,000 miles away, more and more New Hampshire records are being published. Heritage Books has published the *Vital Records of Rye, New Hampshire: A Transcript of the Births, Baptisms, Marriages, and Deaths in This Town to the Year 1890,* by Kathleen E. Hosier. The facts supporting this book are taken from microfilmed copies of the original town records, genealogical records of town clerks, and records of the Congregational Church, which was organized in 1726. Could be that your Rye ancestor is listed somewhere in the 336 pages of this paperbound book. The book can be ordered from Heritage Books, 1540-E Pointer Ridge Place, Bowie, MD 20716, 800-398-7799. The same book publisher is offering the *History of Rye, New Hampshire, From Its Discovery and Settlement to 1903,* by Langdon Parsons. This 675-page, 1905 reprint is indexed and can be ordered for $38.50 at the phone number above. Every month Heritage offers several more titles in its free catalog. Request one at 800-398-7709.

Most genealogical libraries have several reference books relating to New Hampshire families, history and records. The New Hampshire answers you seek might well be obtained right in your own local library.

TODAY'S TRIVIA: The New Hampshire Office of Travel and Tourism offers a free *Guidebook to New Hampshire.* Call that office at 800-944-1023 to request your copy. This book will help you lay the groundwork for a perfect trip to the Granite State.

The NGS offers a home-study course that teaches genealogists how to better use cemetery records, courthouse records and to do more effective genealogical research. The course costs about $300. For more information, contact the NGS.

CENSUS BUREAU PROVIDES SPECIAL SERVICE

Genealogists should take advantage of a special service provided by the Bureau of the Census through its Age Search office. This office, a small branch of the Census Bureau, until recently was in Pittsburg, KS, and now is located in Jeffersonville, IN.

Any person can request a personal search of census records, including the 1930 through 1990 censuses currently closed to the public. The basic search fee is $25.00, and the Age Search office will search any two censuses for a person appearing in the schedules. For example, you can request a search of the 1930 and 1940 censuses for your father or mother, or search the 1970 census for yourself. The person who is the subject of the search must be yourself or a direct ancestor. You must provide proof of death for this ancestor.

The search is limited to the person for whom you are requesting information, but you can ask for information on other family members for $2.00 per extra person. You can also request the full line of information from the census schedules for $6.00

per extra person. Unless so stated (and so paid for) a basic search for one person will be conducted per request. If successful in locating the person, the Census Bureau will return to you an official document giving the person's name and answers to all census questions taken on that census.

The document you'll receive from the Age Search office will be certified by the Census Bureau as accurate, and this certificate can be used to obtain passports, Social Security cards, etc., for persons without a recorded birth certificate.

If you wish to submit a request for a collateral relative, you need to declare your relationship to the person and provide evidence of the death of that person as part of the application form. The chances are good that by stating your purpose as "genealogical research," and providing evidence of death for a person, just about any deceased person's census record can be received through this service.

The special service must be requested on the Census Bureau's form, one of the better government forms around because you can actually read it and understand the steps involved. Since the primary use of this service is for persons applying for Social Security who need evidence of their age, any Social Security office is your best source for obtaining an application form. Ask for Form BC-600, titled "Application for Search of Census Records." There is a place on the form to indicate the purpose of the census search. Family researchers should indicate "genealogical research" as the purpose. You can also request an application form to be mailed to you by writing to the following address: Bureau of the Census, "Age Search," P.O. Box 1545, Jeffersonville, IN 47131. (Thanks to Bill Dollarhide, his January-March 1992 *Genealogy Bulletin*, for the above information.)

TODAY'S TRIVIA: A genealogist's work is never done, and here's the reason why. You begin your genealogy with yourself and two parents. Soon you're learning about four grandparents, eight great-grandparents, 16 great-great-grandparents, etc., etc., doubling each generation backwards.

Assuming 25 years more or less to a generation, you'll get back to your 16 great-great grandparents of 100 years ago, in four generations.

The figures doubling each generation would generate 256 ancestors 200 years ago, and would involve for many of us our Revolutionary ancestors in this country. Going back 300 years, our ancestors of 12 generations total 4,096. From here back the figures really begin to skyrocket. Sixteen generations, or 400 years ago, our ancestors numbered 54,536. Beyond that at 500 years, or 20 generations, you have 1,048,576 ancestors; 600 years, or 24 generations, you have 16,777,216 ancestors; 700 years, or 28 generations, you have 268,435,456 ancestors.

If you could document your lineage back to the time of Christ, you would have well over 3 billion ancestors. Logic tells you, however, that there were not 3 billion people living at the time of Christ, so know that many, if not most, of us have common ancestors somewhere in the past 30 generations.

To say it another way, many of us are no further apart than 30th cousins. But it's still a mountain of names to research, even with all the sharing, and so it's true that a genealogist's work will never be done — and most of them like it that way!

ANCESTRAL FILE COULD USE YOUR ASSISTANCE

You are invited to contribute your family information to Ancestral File, a computerized collection of genealogies. This file links individuals into families and pedigrees, showing their ancestors and descendants.

The file contains genealogical information about millions of people from throughout the world. This information includes names of individuals; their family relationships and pedigrees; and dates and places of birth, marriage and death.

Ancestral File is part of FamilySearch, an automated system that simplifies the task of family history research. FamilySearch is available through the Family History Library in Salt Lake City, and all the branch Family History Centers throughout the world.

Ancestral File is a community effort, depending almost entirely on individuals and families contributing their genealogical information to it. The file has enormous potential, having grown from 7 million to 13 million names in less than two years. By contributing your family information to Ancestral File, you will benefit in the following ways: You will share your discoveries with others; you will link your information to other information in the file; you will coordinate your research with others; and you will preserve your genealogy permanently.

You can search the file free of charge at any Family History Center. You can also print copies of records and charts for a minimal fee, or copy them to a diskette to use on your home computer and to share with other family members.

To enter your family information into Ancestral File, you first need to computerize your data on any software program that is registered for contributing information to the file. PAF (Personal Ancestral File) is the preferred program, and this program is available for $15.00 through the Family History Centers or by calling 800-537-5950 to order. If you do not own a computer that runs a registered program, PAF is available at the Family History Centers for you to use.

I recommend you call for the hours and for an appointment to use Ancestral File at the center nearest you. The reason for needing an appointment is that there are so many folks wanting to use the few computers at the centers that without an appointment you may not get a turn.

Ancestral File depends on genealogical contributions from individuals and families. The more information you and others contribute, the more useful the file will be. I hope you'll "catch the vision" and consider sharing your family information with Ancestral File.

As long as we're on the subject of the Family History Centers, you should know that in 1991, more than 110,000,000 pages of genealogical information were added to the collections of the Family History Library. This information came from the United States and 38 other countries of the world. For instance, 353,000 pages of genealogical records from Peru were added, as were 49,000 pages from Yugoslavia. This material came from microfilmed records and purchased records. The rate of acquisition continues today. Keep that in mind as you ponder your pedigree; might the Family History Library have some records for you?

LIKE NSDAR, MEN'S GROUP HAS OWN LIBRARY

The National Society Daughters of the American Revolution, their goals and their library, are given considerable coverage in the genealogical journals. But did you know that there is a Sons of the American Revolution organization for men who are descended from a Revolutionary War patriot?

The Sons of the American Revolution, or SAR, is a much smaller group, but entrance into the SAR is obtained in the same way as the ladies join the NSDAR. To join the SAR you must document your lineage back to a Revolutionary War patriot. Either a paternal or maternal lineage is acceptable.

Just like the NSDAR, the SAR maintains a genealogical library, and theirs is in Louisville, KY, at its national headquarters. In 1978, the SAR moved from Washington, DC, into a former Masonic building in Louisville, where an entire upper floor was given over to the society's impressive library. The library attracts researchers who are hoping to prove their patriotic descent and thus qualify for membership in the society, but it is also an excellent resource place for any kind of genealogical exploration. SAR members may use the library free of charge; for other researchers the charge is $1.00 per day. An article in the July-August 1991 publication *Southern Queries* quoted SAR librarian Mike Christian. Calling the library "a place that seems to be a well kept secret to all but members, would-be members, and the occasional researcher," Christian said it averages only 15 researchers per day.

Besides the 4,500 volumes of family history, the SAR library has a significant collection of regional histories and periodicals. The library's biggest strength is its Revolutionary War records, which contain an abundance of material to aid folks tracing their patriot ancestor.

First-time visitors to the library usually have a target name in mind and should ask the librarian for help: A computerized patriot index can be checked, and the library owns a complete set of the Revolutionary War pension records on microfilm, and a compiled index to military service records by states and regiments. Stored in a back room, jokingly called "the vault," are a number of older SAR applications on microfilm.

Christian also says that increasing numbers of visitors come to look at the George Washington Room, furnished to look like Washington's own study at Mount Vernon. This room houses one of the best collections of materials in the country on the first president.

The SAR library is open Monday through Friday, 9:30 a.m. to 4:30 p.m. The address is 1000 S. Fourth St., Louisville, KY 40203, and the phone number is 502-589-1776. It is strongly suggested you call before your planned visit to verify the days and hours. Staff members cannot perform research for people, but they will make photocopies of specifically requested items. They also have a list of local professional researchers which they will send upon request.

Southern Queries is an informative new publication carrying queries on Southern ancestors as well as helpful articles. The information on the SAR library which I quoted above was obtained from this periodical. The article also told about the other genealogical libraries in Kentucky: the Filson Club in Louisville, the Kentucky Historical Society and the Kentucky State Archives in Frankfort. If you'd like to subscribe to *Southern Queries* ($24.00 per year, queries free to subscribers), write to P.O. Box 23854, Columbia, SC 29224-3854.

TODAY'S LAUGH: Our teenage grandson was curious about his family tree, and when we got through listing the mixture of German, English, Scottish and Indian, he threw up his hands and said, "Boy, if I were a dog, I'd be a mutt."

1993

NOW IS A GOOD TIME TO RECHECK YOUR GENEALOGICAL DATA

W elcome to 1993, and the start of another great genealogical year. Let's begin our year by evaluating our genealogical data — where we are and where we need to go next in our quest for family history information.

If you're like most working genealogists, you have boxes, shelves, drawers, file cabinets and often rooms full of material you have gathered through the years on your family lines. All of this "stuff" represents a pool of genealogical information, and you may have entered some of it onto your pedigree charts and family group sheets, and you even may have entered it into a computer program. But when was the last time you really took the time to evaluate each date, event and family connection? You might just be surprised at the answers if you do this little exercise.

Many times in our genealogical searching, we copy and recopy records and information and all too often never stop to ask ourselves if the information is logically correct or if we have miscopied dates or events ourselves. A good thing to do; and especially so at the beginning of a new genealogical year, is to take your family sheets one by one and go through the test below. By rechecking your data you may find some errors and you may find some areas you have not thoroughly covered. Here's a list of questions:

1. Are all dates in the proper order: birth, marriage and death?

2. Are all abbreviations correct: city, county, state and country?

3. Do you have proof of each birth, marriage, death and each event place?

4. If the family arrived in America in the latter half of the 19th century, did you check the 1900 and 1910 censuses for the year of their arrival and whether they were naturalized citizens?

5. Did they seem to be a part of any large migration, either to this country or within this country?

6. Do the dates make sense? (Hard for a woman to have children at age 8.)

7. Do all the children belong to the same wife?

8. Is there any big age gap among the children, suggesting two wives or that the father was away on military service?

9. Does the naming pattern for the children follow any ethnic system of naming?

10. Did the man serve in the military? Did he receive a pension?

11. Did the man own property? Or pay taxes?

12. Do you have the correct birth order for the children?

13. Have you researched the descending lineages for the children?

For the more advanced genealogist (meaning one who has been at this sometimes frustrating hobby longer!) here are some suggestions:

1. Have you found each person on your pedigree chart on each census of his or her life?

2. Have you listed where you either have sent for or can send for birth, marriage, and death certificates for each person on your pedigree charts?

3. Have you compiled a documentation list for every single fact that you've listed on your pedigree charts?

4. Have you turned the bare facts about your ancestor into prose, and written the story of his or her life? Your genealogy is not done if all you've done is collect the facts; you must compose these facts into a life narrative. (I say in my classes that you don't have a sandwich with the ingredients out on the counter and not compiled!)

If none of the above ideas has any meaning to you, here's a suggestion: Have you completely gone through all your genealogy "stuff" and listed out what is pertinent to your actual family history and what is just gathered, miscellaneous "stuff?" If an accident were to befall you, would your family know what to keep and what to donate to the local genealogical society? (My husband often says he'll take a huge load to the dump! I'd better leave good instructions!)

ILLINOIS ARCHIVES CAN BE A REAL GOLD MINE

Deanie Binsfield is our local Illinois research specialist. She was a presenter at the Eastern Washington Genealogical Society's fall workshop last October, and gave an eager crowd all sorts of great information on researching your roots in Illinois records.

One resource that she told about was the Illinois Regional Archives Depository System, or IRAD. Sponsored by the Illinois State Archives, this program has collected local records into seven regional repositories. These local records could be birth, marriage and death records, land deeds, mortgages and tax sale records, assessors' and collectors' tax books, poll books and voter registrations, naturalization records, probate records, and miscellaneous county records. IRAD also has an extensive collection of records for the city of Chicago. A computerized listing of all these local records has been created by IRAD, and is available to all researchers. This means you can write to IRAD and request a printout of their holdings for a specific county, and they will send it to you free of charge.

Deanie told her class that "A Summary Guide to Local Records in the Illinois State Archives" was reprinted recently and is available for $6.00 from the Illinois State Archives (Archives Bldg., Springfield, IL 62756).

IRAD welcomes letters from genealogists. They ask that you include the full name of the person you are researching, the approximate year this person is expected to appear in a record, the name of the county, and the record title or type to search. Please limit two names per request, and you DO NOT have to send a stamped envelope.

Two brochures were passed out at Deanie's class. These were "Discovering Family and Local History at IRAD" and "Mapping Your Past: Genealogy at the Illinois State Archives." If you'd like a copy of these brochures, drop a postcard to the Illinois State Archives (address above). You will need these brochures to know which branch of IRAD to write to, i.e., to know which county records have been placed in which repository. There's a map on the brochure showing these boundaries very clearly.

Since Deanie is our area's Illinois specialist, she welcomes calls from folks needing answers to questions about Illinois research. She belongs to the Illinois State Genealogical Society (ISGS), and has an extensive collection of its publications. These include the seven volumes of ancestor charts of the ISGS members, volumes one and two of the "Prairie Pioneer" series, and volume one of the collected Bible records. Her phone number is (509) 466-8006, and she'd be happy to check these books for the name of your Illinois ancestor.

On another note: In 1979, Audrey Megerian was commissioned by a group of Armenian people to determine what Armenian family records still existed. She went to Armenian centers throughout the world, seeking and collecting this information. As a result, the Armenian Genealogical Society has been able to microfilm records in 23 countries, including Armenia, Egypt, England, Greece, Israel, Italy aid Turkey. As a result, this society is now a recognized authority in Armenian genealogy. The microfilmed records are available through the Family History Library in Salt Lake City, and at the Armenian Family Heritage Center (6470 Foothill Blvd., Tujunga, CA 91042). In addition to the microfilmed records, at the Heritage Center you'll find a full library of materials relating to Armenian families. Dr. Nephi Kezerian is the coordinator of the center, and welcomes your letters or phone calls (818-352-2491).

TODAY'S TRIVIA: Be glad you didn't live before 1883 when there were more than 50 time zones in the U.S., not just four as today. In those days there was no such thing as standard time; noon was whenever the sun crossed the meridian overhead. When it was noon in Washington, DC, it was 12:24 in Boston and 11:43 in Savannah. By the 1860s, as the railroads expanded, confusion and missed train connections reached nightmare proportions. In 1878, Canadian engineer Sanford Fleming proposed a worldwide system of 24 time zones, the same time to be observed throughout the zone. On Nov. 18, 1883, the railroad adopted the system and sanity was restored to travelers. But Standard Time didn't become law until 1918.

GRAVE MARKERS ARE AVAILABLE FOR ALL VETERANS

Did you know that the Veterans Administration will furnish, upon request and at no charge to the applicant, a government monument to mark the grave of an eligible veteran buried in a national, military post or base cemetery, or state veterans' or private cemetery?

The grave of the veteran must be unmarked in order for a monument to be furnished at government expense. Also, "In Memory Of" monuments, known as memorial monuments, are provided for eligible, individual veterans whose remains are not buried.

Local genealogist Ronald Miller recently sent a brochure explaining this program. He said he picked it up at the local Veterans Affairs office. Ron thinks that any ancestor who served in the Revolution, the War 1812, the Civil War or any other conflict in which America was defended, might qualify for a free monument.

The brochure states that qualified veterans include those discharged from honorable duty prior to Sept. 7, 1980. The brochure also clearly states that documented proof of military service must be submitted along with any applications.

The pamphlet is titled "The Veterans Monument Program," #40-107. If this policy of placing free government markers on unmarked veterans' graves is of interest to you, contact your local Veterans Affairs office.

Planting more roots: Here's something really new and very different. The Ellen Payne Odom Genealogy Library in Moultrie, GA, has announced that it has joined the efforts of Famous & Historic Trees and has become a Global ReLeaf partner. This organization has collected seeds from a red maple at Mount Vernon, George Washington's home, and grows them up to shipping and planting size. Upon receiving an order, they will ship you a small tree, complete with everything you'll need for successful growing. The idea is that as your tree grows, you'll feel a closer link to America's past, and you'll be helping to preserve the environment. Should you like to order this $42.00 kit, call 800-677-0727, or write to Famous & Historic Trees, P.O. Box 7040EP, Jacksonville, FL 32238-7040 for a copy of their catalog listing over 140 historic trees. With the tiny red maple tree comes the promise that "your family tree can be traced back to George Washington." (Isn't this a cute idea? And it proves that genealogy can invade all areas of our life!)

HELP FINDING CANADIAN TIES IS AVAILABLE

Many folks in Eastern Washington can trace back to ancestors who came through or lived in the Atlantic province of Nova

Scotia, Canada, and are seeking to know more about the records there. Genealogical Publishing Co. has published two reference books for Nova Scotia.

Nova Scotia Immigrants to 1867, compiled by Leonard and Norma Smith (1992), attempts to pull together all the sources documenting emigration from Nova Scotia into New England before Confederation in 1867. This work is an index to the names in all those other reference books. This book will help those of us who are trying to find where in Nova Scotia our ancestors came from. The cost of the book is $37.50.

Yarmouth, Nova Scotia, Genealogies, by George Brown (1993), is a book compiled from genealogy columns that appeared in the Yarmouth Herald between 1896 and 1910. Brown's columns focused almost exclusively on New England families who migrated to Nova Scotia around the time of the Revolutionary War. The cost of this nearly 1,000-page book is $60.00; both books may be ordered by calling GPC at 800-727-6687.

The September-October 1990 issue of the Ancestry newsletter contained a two-page article on beginning research in Nova Scotia. This article, written by Denise K. Fourie, M.L.S., tells of her personal experience in using records from this province, and particularly in the Public Archives of Nova Scotia. She also gives a short bibliography of "where-to-begin" books on researching in Nova Scotia. For a copy of this article, call at 800-ANCESTRY.

Researching in Nova Scotia appears to be a bit easier than in some Canadian provinces. Tombstone inscriptions from many cemeteries have been copied and are on file at the Public Archives of Nova Scotia. Fifteen censuses were taken from 1671 through 1881. Protestant church registers covering the period 1780 to 1914, and Catholic registers from 1679-1914, are held by the Public Archives.

Passenger lists of immigrants arriving at Halifax are available from 1881 to 1900. The Public Archives has an alphabetical file of draft land grants and petitions from 1775 onward. Probate registration began in Halifax in 1749. Poll tax records exist for the 1770-1827 period, when the censuses are the weakest. The Public Archives has marriage records from about 1850 for all towns in the province.

The Family History Library in Salt Lake City has prepared a series of guides for researching in all the various Canadian provinces. These four- to six-page guides present the sources and addresses for using all the major record groups in each province. The guides can be ordered from the Family History Library at a cost of $1.00 for two, and the address is 35 N. West Temple St., Salt Lake City, UT 84150.

A free brochure titled "Tracing Your Ancestors in Canada" may be requested from the Public Archives of Canada, 395 Wellington St., Ottawa, Ontario KLA ON3. This brochure outlines what is available in the national, provincial and private archives of Canada, and gives information on censuses, vital records and immigration and naturalization.

TODAY'S TRIVIA: Would you like to see a genealogy postage stamp? The New England Historic Genealogical Society is encouraging its members, and I encourage all of you, to support a U.S. postal stamp honoring genealogy. Folks should voice their opinion to the Citizens' Stamp Advisory Committee, U.S. Postal Service, 475 L'Enfant Plaza, SW, Washington, DC 20260-6753. Probably a postcard sent to them would suffice.

MILITARY RECORD INFORMATION IS AVAILABLE

Sooner or later, most genealogists have the need to find military records on their ancestors. The U.S. Army Military History Institute in Carlisle Barracks, PA, is an important repository for anything pertaining to American military history. If you have tried writing to the state adjutant general's office, the state archives, and the National Archives for information on your soldier, and still desire more information, write to "Carlisle Barracks," as it is commonly known. The U.S. Army Military History Institute collects, preserves, and provides to researchers source materials of American military history. The institute is housed in Upton Hall, built in 1941, and named for Brevet Major General Emory Upton (1839-1881). The facility was formerly the academic building for the Army Medical Field Service School and for the Army War College, prior to becoming a home for the U.S. Army Military History Institute in 1977. The institute's collections contain more than one million items relating to military history, including 120,000 books, 9,000 periodicals, 730,000 photographs, 40,000 audio/visual items, and over five million manuscript items (diaries, memoirs, letters, etc.). The institute also strives to perpetuate the history and traditions of the Army, the Army's role in the development of the United States, and the lists of the men and women involved in its development.

The institute cannot do extensive genealogy by mail, but will gladly provide research and reference assistance. This means that you cannot write and ask for information on your specific Civil War ancestor for instance, but can request information on his unit, and what battles his unit was in. Or you could request information on what his uniform might have looked like, or the weapons he might have carried.

The institute does participate in the national inter-library loan program. This means that if you write to them asking about books on a certain subject, and they reply that they have the books you seek, you can possibly borrow these books through inter-library loan.

I have done this, and it's a good system. Working on an article about the Balloon Companies stationed near Port Townsend in Jefferson County, WA, I wrote to the institute for information on these companies. In reply, they sent several copied pages of information, some bibliographic lists, and offered to inter-library loan to me several of the items. All at no charge!

The institute is open daily to the public for research, or you may write to this address: U.S. Army Military History Institute, Carlisle Barracks, PA 17013-5008, or call 717-245-3611 for more information.

On another note, while I was working on the above mentioned article on the Balloon Companies, I wrote to the Wright Patterson Air Force Museum in Ohio. Besides sending what I'd requested, they sent a two-page list of addresses for all sorts of different military related archives, museums and repositories. You might still be able to obtain this list from them.

Did I pique your interest with mention of Balloon Companies? During World War I, aerial balloons were used successfully to spot enemy positions along the front in France. After the war, and thinking that use of aerial spotting balloons would be a good idea for coastal defense, the stationing of balloon companies along American coasts was authorized. In May 1920, three balloon companies unloaded at Port Townsend, WA, and immediately began making ascents and performing tests. These tests were designed to determine the feasibility of permanently stationing balloons in Jefferson County. Many of the ascents were made from the parade grounds of Ford Worden (remember the movie "An Officer and a Gentleman?"). The tests proved that balloons could perform sighting missions, and authorization was given for two balloon hangars to be constructed, and two companies to be permanently stationed there. The hangars were completed by 1921, but by then newer and more effective technology was emerging, and the idea of balloon reconnaissance was outdated; the whole idea just melted away. Did one of your ancestors serve in a balloon company?

TODAY'S TRIVIA: The original Indian name for Connecticut was Quinnehtukqut.

My favorite quote from Abraham Lincoln reads, "The written word allows us to communicate with the dead, the absent and the yet unborn."

NORWEGIAN CENTER HAS HISTORIES GALORE

It certainly seems to me as if the folks searching for Scandinavian ancestors have all the luck. There are so many organizations available offering information and help finding the Swedes and "Norskies," that it's not fair to those of us with Spanish or German ancestry for whom there is much less help. I think Scandinavians were more interested in keeping records than some ethnic groups.

The Norwegian Emigration Center in Stavanger, Norway, offers a lovely brochure (written in English) detailing what it offers by way of genealogical research help. It was established in 1986 as a research and information center with the objective of developing contact between Norwegians around the world. The center has a large library and reading room, and will do research by mail, mainly in the large collection of emigration indexes. These indexes contain the names, ages and birth places of emigrants, and the source of the entries are the Norwegian Church records. The center also has 19th-century censuses for Norway, and "hundreds of local Norwegian history books having detailed information on families through the centuries." The fee for help by mail in 1993 was $25.00 (U.S. funds), and should be sent to P.O. Box 307, N-40001, Stavanger, Norway.

It is too bad that we all can't visit Stavanger in the summer. That's when the annual Norwegian Emigration Festival takes place, with exhibitions, concerts, folk dancing and seminars. The highlight of the celebration is the performance of a play about the first Norwegian Emigration to the U.S., July 4, 1825, and is staged in the Stavanger harbor. If you would like more information about Norway, Stavanger or this festival, contact the Norwegian

Tourist Board, 655 Third Ave., New York, NY 10017, or your local travel agent.

Descendants of Swedish ancestors have a place to visit that's much closer to home. The Swedish Finn Historical Society, 7400 Woodlawn Ave. NE, Seattle, WA 98115, (206) 483-2991, exists for the preservation of Swedish-Finnish heritage, especially that of the Pacific Northwest.

Emigration from the Swedish-speaking section of Finland to North America began in earnest around 1870. The majority of these so-called "Finlandssvenskar" settled in the northern areas of the U.S., and a large population settled in the state of Washington. An archive has been established for the collection of newspapers, genealogies, histories, photographs, printed matter and other memorabilia. If you are of Swedish or Finnish descent, perhaps a visit to the Swedish Finn Historical Society in Seattle should be part of your summer travel plans.

Welsh ancestry: If you are interested in genealogy and have Welsh roots, then you might be interested in linking with others of similar background and interest. The Welsh-American Genealogical Society (WAGS) was formed in 1990 and is based in Poultney, VT. This is a nonprofit organization that has big plans to help folks with Welsh ancestry. So far, it has begun publishing a quarterly newsletter that will carry Welsh-related queries. Membership is $10.00 per year, and you may write directly to WAGS, RR No. 2, Box 516, Lewis Road, Poultney, VT 05764-9317.

Map guide reissued: You cannot effectively do American research without using Bill Dollarhide and William Thorndale's *Map Guide to the U.S. Federal Census, 1790-1920.* This 445-page book was recently reissued in paperback, costing much less, so now all researchers can afford a copy.

The *Map Guide* has a history of census growth, an explanation of the technical facts about each census, an essay on the sources available for identifying each state's old county lines, and a map of the state for each census year showing how the county boundaries have shifted.

You can use this fine research aid at any area genealogical library, but if you would like your own copy, if may be ordered from Genealogical Publishing Co. for $39.95; call 800-727-6687. Individual state packets may be ordered from American Genealogical Lending Library for $5.95 each; call 800-760-AGLL.

NORTH CAROLINA IS TOUGH ON RESEARCHERS

Dr. George Schweitzer, nationally known speaker and author, says that North Carolina is the toughest state in which to do research.

He gives the following reasons:

North Carolina had no major immigrant ports; in fact, her treacherous coastline prevented ships from coming close.

The majority of people who settled in North Carolina trickled down the valleys from the north.

The folks in North Carolina became Baptist very early, and early frontier Baptist churches kept very poor records.

The last reason Dr. Schweitzer gives is the most revealing. "Scotch-Irish came in droves to North Carolina, and these stubborn, hard-driving people had little regard for the law and little use for registering their affairs with the law."

He sums up his remarks by saying that if you could do successful ancestor-finding in North Carolina, you could do it anywhere.

His book, *North Carolina Genealogical Research*, is a 190-page guide to researching in this difficult state.

The book includes chapters on types of records, record locations, and county listings of records available. You may order this $12.00 book postpaid, from the author at 407 Ascot Ct., Knoxville, TN 37923-5807.

Still on the topic of North Carolina research, you'll be happy to learn that the Family History Library has published a research outline for North Carolina.

This 11-page booklet lists the addresses for the major libraries and archives of this state, a bibliography of books on the history of North Carolina, cemetery records and church records.

In short, you'll learn about everything you'll need to know about beginning your research in the Tar Heel State. (This booklet is part of a series of research outlines covering all the states, and may be ordered by sending $1.00 for two states to the Family History Library, 35 N. West Temple Street, Salt Lake City, UT 84150.)

North Carolina Wills: A Testator Index, 1665-1900, by Thornton W. Mitchell, is a newly published index to more than 75,000 people who died and left wills in North Carolina between 1665 and 1900.

This book will be a valuable research aid in North Carolina, because ordinarily the researcher would have to check the files of over 100 counties for their ancestor's name, and here is an alphabetical listing of all names from those counties.

This book may be ordered from Genealogical Publishing Co. for $49.50; call 800-727-6687. (Perhaps this would be a good book for your genealogical society to purchase with some acquisitions money? Let your society know you would like this book.)

Family Bibles: If you know of a family Bible, either of your own family's or that of a friend or neighbor, would you consider giving a copy of the information pages to the genealogical society? Many genealogical societies are seeking to collect Bible records with an eye toward publishing the information, and thus making the information available to other genealogists.

These societies do not want your Bibles; please send photocopied, written or typed copies of the family information, usually found in the center pages of the Bible.

Please include the publishing company for the Bible, and the publishing date. (The publishing date is important. If the Bible was printed in 1922, and the family information dates back to 1889, then it is obvious that the old info was recopied into the newer Bible.)

I know that this is a valuable thing to do. I know that a Potter family Bible of mine was in Latah County in Idaho in 1922 — where is it now? I wish whoever has it would turn in a photocopy of the family pages, and hopefully I'd eventually find that information.

TODAY'S TIP: Have ancestry in Louisiana? Try sending a query to the "Louisiana Ancestors" column in *The Times-Picayune,* 3800 Howard Ave., New Orleans, LA 70140.

Queries are free, and can be any length, but must have a Louisiana connection by heritage or residence, says columnist Damon Veach.

Harry Wrangham of Kennewick sent me a December 1992 column, and it gives the address for the Louisiana Genealogical and Historical Society as P.O. Box 3454, Baton Rouge, LA 70821-3454. You might also write to them with your Louisiana ancestor problem.

DATA MAY HELP YOU FIND GERMANIC ANCESTORS

Henry Z. Jones Jr. has spent years pursuing the 847 families that in 1710 left the Palatine area of what was to become Germany to immigrate to England, Ireland and colonial America. In seminars all over the United States, Hank tells eager groups all about this project and why his findings are important to anybody having Germanic ancestors who came to America before the Revolutionary War.

Most of the folks in the large audiences don't realize, but Hank explains that while there were 847 families that emigrated from the Palatine area, often any Germanic immigrant of the colonial period was said to be a "Palatine." We learned that his series of books are a wonderful database of names, and that if we have German roots dating back to before 1776, we should check them.

Check your local library for these books: *The Palatine Families of New York, More Palatine Families* and *The Palatine Families of Ireland.*

Genealogical Publishing Co. Inc. has published four volumes of "German Immigrants Lists of Passengers Bound from Bremen to New York," covering the years of 1847 to 1871, and they are available in many genealogical libraries. These books represent the reconstructed passenger lists made from the arrival lists in New York, as the original emigration lists housed in Bremen were destroyed by the bombings in WWII. The four volumes provide the place of origin of over 100,000 immigrants. The books cost about $23.00 each and can be ordered from GPC at 800-296-6687.

Another new source of help for finding those German ancestors is a compilation by Barbara Manning: She wrote me that her book, *Genealogical Abstracts from Newspapers of the German Reformed Church, 1830-1839,* is a collection of all kinds of vital records information and news tidbits about German families in Pennsylvania, Maryland, Ohio, New York, Virginia, the Carolinas, Illinois and Indiana. Barbara also said that these newspapers were not microfilmed or previously indexed, and so were virtually impossible to access. Her book costs $27.50, plus shipping, and is available from Heritage Books Inc. at 800-398-7709.

While we're on the subject of German ancestors, I recently read in a ten-year-old *Christmas Genealogical Society Quarterly* an explanation of the difference between High and Low German.

The article said that about the eighth century, there was a language break into High and Low dialects, "a difference in the sounds of the consonants." It isn't known why this happened, except that it seems related to geography. Low German is spoken in northern Germany where the terrain is very flat. In the mountainous parts of southern Germany, High German is spoken. "There is a theory that people of a mountainous area have to breathe harder; therefore, a stronger pronunciation. Thus, High German."

Martin Luther took the dialect of an area of east-central Germany for his translation of the Bible, and so from him came a "Middle" German dialect, not so far from either High or Low, but one that everyone could understand. This "Middle" German became the universal written language, which people studied and understood, even though they spoke in a different dialect. Is this so? I'm not sure. I'm just reporting something.

TODAY'S LAUGH: Recipe for Genealogy Stew: Take 1 curious beginner. Add 1 age discrepancy, 1 unreadable microfilm, and 1 census record written in disappearing ink. Fold in 1 ton of correspondence. Simmer while awaiting answers. That's enough to make any genealogist stew!!

WWI DRAFT CARDS ARE AVAILABLE ON MICROFILM

If your male ancestor was born between June 6, 1886, and June 5, 1896, he was between 21 and 30 on Tuesday, June 5, 1917, and according to a newly passed law, had to register for the draft. Only those persons already serving in the military were exempt from registration. That day, June 5, 1917, was declared a national holiday! The registration was so effective that by June 16, 1917, some 10 million men were recorded. In subsequent phases of the World War I draft registration the rules and questions were changed somewhat, and by the waning years of the war the draft was conducted on a regular quarterly basis. By the end of WWI, a total of 24 million men had been recorded, including all men (whether native born or alien) between the ages of 18 and 45.

Not all of the men who registered actually served in the military; not all men who served in the military registered for the draft. The draft cards are not military service records; they have information about a person's military service. About 4.8 million men actually served in the U.S. armed forces between April 1917 and November 1918.

The project of microfilming these 24 million cards has recently been completed. The films are available through the Family History Centers, arranged by states and counties, and then alphabetically by surname. To look for your ancestor in these WWI draft registration cards, you must know at least the state where he was living when he registered. It would narrow your search considerably if you knew the county, too. If you'd like to use these records, ask for help ordering the right microfilm at your nearest Family History Center.

Another new database of names is also available through the Family History Centers. The Chicago and Cook County Voting Registers for the years 1888, 1890 and 1892 were recently discovered, microfilmed and are now available for genealogists to use. Here's the story:

The record series, "Record and Index of Persons Registered and of Poll List of Voters," was created and maintained by the Board of Election Commissioners in Chicago. The series was produced to comply with an 1885 Illinois law requiring registration of voters in each precinct some four weeks prior to elections. In 1888,1890 and 1892, unknown persons at the Chicago Board of Elections collated these precinct lists, thereby creating a complete alphabetical listing of every registered voter in Chicago. These lists of voters form a unique source of information and differ greatly from the Chicago city directories of this period. They show 133,236 voters in 1888; over 138,000 in 1890; and approximately 276,300 in 1892. The record shows the voter's address, term of residence, country of birth, whether naturalized or not, and if so the court and date in which the papers were obtained.

These records were discovered in the Voters' Registration Department nearly 10 years ago by Tom Burke who was doing some genealogical research. In a back room, high on a shelf, he noticed a stack of 25 old books. The attendant did not know what they were and gave Burke permission to get them down. One can only imagine his amazement and the thrill of the discovery of such an unknown source. After months of trying to get the records available for researchers, they were finally microfilmed by the Illinois Regional Archives Depository (IRAD), and made available to all researchers.

In 1992, these microfilms became available through the Family History Centers. If you're seeking a "lost" ancestor in the

1888 to 1892 time period in Chicago, here might be a new place for you to look.

Boundary history: The busy genealogists up in Boundary County, ID, have completed their project of producing the *History of Boundary County, Idaho,* listing 1,335 family histories. The book costs $45.00 and may be ordered from Boundary County History Book, P.O. Box 808, Bonners Ferry, ID 83805.

TODAY'S TRIVIA: Did you know about these Washington towns that had their names changed? Virginia City became Brewster. Poulsbo means Paul's Place in Norwegian. Sidney was renamed Port Orchard. Neppel was founded in 1910, but was renamed Moses Lake in 1938 in honor of Chief Moses. Park Place is now the city of Monroe, named after President James Monroe in 1891. Remember that when you are researching your pioneer Washington ancestors, and realize that similar naming stories exist for all states.

EUROPEAN DESCENT?
HAMBURG LISTS MIGHT BE OF HELP

What are the Hamburg passenger lists? Would they be of help to you in your genealogical research? The answer is probably yes if you had ancestors who left from the port of Hamburg during the 100 years of emigration activity.

The Hamburg passenger lists contain the names of millions of Europeans who emigrated through the port of Hamburg between 1830 and 1934 (except 1915 to 1919, during World War I). Nearly one-third of the people who emigrated from central and eastern Europe during this time are included on these lists. If you have ancestors who emigrated from these areas, the Hamburg passenger lists could provide important genealogical information about them, including their hometowns. Extensive indexes make these records easier to use than most other passenger lists and emigration records.

The Hamburg passenger lists are made up of two sections. The Direct Lists show passengers who left Hamburg and sailed directly to their destination without stopping at other European ports. The Indirect Lists show passengers who stopped at another European port before sailing to their final destination. (About 20 percent of the immigrants leaving Europe took indirect routes.)

The Hamburg passenger lists and indexes are on 486 rolls of microfilm available through the Family History Center. To find film numbers, search the Locality section of the library catalog under GERMANY, HAMBURG, HAMBURG-EMIGRATION AND IMMIGRATION. If you are using the compact disc version of the catalog, select the computer number search and enter 11064. For more information on the Hamburg passenger lists and how to use them, have the Family History Center order a special microfiche for you. Fiche No. 6000034 will give you pages of useful information on this topic.

NEW BOOKS: Ed Peters of Manson, WA, has compiled *Some Descendants of Michael Peters.* This 600-page book (of which 90 are index pages) is done in the Modified Register System on computer, and begins with Michael Peters, who died in 1847 in Franklin County, VA, and his wife Hannah Dillinan. With their five children, the family migrated from Virginia into the Midwest, then south to Texas, north to Canada and some to Washington state. Ed was born in Wenatchee. The book's most impressive feature is the beautiful 1917 photo of a 50th wedding anniversary family group, and all the faces are identified. If you are of this family, and would like to order this $40.00 book, write to Ed Peters, Rt. 1, Box 432, Manson, WA 98831.

Richard Gilberg of Port Angeles has compiled *Charles Yerkes Supplee, His Ancestors and His Descendants.* This 27-page book begins with Andris Souplis who was born in 1634 in France and died in 1726 in Philadelphia. His son Andrew took the surname spelling of Supplee, and eventually merged with the Yerkes family of Pennsylvania. In the foreword, Richard calls for reader comments or suggestions. Contact him at 1311 Second St., Port Angeles, WA 98363. My good friend Betty Engelbart of the Heart of America Genealogical Society sent me a copy of their new book, *Death Records of Kansas City, Missouri, Book A, 3 Aug 1874 to 31 Jul 1889.* The society has spent the last three years abstracting the death records and getting them ready to publish. This book contains 14,470 death records! The information was taken from a microfilm of which only three copies are known to exist, so this group has performed a wonderful act of service for the rest of us. For a copy, send $18.00 to the H.A.G.S., c/o Kansas City Public Library, 311 E. 12th, Kansas City, MO 64106-2412.

TODAY'S TIP: *Reunions*, the magazine, offers to help you with your family reunion planning. If you will register your reunion with them, they will announce the big event in an upcoming issue of the magazine for free. This magazine is full of reunion helps and ideas, and not just for family reunions. Military, school and adoption reunions are featured. For more information on this fine publication, write to them at P.O. Box 11727 Milwaukee, WI 53211-0727, or call 414-263-4567.

TODAY'S LAUGH: Newspaper ad: "Beware of bargains in parachutes, life preservers, fire extinguishers, brain surgery and genealogical research!"

COURTHOUSE RECORDS ARE A REAL TREASURE

Last May, JoAnn Gemmrig and I spent an entire morning in the records vault of the Union County Courthouse in La Grande, OR. And it was a glorious experience, as any real genealogist would agree. JoAnn was looking for some particular ancestors; I was just poking around and having fun.

Neophytes would not believe what you'd find in the vault of the courthouse. Besides books and books and BOOKS, I found one very dusty cupboard containing items tagged as evidence in trials of decades ago. One item was a corked bottle clearly labeled with the skull and crossbones and a "POISON" warning. What a story that bottle might tell!

We approached clerks in the Union County Courthouse with a request to look at their marriage index records. Without hesitation, the smiling clerks showed us to the vault ("duck your heads here") and said we could have all the time we wanted. (I begged them not to shut the huge steel door on us as our lunch was out in the car.) Within minutes, JoAnn had found the large leather-bound marriage register containing the marriage documentation for her great-grandparents.

She was even more buoyant than usual because she had written twice for this record with negative results.

I confess to my readers that this was the first time I'd really spent more than 30 minutes in a courthouse, and I quickly became fascinated by the enormous variety of records that were carefully kept there. There were registers containing the expected records of marriage, probate, wills, deeds, mortgages and naturalizations. But there was an entire wall of little metal drawers containing probate *packets*, string-tied bundles of papers, each the final business for a life spent on earth. Now I finally understood why probate packets are never microfilmed. Let me list some of the other records that I found:

- Register of Scalp Bounty Claims (not people scalps, but cougars and coyotes)
- Records of Marks and Brands; Records of Stallion Licenses
- Records of the Paupers and Insane; Records of Road Viewers
- Judgment Docket Books; Books of Trial Testimonies
- Coroner's Inquest Records; Bills of Sale; Victory Tax Records
- Military Records (discharge certificates); County Military Lists
- Juvenile Court Records; Hospital Lien Records; Chiropractic Records
- Records of Dentists Certificates; Records of Nurses Licenses
- Optometry Records; Adoption Registers; Dog License Register
- Records of Water Rights; Guardianship Records
- Defendant and Plaintiff Indexes to Court Trail Records
- Sheriff's Attachment Records; County and Federal Tax Lien Records
- Miners' Claims Records; Estray Records; Dance Permit Registers

I kept thinking, as my arms ached and my hands turned black from lifting down and putting back all those "dirty old books;" was this a typical courthouse? And this was little, rural Union County, OR. Think what the King County, WA, Courthouse must be like! (I'll never find out: larger courthouses do not let folks just roam at large among the precious records, and that's OK.)

JoAnn and I both made some copies. Putting half of a 30-pound, 11-by-18-inch book on a copy machine is no joke. But she gathered ancestors and I gathered copies to illustrate my lessons.

Knowing the policy in most courthouses, we both fully expected to be charged $1.00 per copy and while ready to do so, cringed at the thought. With a straight face, the clerk said that on Wednesdays the fee was $5.00 per copy; I'm sure she said that just to watch our faces. We were charged only 25 cents per copy and went out to dinner with our savings.

A valuable lesson was learned by both of us that day. Nothing substitutes for going in person to a courthouse.

You can write until you run out of ink, and may repeatedly get a negative answer. This is not because the clerks hate genealogists (although some do and deservedly so), but because they are busy eight hours a day processing current records. Their demanding jobs leave little time to answer letters.

While most will do their best, I could see for myself that there was no way a clerk could check all those different county records for mention of my ancestor.

So if you are really stuck, and really need need help in a particular county, take a vacation and go in person. Or hire a local agent (a fancy term meaning local genealogist) to go in your place. There is no other way.

PINPOINT PARTICULARS BEFORE SEARCH STARTS

The subject of "immigration," as related to genealogy, is vast. It is too broad a topic to be dealt with adequately in an all-day seminar, much less one workshop session, and certainly too big for one newspaper column. The subject easily breaks down into six areas, and any of these more-defined topics can be studied as the need arises. When you are ready to begin researching your immigrant ancestor, ask yourself which of these six areas you want to know more about.

1. Do you want to know what caused your ancestor to emigrate?

2. Do you want to know more about the conditions or particulars of the voyage or journey?

3. Do you want to locate your ancestor on a passenger list?

4. Do you want to find his naturalization and citizenship papers?

5. Do you want to learn how and why he migrated through America after arriving?

6. Do you want to study the reasons why his name has changed?

Addressing No. 1, the history of the country must be studied to learn why your ancestor emigrated. Was it the potato famine in Ireland? Was it because of military conscription in Germany? Was it that he was driven out because of his religious beliefs? All of this can be learned from history books.

To learn more about the voyage, I recommend *Going To America,* by Terry Coleman. Published in 1987 by Genealogical Publishing Co. (GPC), this book zeroes in on the grim story of the British and Irish immigrants who came between 1846 and 1855.

But to me the book would apply to all ocean-crossing immigrants, because the author vividly describes the conditions on the ships during the long voyages. (And they weren't pretty; we should be ever thankful that we weren't the ones who had to blaze the trail to America.)

Do you want to locate your ancestor on a passenger list? This is the hardest one; it can be a daunting task to find your family names out of millions of family names on a passenger list. I've read that you can find your name only if you know the port, the arrival date and the ship. (Of course, if you knew that you wouldn't be looking, right?)

To find those names, you'll have to learn about passenger arrival records, ships and prominent ports. *American Passenger Arrival Records,* by Michael Tepper is the definitive work on American ships' passenger lists, and is a splendid history and guide. This book, more than any other, will teach you the skills necessary to tackle those millions of names.

Another fun book is *Ships of Our Ancestors,* by Michael Anuta. This book shows pictures of the nearly 900 steamships that carried our ancestors across the Atlantic. How could the biography of our immigrant ancestor be complete without a picture of the ship on which he came?

Do you want to find his naturalization and citizenship papers? I recommend two books to teach you the basics of that topic. *American Naturalization Processes and Procedures, 1790-1985,* by John Newman explains all the steps, and shows all the forms, that your ancestor had to deal with in the process of becoming a citizen of his new homeland. Another source would be *Locating Your Immigrant Ancestor,* by James and Lila Neagles. This little book explains where all these papers may be found, and shows by a graph what records still exist in the counties.

(In 1996, Christina K. Schaefer compiled a *Guide to Naturalization Records of the United States.* Available from GPC for $25.00, plus postage and handling, this book promises to become "the" guide for this subject.)

Would you like to learn how and why he moved from the Atlantic port city to Indiana or Washington or Canada where he settled? This information can often be found in family histories, but failing that, you can try area histories.

Those local histories might not mention your ancestor specifically, but will explain when and why certain ethnic groups came to that area.

Another great source to answer this question is to read good-quality American history novels. Allen Eckert has written many superlative novels about the settling of early America. Vilhelm Moberg's *The Emigrants*, about Norwegian immigrants to Minnesota, was so good a movie was made from the story. Anya Seton's *The Winthrop Woman* tells about the Puritan Winthrop colony in colonial Massachusetts. I could fill this paper with a list! Ask your public librarian to help you find good novels written about your ancestor's place and time in history.

Many of the books mentioned above can be found in your local genealogical collection, and most can be ordered from GPC by calling 800-296-6687. If you'd like to know more about a certain book, call GPC and ask for a flier.

Civil War Sites Are Rich With Information

While it is winter here in the Pacific Northwest, our thoughts turn to next summer's vacation. For genealogists, our thoughts often turn to including Civil War sites in our vacation plans. The reason for that is that 33 million Americans fought in the Civil War, and many family historians count one of these veterans in their family tree. If you are planning to visit a Civil War site next summer, let me share some ideas with you.

While the Civil War was fought in more than 10,000 places, most sites have been lost to time and circumstance, and many that survive are privately owned. Yet scores of sites are accessible, including 31 battlefields and related sites administered by the National Parks Service. An article by Robert A. Webb, "Visiting Sites of the Civil War," was published in the March/April 1992 issue of *National Parks* magazine. This article is a great overview of how to best prepare for a visit to a Civil War site.

Before you go, write to the Office of Public Information, National Parks Service, Washington, DC, 20240, for a free battlefield tour map and brochure. Call the battlefield park for information on special events that will be scheduled during your visit. Read about the battle and the broader context — the political situation and the personalities involved.

When you arrive, stop first at the visitors center to become oriented to the land and the battle. Be sure sure to see the orientation film if there is one. Visit the bookstore for books and information on the site and the Civil War in general (more than 50,000 volumes have been written about this conflict).

Plan to visit the national cemetery if there is one at the park; plan to drive or walk around the park early in the morning trying to imagine the scenes of 130 years ago.

The article reminds readers that the end of the park visit may be only the beginning of your search for an ancestor who fought at one of the battlefield sites. Organize your materials, visit nearby libraries, and learn more about this part of U.S. history and your ancestor's involvement.

More detailed information is available in a brochure, "Visiting Civil War Battlefields: How to Have a Quality Experience," which you may have for free by writing to Park Education Center, NPCA, 1776 Massachusetts Ave., NW, Washington, DC, 20036.

Perhaps when you visit a Civil War battlefield administered by the National Parks System next summer, you will want to use the new "Civil War Soldiers System." This is a computerized database containing very basic facts about soldiers who served on both sides during the Civil War. The facts about these soldiers were entered from records that are indexed and will lead you to hundreds of other documents about Union and Confederate soldiers maintained by the National Archives and Records Administration.

When you visit the battlefield park, you will be able to use a computer to discover if your ancestor fought at that (or any other) battlefield. You may actually do the typing, or in some cases, a park interpreter may operate the system. The system is easy to operate and requires no special computer knowledge.

Eventually the system will be expanded to provide all sorts of other information on "your" soldier, such as regimental histories, descriptions of battles, and burial locations.

This project is being accomplished with the cooperation of the National Park Service, the Federation of Genealogical Societies, and the Genealogical Society of Utah. This team has had to develop the software necessary for the project, obtain the films of the indexes, and do the labor of data entry.

Volunteers are needed to help in this project by doing data entry. Much of the work is being done at special locations around the country (National Archive branches), but data may also be entered on IBM-compatible home computers. If you would like information on how you can volunteer to help with the Civil War

Soldiers Index, write to that designation, P.O. Box 3385, Salt Lake City, UT 84110-3385.

TODAY'S THOUGHT: How did this happen? In the Walla Walla County, WA, Courthouse, I found a marriage certificate dated April 5,1910, for Matthew Brown, a Salvation Army officer from Austin, Texas, and Helen Lindsay from Denver, CO. How did they come from so far away to marry in Washington? And how will descendants ever find the record of their marriage?

HOBBY OF GENEALOGY TRAVELS WELL

Many genealogists who live in the northern regions of the United States are also winter snowbirds, escaping wintry places for sunny places. Whether they go for a few days, weeks or months, seasoned snowbirds take their favorite hobby with them and seek out genealogical libraries wherever they happen to spend the winter. Fledgling snowbirds are eager for guidance — "Is there a genealogy library in Yuma? Mesa? Bullhead City? If we stop off in Salt Lake, what can I accomplish there?" I have been asked these questions numerous times, and a letter from Patricia Rice of Almira, WA, finally prompted this column.

Pat wrote, "My husband and I usually go to Arizona for some time during the winter, and we were thinking of stopping in Salt Lake for a couple of days. Here's where we need help. We've never been to the library there before and imagine it will be quite overwhelming. What would you tell the first-time user to do to be prepared? What should we not forget? Should we sit through their introduction to the library?"

Yes, first-timers to the Family History Library in Salt Lake City should take advantage of the brief introduction. Volunteers stand ready at all hours that the library is open to introduce visitors to this four-floor library. How else will you know where the British Isles collection is? The books on Missouri? The census indexes and films? The snack room? The restrooms?

The very best thing you can do before you go to Salt Lake is to visit the Family History Center nearest you. These are small, local branch libraries of the Family History Library. The exact same computer program is used in both places, so you can learn FamilySearch at your local branch and then use it there.

FamilySearch consists of two main divisions: databases of previous research and the card catalog which will guide you to original documents. You do not need to go to Salt Lake to check for your family names in the many different databases of FamilySearch (like the Ancestral File and IGI), but many of the items listed in the card catalog that you will want to look at can only be used in Salt Lake, i.e., they are not microfilmed. These would be things like cemetery records, probate records and family histories. Whether at your summer home or winter home, you must learn how to use this *easy* computer program to take full advantage of all the Family History Library has to offer. So before you fly south for the winter, spend some time in your nearby Family History Center.

When you go to Salt Lake, or to Arizona, take only what you need. Everything should fit into a three-ring notebook; put all your information on pedigree charts and family group sheets in this notebook. Do not take your documents or photographs. A waist pouch, or fanny pack, is the safest way to keep your valuables with you, and don't forget a roll of dimes for the copiers.

If you are not stopping off in Salt Lake, but are heading straight south, then plan to visit the Family History Center wherever you are spending the winter. These centers are scattered all over! Ask your neighbors where the nearest one is — chances are they're into genealogy, too. If they don't know, ask someone at the local public library. You can look for your ancestors in the FamilySearch databases in any Family History Center. Some centers have large book collections, too. So if you are a snowbird and a genealogist, you can take your favorite hobby with you.

TODAY'S TRIVIA: The New York Municipal Archives has 10 volumes of records from 1859 to 1894 titled "Bodies in Transit." These are the names of deceased persons whose remains arrived in Manhattan by ship, train and local ferry. A law required their registration to prevent communicable diseases. Data on the forms included date of arrival in New York, name, age, nativity, place and date of death, disease, place of interment, and name and address of the person having charge of the body. Write to the New York Municipal Archives at 31 Chambers St., Room 103, New York, NY 10007. Don't forget your stamped, self-addressed envelope.

The Indiana State Library's Genealogy Division has completed an index to Indiana marriages through 1850. The file is alphabetically arranged by bride and groom and gives date and county of the marriage. The library staff will search the index only if specific information is provided (full names, and if a common surname, include the county). Write to: Genealogy Division, Indiana State Library, 140 N. State St., Indianapolis, IN 46204.

Pennsylvania County maps which include cemetery locations may be obtained by writing to: Pennsylvania D.O.T., Public Sales Section, P.O. Box 134, Middletown, PA 17057. Specify the name of the county, and ask for General Highway Service Map No. 10.

In March 1990, the Ellen Payne Odom Genealogical Library opened in Georgia. This library expects to be a major repository for Scottish clan records in the U.S. The address is: P.O. Box 1110, Moultrie, GA 31776. It offers a nice newsletter full of clan "doings," genealogical tidbits and queries. The newsletter is free, but postage donations are appreciated.

Barbara Van DePete has access to an index for the 1910 census of Montana, but only for counties beginning with letters A-L. If you are searching in those counties, send $1.00 and an SASE to Barbara at 8430 Highway 2 West, Havre, MT 59501. Also, the Havre-Hill County Library at 402 Third St., Havre, MT 59501, houses the books of the Fort Assiniboine Genealogy Society. They will check their genealogy holdings and make two copies if you'll send $1.00 and an SASE to them.

LAND RECORDS CAN AID GENEALOGISTS

Bill Dollarhide, co-author of the *Map Guide to the U.S. Federal Censuses, 1790-1920,* is an expert on American land records, and a crackerjack genealogist. He began publishing the new *Genealogy Bulletin,* a bi-monthly bulletin showcasing the Dollarhide Systems and always carrying several helpful articles. Bulletin No. 19 had a great explanation of the BLM records project, and I quote from that article here. If you'd like to subscribe to the *Genealogy Bulletin,* now published by American Genealogical Lending Library, call 800-760-AGLL.

"The Eastern State Branch of the Bureau of Government Land Office's Automated Records Project is aimed at electronically scanning the images of original land patents into a computer form, and at the same time providing an index to the names of every patentee (the person to whom the patent was issued).

"A patent is the document issued by the old Government Land Office to an individual purchasing land from the federal government in the public domain states, representing the first transfer of land by the U.S. government to a private party.

"The Eastern States Office of the BLM is the largest of several branches, and covers the 13 public domain states of Alabama, Arkansas, Florida, Illinois, Iowa, Louisiana, Michigan, Minnesota, Mississippi, Missouri, Ohio and Wisconsin.

"As of June 1993, eight of the 13 states have a completed computerized index to every patent issued (by name of the person buying land), and it is now possible to receive a facsimile copy of GLO land patents issued in Arkansas, Florida, Louisiana, Michigan, Minnesota, Mississippi, Ohio and Wisconsin.

"If you had an ancestor who was an early settler in one of these eight states, the chances are very good that he took out an original entry of land, which means that a copy of the patent is available.

"The patent shows the name of the patentee, date of the sale, the GLO field office which issued it, and a description of the property. A copy of a patent may also give you an actual signature of the president of the U.S. prior to about 1850, and a signature of an assistant signing for the president thereafter.

"For genealogists, the patent is the first step in finding more records relating to the land transaction. The patent gives a 'file number' for the transaction which is very important to learn since other papers that were associated with the land purchase are now stored in the Suitland Branch of the National Archives, and these 'Land Entry Files' may contain significant genealogical information. For decades, it has been a difficult task to access the Land Entry Files without knowing the file number. Having a copy of the patent your ancestor received is an important historical document, but the real genealogical information is sitting in a different repository.

"With the patentee's name, place of sale, type of sale, and the file number (all items you can get from the patent), you can write to the Suitland Branch of the National Archives and request copies of the 'Land Entry Files.' In most cases, the land entry files will reveal important genealogical clues, such as dates, names, signatures, receipts, etc., but in some cases, you may be fortunate to learn that your ancestor mailed in a copy of his marriage certificate (which he never got back), a copy of a naturalization certificate, or even a page from a family Bible. All these documents were submitted by the applicant as proof of marriage or citizenship, and are part of the Land Entry Files.

"To obtain a copy of a land patent from one of the eight indexed states, you now only need to provide the patentee's name. For the yet-to-be-indexed states of Alabama, Missouri, Iowa, Illinois or Indiana, you need to provide the person's name, along with an exact range/township property description.

"Before you can obtain copies of the patents, you need to establish an 'account' with the BLM by sending a check for $25.00 (payable to 'BLM'). The fee ranges from $4.00 to $20.00 for most searches, depending on the number of names involved, and any money left over will be refunded. Write to the Department of Interior, Bureau of Land Management, Eastern States, 7450 Boston Blvd., Springfield VA 22153.

"To obtain copies of Land Entry Files, write to: Suitland Reference Branch (NNRR), Textual Reference Division, National Archives and Records Administration, Washington, DC 20409. Send a request letter along with a copy of the patent. They will quote you a price."

(For an update on this project and the newest and easiest way to access these land records, I recommend reading *Land and Property Research In The United States*, by E. Wade Hone, published in 1997 by Ancestry.)

TODAY'S TRIVIA: May I close the year by offering a poem by Johann Long, as found in *The Sunny Side of Genealogy*, by Fonda Baselt:

Another year of climbing the genealogy tree.
I've looked under the leaves and what do I see?
You coming up, while I'm going down,
We compare notes on what we have found.
At times it's not much, just one name or two,
It's better than nothing, I know that is true.
Still we search on, through films and a book,
Hoping our family's in the next one we look.
May next year be fruitful, our lost one we find,
And soon all our families will be intertwined.
I ask Santa to send us to all the right places,
To guide us and lead us to see smiling faces.
May each of you find your lost pioneer,
I wish you Merry Christmas and a Happy New Year!

1994

MOTIVES BEHIND GENEALOGY RUN DEEP

In this first column of a new year, I'd like to present some thoughts to you penned by Carolyn J. Nell, president of the National Genealogical Society. In a recent *NGS Quarterly* article, Carolyn asked the questions that most genealogists ask at some time or another. "What's in it for me? Why do I do genealogy? Why should genealogy be kept alive? What is the value of doing genealogy?" These are valid questions, and a great New Year's idea for discussion.

Here are the thoughts that Carolyn included in the article to address those questions:

- To gain knowledge, have fun, and meet other people with similar interests.
- To satisfy an inherent desire to answer the questions, "Who am I?" and, "Where did I come from?"
- To establish the roots of family history and to create a sense of personal pride and understanding.
- To bridge generation gaps through communication and exploration.
- To educate children by bringing history to life (genealogy being taught in the schools).
- To extend and connect family units that have been fragmented and separated by a mobile society.
- To leave a family history legacy for future generations.

I have often asked myself, why I do genealogy. How did this obsession begin? As I've talked with other genealogists, they echo the same thoughts. The answer can be given in a few words. "Everybody has a family, and every family has a history." I do genealogy because I have always been fascinated by history, especially American history, and recognized very early that it was my ancestors who helped make that history. I do genealogy because I remember the stories of my grandmother Clara, whose parents were born in Germany, and who came to Illinois during

Civil War times. I do genealogy because I discovered that one ancestor was William Bradford, who came on the *Mayflower*. I do genealogy because I cannot find out where Charles Robert Phillips came from in Georgia!

Perhaps Alex Haley said it best in a *Readers Digest* article back in May, 1977. He said, "In all of us there is a hunger, marrow-deep, to know our heritage — to know who we are and where we have come from. The whole business of family quest...is a great common denominator, a leveler in which a king is no more than a peasant. It reaches into something subliminal in people, and I have been most astonished that the response to it transcends all lines — color lines, age lines and ethnic lines. To me (this)...can be explained only by something that is beyond ordinary comprehension, something spiritual. We all have lineage and forefathers." I would add to his words that to search for one's forefathers and lineage is akin to a spiritual quest for many genealogists.

Outwardly, doing genealogy is putting names and dates on paper, visiting libraries and attending workshops and meetings. But really "doing" genealogy is trying to relive your ancestor's life, focusing your thoughts on his life to learn or imagine how his life and times really were. It is visiting the places where he worked and lived, and trying to "hear the ghosts." And the turning of our hearts and minds to our forefathers is a very good thing for us individually and as a people. I cannot think of another "hobby," for so the world deems it, that is as soul-satisfying as doing genealogy and establishing connections to those who made us possible.

I invite you all into membership with your local genealogical society. I invite you all to visit your nearby Family History Center. Meet with and begin learning genealogy from others of like mind. You will quickly find, as millions of others have, that doing genealogy is an infectious business; like eating popcorn, once you start, you will never want to stop!

TODAY'S THOUGHT: Charles Osgood, TV commentator, has said, "If you wish to travel back in time, music is the surest and most gentle of all roads."

ANCIENT PEOPLES PRACTICED GENEALOGY

Ever thought much about the history of our favorite hobby, genealogy? In one way or another, and for one reason or another, people through the ages have been keeping a record of their forefathers.

The Egyptians carefully recorded pharaohs into dynasties. King Tut was a ruler in the 18th Dynasty. The Assyrians, who dominated the 7th and 8th centuries in the Mideast, kept records on clay tablets. Some 20,000 of these tablets were discovered in the 1840s. The Bible preserves many genealogies, including two of Jesus Christ (which differ from each other!). The Greek and Roman peoples did genealogy to "prove" their descent from a particular god, and to distinguish themselves as patricians. The Chinese actively worshipped their ancestors, so they had to keep track of who they were. Some Chinese genealogies go back thousands of years. The Maori people can repeat their pedigree back to the time they first arrived in New Zealand. The ancient Inca peoples kept picture genealogies. The Native Americans of the Pacific and Canadian coasts carved totem poles which were visual genealogies. Admittedly, many records kept were of the ruling class and not the average folks. But the principle of genealogy was there.

During the Middle Ages, questions of kinship and descent became of great political importance. This was especially so when the hereditary transmission of kingdoms and fiefs became established. Many privileges of the nobility and gentry depended on birth. A candidate for knighthood had to furnish proof of ancient nobility. During this period, a hereditary system of personal recognition developed. This system, employing symbols on a shield, developed among nobles in the 12th century and was called heraldry. Highly ranked persons wanted to be able to be recognized, even with their helmet visors down.

In 1538, genealogy records began to be kept in England, thanks to King Henry VIII. It was during his reign that the law was passed requiring ministers to keep records of christenings, marriages and burials from their parishes. These church records were the only "genealogy" records kept until 1836, when a civil law was passed in England making it compulsory for all births, marriages, and deaths to be recorded and provided central repositories where these records would be kept.

The American Revolution in 1776 signaled that the colonies wanted to break away from England to become their own country, but from a genealogical standpoint the new nation did not want to entirely disregard its roots. The New England Historic Genealogical Society was formed in Boston in 1845. Interestingly enough, it was some years later that the first genealogical society in England appeared.

The very word "genealogy" comes from two root words. "Genos" means family, and "logos" means books or records, in a loose translation. Isn't it grand to know that you are engaged in a pursuit that has been going on nearly since our civilization began?

If you think that your genealogy "plugs in" to the early and royal lineages of England, then you might be interested in these books from Genealogical Publishing Co. Call them at 800-296-6687 if you would like a descriptive flier on any of the titles listed below.

Royalty for Commoners, The Complete Known Lineage of John of Gaunt.

The Magna Charta Sureties, 1215 (list of the barons named in the Magna Charta).

The Plantagenet Ancestry, Tables Showing the 7,000 Ancestors of Elizabeth, Daughter of Edward IV and wife of Edward VII, 1465-1503.

Emperor Charlemagne's Descendants, Vols. 1, 2 and 3.

My Ancestors Came with the Conqueror, Those Who Did and Did Not (come with William the Conqueror in 1066 from Normandy to England).

Queen Victoria's Descendants.

Americans of Royal Descent.

Prominent Families of the United States of America.

English Origins of American Colonists.

Ancestral Roots of Certain American Colonists Who Came To America Before 1700.

American Ancestors and Cousins of the Princess of Wales.

Heritage Books, Inc., 800-398-7709, offers *Blood Royal* and *Colonial American of Royal and Noble Descent,* among others in their free monthly catalog.

TODAY'S THOUGHT: "Let every man honor and love the land of his birth and the race from which he springs and keep their memory green. It is a pious and honorable duty..." (Henry Cabot Lodge)

NEW INDEX HAS 200 MILLION NAMES

Kory Meyerink was the speaker at a banquet I attended in December in Salt Lake City. Meyerink is the coordinator of publishing for the Family History Library, and is responsible for all the resource guides in the library. He is also a nationally known teacher and lecturer, and as a library employee spends some of his days at the U.S. reference desk in the library.

The theme of Meyerink's talk was "What's New at the Family History Library?" This talk applies to genealogists everywhere, for almost all the resources at the big library in Salt Lake are available to us via the branch libraries, or Family History Centers.

Meyerink announced that the 1993 edition of the International Genealogical Index is ready to use. This new IGI contains over 200 million names, 33 percent more names than can be found on the 1991 CD-ROM version, and 13 million more names than the 1992 microfiche edition. He also explained that the Ancestral File has "tightened up" eliminating duplicates of parents and children, and is actively requesting original submissions or corrections from all genealogists. Meyerink called the Ancestral File an "opinion file," for in this file, "folks have submitted their opinions (or families), and you hope that their opinion intersects with yours."

The Family History Library in Salt Lake City now has a data center, a separate room where CD-ROM disks produced by commercial firms may be used. This would include PhoneDisk, and CDs from Automated Archives Inc. and other commercial firms. Library patrons also can access four of the five national genealogical bulletin boards in the data center. New resources will be added as they are available.

Meyerink also announced the publication of a whole list of new resource guides. These inexpensive leaflets are guides to researching in the U.S. as a whole, to each of the 50 states, to most foreign countries, as well as a guide to U.S. military records and one titled "Tracing Your Immigrant Ancestor." These very helpful, inexpensive, 8 1/2 x 11 leaflet guides are a "must" for any family researcher.

The Family History Library's growing collection of microfilmed records, especially those from most European countries, coupled with the library's limited storage space has necessitated that some European films be stored at a site away from the main library. The records kept in the main library would be the most-used films, things like church records and civil registration records. But any films can be brought in from storage for patron use.

Meyerink counseled that those planning to come to Salt Lake to do comprehensive research in a particular country do some homework first. Using the FamilySearch program at the local Family History Center, patrons should ascertain what records they would like to use during their visit to Salt Lake, and then they should write and advise the library of their arrival dates and requests for films. Then the library staff can have the proper research materials ready when the patron arrives. Otherwise, the patron may have to wait a day while these materials are brought into the library. This situation does not affect local Family History Center patrons; any film in the catalog can be ordered into any center.

Banquet attendees laughed as Meyerink finished up his talk with some items from his quote file. The first was from Abraham Lincoln: "I don't know who my grandfather was; I'm much more interested in knowing what his grandson will be." Then, "God gave us our relatives; thank goodness we can choose our friends." "You can't choose your ancestors, and neither can your descendants."

TODAY'S LAUGH: A wonderful Family History Library patron from New Jersey, researching his Jewish family, taught me a new word: "yamash." He said that's what you can say, and with fervor, when the computer is doing what you tell it to do; not what you want it to do.

TODAY'S TIPS: Many Iowa tombstones were carved from sandstone which over the years has eroded and/or crumbled.

However, during the 1930s, the WPA made a survey of Iowa cemeteries, preserving the tombstone data from further weathering. If you are seeking an ancestor's tombstone in Iowa and are having troubles finding it, write to Information From Iowa, Capitol Complex, Des Moines, IA 50319. Be sure to give the county in which your ancestor's cemetery is located.

♦ Angel Island in San Francisco Bay is to West Coast immigrants what Ellis Island was to East Coast arrivals. In the early 1900s, many immigrants from Hong Kong entered the United States there. Descendants of those Chinese immigrants are undertaking a campaign to raise three million dollars to restore the old detention center on the northeastern edge of the island. They eventually hope to have a database of names, too.

♦ The Concordia Historical Institute is collecting genealogies of Lutheran families who emigrated to the U.S. Genealogists are invited to deposit copies of their research in the institute's collection. Write to 801 Demun Ave., St. Louis, MO 63105.

♦ Over the next five years, 54 teams of camera operators from the Genealogical Society of Utah will be filming in the 200 regional archives in the former Soviet Union.

RESEARCH STILL TRICKY IN EAST GERMANY

According to the statistics that I've seen, about one-quarter of our collective ancestry (meaning of most Americans) comes from the country known since the mid-19th century as Germany. That explains why so many genealogists seek to better understand how to find their German ancestors. And especially those ancestors living in the area of eastern Germany.

Maralyn Wellauer wrote an article for the National Genealogical Society Newsletter in 1993 explaining how the reunification of Germany continues to affect genealogical research. The first part of her article explained how some of the social changes will affect genealogical researching, i.e., reunification has almost doubled the size of the territory served by the federal postal service. East and West Germany had over 8,000 cities with the same postal codes, and new ones have been assigned. In some cases, new names have had to be chosen for streets and even towns. Also, new telephones are being installed at the rate of 50,000 per year in the East. These changes will have an impact on those trying to find living relatives.

Access to church records, the primary resource for German genealogists, is still in the hands of individual ministers in the East. A greater number of special church archives, both Catholic and Lutheran, have been established to house parish registers in the West; there are fewer in the East. The majority of the extant parish registers have not been filmed by the Genealogical Society of Utah teams, who are still negotiating for filming rights.

Church authorities formerly were reluctant to share information from their books because of the government's attitude. In the words of an East German archivist in the early 1980s, "The ministers are not discouraged from supplying information to the West but they are not encouraged to do so either."

Often in the past, letters sent to archives and parishes were not answered. Attempts to obtain information more than three years ago may be repeated today with the expectation of better results.

According to law, archives and churches must charge for genealogical services and information. This mandatory charge amounts to approximately $35.00 per hour; it may be more in some jurisdictions and less in others.

One thing hasn't changed since 1990. There are many itinerant ministers serving German parishioners. They are young, and many are unable to read the old script. Due to their extended duties, they have little or no time to undertake genealogical searches. It is also important to remember that an entire generation of young people has been brought up with no religious influence, so church records of 20th century Germans may be hard to find for many reasons.

Wellauer's article continued with an explanation of German archives. She wrote that the German archives most consulted by U.S. genealogists are the state archives, town or city archives, church archives, city registry offices, nobility archives, military or federal archives, and university archives.

For the most part, archives in both the East and West are at the same locations as before 1990. Some archives have changed names, again due to the reunification. Many longtime archivists retired after reunification, prompting policy and administrative alterations. It has been reported that the archives have become more "user-friendly."

New appointees have proved to be well organized and interested in disseminating information about their holdings. These archival collections have been newly inventoried and described in several new catalogs such as: "Church Records in the German Central Office for Genealogy, Part I: Church Records of the Former German Provinces of Posen, East and West Prussia, Pomerania and Silesia" (revised by Martina Wemes, et al. Neustadt/Aisch: Verlag Degener & Co., 1991). Writers receiving negative replies before 1990 are advised to write again.

Archives in Germany remain understaffed and have major storage problems. In anticipation of an on-site visit, it is important to write ahead.

State your reason for coming, what sources you wish to consult, and how long you intend to stay. Give specific dates. There are several reasons for this courtesy, but mainly it will allow archivists time to retrieve records in storage. Bear in mind that August is vacation month, and many offices are closed.

There is renewed concern by Germans about data protection and the right to privacy as the rush to uncover information gains momentum. Access to some records, particularly civil documents, may be limited to direct descendants. If so, a notarized statement to show descent may be required before information is released. In Germany records are protected for a period of 30 years.

Reunification has resulted in the filing of approximately 1 million court cases. West Germans are filing claims for property in the former GDR. Many in the East fear losing their property to West Germans with previous owner's rights. It will likely be years before all the cases are settled. In the meantime, inquiries from genealogists about property may be met with suspicion. Access to court records, an increasingly important genealogical source on emigrants, may also be affected.

Wellauer ends her article by posing some questions about the future. For instance, will the republics of the former Soviet Union return German records held in their archives? Will there be centralized administration of archives in Germany? If so, Leipzig has been suggested by some as a likely hub. It was the publishing capital of Germany before the two world wars and is now the center of a new genealogical society which issues a newsletter dealing with the new Germany.

There seems to be more genealogical activity, in a shorter span of time, than in any other period during this century, particularly in efforts to document emigrations. This activity will likely result in a plethora of new publications and periodicals. To keep abreast of the latest genealogical developments in the new Germany, you should consult current German and German-American periodicals.

Maralyn Wellauer is a nationally known lecturer and is author of several publications on German and Swiss genealogical research. You may write to her requesting a flier on her services and publications. Her address is 2845 N. 72nd St., Milwaukee, WI 53210. Do include an SASE (stamped, self addressed envelope).

Periodicals Help Find German Ancestors

Today's column is the second of two parts giving new tips and understanding for doing research on our German ancestors.

Maralyn Wellauer, nationally known author and lecturer on German research topics recognizes that most genealogists will have some ancestors coming from the areas that up until 1990 were called West and East Germany. She recommends reading current German and German-American periodicals to know "what's new" for researching these areas.

One of the best German periodicals that I know of is the *German Genealogical Digest,* now in its 10th year of publication. This quarterly consistently lets readers know what new records have been made available via the Family History Library, and from what areas these records are coming. Here are some of the things that the *German Genealogical Digest* can do to help your German research:

♦ Help you identify your German ancestral home;
♦ Help you locate your place names on maps and in gazetteers;
♦ Help you determine what sources exist for your areas of research;
♦ Help you find the current location of the records you need;
♦ Help you to read the German records;

♦ Help you learn correct research procedures;
♦ Help you contact others researching the same ancestral lines;
♦ Help you keep current on new books and sources.

Larry Jensen, author and compiler of the *Digest*, says, "Our primary goal with this publication is to teach others to locate, use and read German- and German-American genealogical sources. Each issue includes sources helpful to all German researchers."

Jensen also is the author of two standard reference works for German researching, *The Handbook for German Genealogy*, Volumes 1 and 2. He lectures nationally on German genealogy, and conducts week-long summer seminars on the Brigham Young University campus in Provo, UT. He is well qualified to produce a first-rate German periodical. Subscriptions are $22.00 for one year and may be sent to the German Genealogical Digest Inc., P.O. Box 700, Pleasant Grove, UT 84062-700.

Bette Butcher Topp has published *German Queries* since 1986. This is a query-only, irregularly published, research series of booklets. You may submit your queries to Topp for free, but she will not do research in the booklets for you. The cost of the booklets is modest. Contact her at W. 1304 Cliffwood, Spokane, WA 99218-2917.

The best entry-level book that I've seen on doing German research is *In Search Of Your German Roots*, by Angus Baxter. Updated in 1991, Baxter's book presents the information needed to begin your research in both the former East and West Germany. This 116-page, indexed book costs $10.95 and can be ordered from Genealogical Publishing Co., 1001 N. Calvert St., Baltimore, MD 21202, or by calling 800-296-6687.

Genealogical Guide to Tracing Ancestors in Germany, by Margaret Krug Palen, is available from Heritage Books, Inc., for $19.50. It describes how to do essential German genealogical research in the United States before beginning your quest in Germany. This practical guide contains maps, illustrations, photographs and historical background about the cities and people of Germany. Call 800-398-7709 to order this book.

I would like to share my own German research success story with you — to give you courage to work on your own German problems.

We knew from his 1900 funeral card that our great-great-grandfather, Henry Goss, was born in Dietenhausen in 1835. We learned this fact some years ago, when I was far too timid in my research to think I could ever do anything with "foreign" research. Besides, wouldn't I have to learn to read German? So we worked on other lines, ignoring our German heritage.

Finally, with a few years of genealogical success under our belts, and fortified with some knowledge learned in resources like the above mentioned periodicals and books, we took another look at our Henry Goss "problem." Where to start? We weren't even sure where Dietenhausen was.

Studying issues of the *German Genealogical Digest,* we decided to take advantage of its $5.00 offer to do a surname search. We sent for the forms, filled them out and sent our check. Soon a letter came back that a record of one Heinrich Goss, born Nov. 6, 1835, in Dietenhausen in the province/county of Hessen was listed on a certain microfilm! Imagine our joy! The microfilm was that of a certain small Evangelical Church record, in a small parish, in the very small town that was Dietenhausen, filmed only three years before by the Genealogical Society of Utah.

On my next trip to Salt Lake City, I descended to the international floor of the library, and found the correct microfilm in the rows and rows and drawers and drawers of other microfilm. Putting it on the reader machine, and turning the crank, I was looking at the day-to-day entries in the official "log book" of the pastor of this small church. There were all the christening records of my Goss family, along with some marriage and death records — all on one microfilm!

The handwritten entries were penned onto printed forms, and with help from the *Digest* and the library itself, I was able to establish what the headings were. It was almost like a miracle that as I looked and looked at this record, it just seemed to come clear before my eyes, enough so that I was able to pick out most of the information without help. When I did need help reading the handwritten notes in the "remarks" column, the library staff was always there to help me.

Now we know that our Heinrich Goss, born on Nov. 6, 1835, was the fourth child of Johann Heinrich Goss and Catharine Elisabetha Lommel. Johann and Catharine didn't get married until 1832, but that's a story for another day. Think what we would have missed without the help of the *German Genealogical Digest?*

CLEARLY DOCUMENT YOUR FAMILY PEDIGREE

Webster's dictionary defines "documentation" as "anything printed or written that is relied upon to record, support or prove something."

That definition says nothing about *what is the source of the documentation*, but that to document something is to write down, or make a copy of printed page, of something that just records a fact, perhaps supports a fact, and maybe even proves a fact. Genealogists are continually enduring lecturers and teachers harping at them to document their charts. In simplest terms, that just means to write down the source for every name, date and place written on those charts. (Where to write it down? The back of the chart would be dandy, or a lined sheet of paper kept next to the chart would be best.)

Without documentation this sort of scenario will arise. You are proudly showing off your pedigree charts and family group sheets to a newly found cousin, or to a grandchild someday, and the cousin or grandchild will no doubt be impressed with all your work. But that cousin or grandchild is sure to say, "Where did you learn all of this stuff? Where did you find it all out? Who told you all this?" Without documentary notes as to the source for every name, date and place written upon those charts, how will you respond to that inevitable question?

Resolve today to change your ways and to DOCUMENT everything that you write on your charts, whether with a pencil or a computer. Here are some rules for good documentation.

- ◆ Document as you go — enter the documentation as you enter the facts.
- ◆ Enter your notes in a consistent format.
- ◆ Use confidential information with discretion and sensitivity.
- ◆ List all the sources you found and used.
- ◆ Identify conflicting or missing information.
- ◆ Avoid using unusual abbreviations.
- ◆ Strive to obtain primary sources for each fact.
- ◆ Indicate additional research where needed.
- ◆ Indicate the location of lengthy documents, rather than restating.

♦ Welcome input and constructive review of your documentation.
♦ Identify all researchers' contributions, including your own. Use your name, not "I" or "me."
♦ Recognize that good documentation requires a process of continuous refinement.

I found a list of "Rules for Good Documentation" on page four of "PAF Documentation Guidelines," 1993 edition. Pages one to four of the booklet list the specific form in which truly dedicated genealogists should list their documentation.

TODAY'S TIP: The American Genealogical Lending Library is alive and well in Bountiful, UT. It recently announced that its new catalog is now available on floppy disk for home computer use. The catalog contains 150,000 titles on film and fiche. It has previously been available in print, on microfilm and on microfiche. One of the advantages of the catalog on disk is the ability of the user to search it by key word in order to locate the film or fiche containing the answer to a research question more quickly.

The catalog on disk will run on any IBM compatible system using MS-DOS. It is self-contained and does not require any additional viewing software. The catalog in any format comes with the purchase of an AGLL membership which entitles the member to rent or buy the film and fiche listed in the catalog for a minimal charge.

AGLL membership is $45.00, with the catalog in paper form or disk form, and $30.00 with the catalog on film or fiche. Membership includes biannual catalog updates and newsletters. If you are already a member of AGLL, you may purchase the new catalog on disk for $25.00. Memberships in AGLL enables folks to buy or rent genealogical records for their own personal or home use.

Additional membership benefits AGLL offers include:
♦ Discounts on book purchases from its 140-page books-for-sale catalog;
♦ Indexes to Censuses and Marriages in paper, film, fiche and disk form;
♦ CD-ROM products at discount prices;
♦ All available censuses and census indexes on microfilm;

- ◆ Many ships' passenger lists on microfilm;
- ◆ Two free film rentals for new members;
- ◆ *Heritage Quest* magazine subscription discounts;
- ◆ In-house searches, including ProPhone, Social Security Death Index, Marriage Records Index, Census Indexes and others.

Call AGLL today for an information packet, sales fliers and membership application form. The phone number for the American Genealogical Lending Library is 800-760-AGLL. Or write to P.O. Box 329, Bountiful, UT 84011-0329.

IMMIGRATION IN 1600S WAS NO CAVALIER JAUNT

Today's column is the first of two parts giving you some basic history of American immigration. I hope that it will help you to understand why your ancestor came to this country.

Will Rogers, in poking fun at those who take pride in their ancestry, used to remark that *his* ancestors were at the dock to meet the Mayflower. Figuratively speaking, he was right, being part Cherokee, and this serves to underscore the fact every American is either an immigrant or is descended from immigrants, with the possible exception of the American Indians. We say, "possible exception" because many anthropologists believe that the Indians themselves were immigrants. The story of American immigration is the story of an estimated 70 million people of many different backgrounds and nationalities.

The first immigrants were the English, who were to lead all other nationalities in immigration until the first half of the 19th century when the Irish and German immigrants began to arrive in large numbers. The early English settled in two different places, the Puritans in Massachusetts and the Cavaliers in Virginia.

Tradition holds that the early colonists were religious refugees from a dictatorial and unyielding monarch who refused to acknowledge their basic religious rights. This tradition is right and wrong at the same time, for most colonists were Protestants fleeing the conformity of England's state church. However, their flight arose from a number of issues other than religion. The economy of Europe and England experienced a kind of disruptive development. New wealth, mostly silver and gold from Spanish colonies, caused tremendous inflation. Laboring classes suffered from this condition. Even the king felt the squeeze, because he had a fixed income and was expected to finance his office and authority from his own pocket. However, the large landowners and merchants were prospering from the inflation. The king was refused the right to tax individuals, so he had to devise various levies and duties to meet his needs. This reached into the pockets of the laboring class. In the early 1600s, this working class, pressed by the rising inflation without work, and often in opposition to the state religion, began to consider emigration; it was the only solution to an intolerable situation.

There were political reasons, too, adding to the unrest of the people. The Puritans saw the New World as an ideal location for their "experiment" in constructive Protestantism. They settled in Massachusetts. John Winthrop, the governor of the Massachusetts Bay Company, established a colonial government in 1629. His community centered around Boston. However, he was too strict for some of his followers, most of whom were simple laborers and merchants. This gave rise to a new migration, this one heading out of Massachusetts and into the Connecticut River Valley.

Later on, around the 1650s, a flood of immigrants to Virginia was a direct result of English civil war. Still having quarrels over taxation and royal finances were the Royalists, who supported the king, and the landowners, who were recruited from the Cavaliers and were, for the most part, wealthy Puritans and supporters of Parliament. A series of wars raged from 1642 to 1649 and many people, Puritan and Royalist alike, left the country for the New World. Virginia appeared to be the only refuge for them. They were certainly not welcome in strictly Puritan New England. This was after King Charles I was beheaded in 1649 and the Puritans were in control of Parliament. A huge migration of Cavaliers settled in Virginia. They found a social and economic system which was already in place, similar to that of the English. Large tobacco plantations were prominent, and as time passed, these plantations took on the aura of the English estate. The colonial gentry was made up of the younger sons of the English families. Because of the legal doctrine of inheritance of the estate going to the oldest son, these younger sons often found themselves without any financial support once they reached their majority.

However, in some cases, the people came because they were forced to come. Vagrants, paupers, thieves and even prisoners of war were deported to America, where they would be out of the way of "decent folks," and could do no harm except to each other. Immigrants were sometimes driven out by the law because they were considered to be undesirables.

The profit motive brought others. There are always those who see economic potential in a new land. There were codfish, tobacco, furs and new ports for trade up and down the coastline. Some wanted nothing more than their own land and a fresh start. Some had to become indentured servants for a time. The indentured servant received free transportation to America and at the end of his contract, which usually ran four years, he received his freedom dues. This payment was usually clothing, a gun, tools, some money and sometimes as much as 50 acres of land. In spite of all the dissimilarities in their backgrounds and reasons for coming, all early immigrants had one experience in common. The common bond was a long, dangerous, extremely unpleasant voyage across the Atlantic.

The vessels were small and often overcrowded. When there was a good breeze and a smooth sea, they might make many miles in a day. On other days they might lose ground. It usually took from 47 to 138 sailing days from London to the Capes. The food was composed principally of ship-biscuit, salt meat, peas and cheese, all of the kind that would keep well for many weeks. Food and water for as many as 100 persons for the length of the voyage would require much space. Storms at sea and sickness aboard ship were a dangerous aspect for a voyage. There were many other trials too numerous to mention.

As a general rule of thumb, you can guess that your immigrant ancestor arriving before the Civil War came in a sailing vessel, taking the six to 20 weeks mentioned above. After the Civil War, more and more immigrants were coming on steamships, cutting the voyage time down to about two weeks. It didn't take long for the shipping companies to realize that more money could be made hauling passengers than in just carrying freight.

English immigration to America continued into the 20th century, but by the first half of the 19th century, Irish and German immigrants had begun to pour into America. Nearly one million Irish came in a five-year period as a direct result of the potato famine in 1845. Many Germans came because of a national reaction against the reform ideas of the French Revolution. Any upheaval in a nation produces refugees, and these refugees in turn can become immigrants to new country. Many of Europe's displaced persons became American immigrants.

The Irish generally arrived "dirt poor," and had no real option but to stay where they had landed — in the cities on the Eastern seaboard, particularly in New York and Boston. The first thing they had to do was to get a job. Contractors actually waited at the docks to sign up Irish laborers as soon as they set foot on shore. (The Erie Canal, opened in 1825, was dug mostly by Irish immigrant workers who arrived in large numbers long before the potato famine.) While they could survive, and did get an economic foothold, they had virtually no mobility.

The Germans, however, could afford to go about the business of settling at a more sedate pace. They usually arrived with some savings, and a clear-cut destination: the rich farm lands of the American Midwest. The immigrants wrote long letters home, and these letters prompted still others to make the long, one-way journey across the Atlantic.

The latter half of the 19th century saw the Italians and those from the various Eastern European countries supplant the Germans and Irish. The Scandinavians began to arrive as the 20th century approached, as did the Greeks and others who had the courage to start a new life. Each group had its own story, its own heroes and villains, and its own peculiar problems of adjustment. All have had to overcome prejudice and hardship. They have all made vast and important contributions to American culture and progress. All have faced obstacles, triumphed with quiet pride and dignity; they have all become Americans and are our ancestors. It is only natural and fitting that one should seek to know more about his immigrant ancestors.

They Came in Ships was recently published by author John P. Colletta, Ph.D., and includes a new chapter focusing on the challenge of finding your ancestor on a ship's passenger list in a year when arrival lists are not indexed. This little 108-page book is still a step-by-step guide through the records that concern your immigrant ancestor's ship of arrival. Order this book for $11.95, postpaid, from Ancestry Inc., P.O. Box 538, Salt Lake City, UT, or call 800-262-3787.

Finding Your Italian Roots: A Complete Guide for Americans is another new book by Dr. Colletta. He realized that in ever-increasing numbers, Americans of Italian descent are becoming interested in tracing their families back to the Old Country and visiting their ancestral villages, but few people know where to begin. This guide explains the resources available here in the United States, and shows how to access records it Italian town halls, archives, churches and libraries. Order this book for $14.95, postpaid, from Genealogical Publishing Co. 1001 N. Calvert St., Baltimore, MD 21202-3897, or call 1-800 296-6687.

Polish Roots is a new book authored by Rosemary A. Chorzempa, national director of the Polish Genealogical Society of America. This book throws cold water on the myth that successful Polish genealogical research is beyond the powers of ordinary people, and steers readers confidently around the obstacles of language and geography to research Polish records in America and in the Old Country. (And remember that the Old Country could be Austria, Germany, the Ukraine, Russia or Lithuania, for peoples in these countries exercised dominion ever Poland at different times over the centuries.) Order this book for $21.95, postpaid, from Genealogical Publishing Co. (address and phone above).

One special group of immigrants to America was the so-called Germans from Russia, and Robert Smick of Spokane is a descendant of a member of this group. Smick wrote to me last October to share his success story.

Smick wrote to explain that he and his wife, Flora, had taken my genealogy class in the fall of 1992, and soon discovered that he had an ancestor who was a German from Russia. He explained a bit of history: "In the 1760s, Catherine the Great, Czarina of Russia and a former German princess, issued invitations to entice German peasants and artisans to migrate to the Volga River area of Russia. Promises of free land, freedom to practice any trade or profession, interest-free loans local self-government, and freedom from military service were powerful inducements to German peoples suffering from some forty years of war.

"In 1766, colonists from the Province of Hesse began the long arduous trip to the Volga where 80 families (269 individuals) founded the village of Yagodnya Polyana in 1767. Over the years they prospered, but in the late 19th century, many of the promised freedoms were lost and this gave rise to migration to the U.S. beginning in the 1880s and continuing until the outbreak of World War I. Many of the 'Volga Germans' came to the U.S. and settled in several areas, including Eastern Washington.

"Both sets of my grandparents arrived in the U.S. in the 1890s, coming from Yagodnaya Polyana and settling in Endicott, a farming community in the Palouse area of eastern Washington. Over the years their contact with family members still in Russia grew less frequent, and in 1933 contact ceased completely. The Communist takeover gave our family in America little hope for those left behind in Russia.

"To shorten the story, in the fall of 1993, the dream of reuniting those families came true, when a small group of descendants returned to the village of Yagodnaya Polyana for an emotional visit. A tour led by Dr. Richard Scheuerman of Endicott enabled descendants to spend two weeks visiting their ancestral village and meet new cousins. It was a wonderful experience, and one we hope to repeat."

Smick ended his story by telling me that his Smick line came from one Anna Smick, who came from Hesse to Russia in 1767 with three young children. Her husband died on the trip. A descendant of one of those children ended up in Endicott, WA. What a wonderful story to share.

TORY HISTORY MAKES FASCINATING READING

Was your ancestor a Loyalist? Was he perhaps a Tory? What was the difference? Should we be proud of our Loyalist or Tory ancestors or be ashamed? Do we want to learn more about these ancestors?

The answer is that "Loyalist" was the term given by the British to their loyal subjects who lived in the Colonies. The term "Tory" was pinned on His Majesty's subjects by those who yearned for American independence. So a Loyalist and a Tory were the same person. As you dig into your family history and find an ancestor who was born in Connecticut or Virginia, and who disappears right before the Revolutionary War, you might discover that you have a Loyalist ancestor. The history of these people and this episode in American history is fascinating.

The setting is colonial America. The British Empire is trying desperately to keep control of its powerful position in the world as the French and Spanish empires jockey for land all over the New World. To finance her empire-spreading operations, the British government needs money, and so her American colonies are hit heavily with new taxes, and discontent spreads throughout the land.

But only about one-third of the colonists favor secession; one-third are neutral, and the remaining one-third would not even think of going against their King, or God would strike them dead.

We know what the outcome was, but we hardly ever hear about the losers, the ones who were the establishment. Keep in mind that the Patriots were the rebels, not the British, and with great luck on their side, the greatest county in the world was born. However, the losers were also Americans, but because of their personal political history they were kicked off their lands and run out of their homes, even after the Treaty of Paris guaranteed them their property and the right to stay in their communities. Bitter over this treaty, each state voted to rescind that section of the Treaty and ran the poor Loyalists out anyway.

While many with Loyalist tendencies were run out of the colonies before and during the Revolutionary War, the great exodus happened mainly in 1783 and 1784. Fleet after fleet left eastern ports and sailed to Nova Scotia, but others went to England, and to Ontario and Quebec in Canada, and even to the Bahamas. In 1786, the new Canadian province of New Brunswick was created because of Loyalist settlement. These poor, defeated and very brave people cut their way into a hostile wilderness to start life all over again. Most eventually filed claims with the British government for compensation of their war losses. I'd say you ought to be proud of your Loyalist or Tory ancestor.

Where can you find out more about these fascinating ancestors? Paul J. Bunnell has written the *Research Guide to Loyalist Ancestors*. This $15.00, 146-page book, can be ordered from Heritage Books at 800-398-7709. The book is a directory to archives, manuscripts and published sources on Loyalist ancestry. Bunnell first lists sources in Canadian provinces, then in all relevant states, and then in other countries. This book is the best resource guide I've seen offering help with Loyalist research.

There have been many other helpful books published lately on this topic. Many are lists of records and names. Alexander Fraser's 1905 work, *United Empire Loyalists, An Enquiry into the Losses and Services in Consequence of Their Loyalty,* was republished by Genealogical Publishing Co. in two volumes. This monumental work of over 1400 pages contains records of the claims for losses of over 1200 persons who found it necessary to flee to Canada during and immediately after the Revolution.

A typical entry from this work tells of the claim of one William Falkner, "late of Tryon County New York." It seems that Falkner came to America in 1772 and settled in Tryon County where he was living in 1775. He never took part with the rebels. In June 1778, he escaped with his family to Niagara and remained in Canada, residing in Lancaster. Further testimony states that he had cleared 45 acres and had built a house, barn and stables. He had three horses, six cows, one bull, and six oxen, plus some sheep and hogs, all of which were killed by the rebels. His furniture, clothing and farming utensils were taken by the rebels. The book tells his descendants of his claim, and tells where to write for actual records. This book can be ordered for $87.50 from Genealogical Publishing Co. at 800-296-6687.

Other good books on this topic are *The Loyalists in the American Revolution,* by C.H. Van Tyne, 1902, republished in 1989 by Heritage Books; *The Loyalists of Massachusetts,* by J.H. Stark, 1907, republished in 1989 by Heritage Books; *The New Loyalist Index,* by Paul Bunnell, 1989, Heritage Books (which includes index of Loyalist names that the author found in many different cited sources); *American Loyalist Claims,* by P.W. Coldham, 1980, published by the National Genealogical Society (lists the claims as found in British courts).

How To Protect Family Stats, Photos

Imagine an advertisement stating: "Genealogical Insurance Is Available!" An ad like that would surely catch the eye of every genealogist, who would welcome some sort of "insurance" to protect his or her life's work.

Carolyn J. Nell, president of the National Genealogical Society, penned an article in a recent issue of the NGS quarterly on this subject. She wrote, "During the past two years, newspaper headlines and radio and television news broadcasts have reminded us of our vulnerability to nature's onslaught. We've been caught up in the heart-wrenching stories of those who have felt the wrath of Hurricane Andrew and the destruction caused by the flooding of the mighty Mississippi River and its tributaries. These tragic events were followed by devastating fires in California. Some of you, our fellow genealogists and friends, were victims. To you, as well as to all of the others, we express our sympathy. For those grateful that it was not happening to you, please take heed because none of us are immune.

"Many genealogists and family historians spend much of their lifetime accumulating family statistics, photographs and memorabilia. Our dedication to researching and preserving our family histories brings great satisfaction to all concerned. But when disasters occur, some things, in addition to the loss of life, are very precious and may never be replaced."

"Family statistics, like homes, might be restructured with much effort. Family stories and interviews may not be so easy to reconstruct because they were probably generated by older family members now deceased. Old family photographs, letters, souvenirs and many other treasured items are irreplaceable. Preventive measures to minimize loss constitute your "genealogical insurance." Here are some simple things you can do NOW to ensure that your precious family data will not be completely lost:"

- ◆ Create a plan to organize your family statistics, photos and stories. Keep it simple so you can accomplish it easily. Disasters are never orchestrated — they just happen.

- ◆ Consolidate your information on family group sheets and pedigree charts, and be sure to cite your sources. If you have a computer, put information on computer disks. It's also important to reproduce this information and share it with family members who live elsewhere. Sharing is the key to the success of genealogical insurance.

♦ Identify repositories that accept genealogical information. Manuscript and photograph collections can be microfilmed by you or by these agencies thereby adding additional insurance coverage.

♦ The Family History Library invites individuals and family organizations who are interested in sharing genealogical information to submit their data to Ancestral File, a database in FamilySearch. Submitting information to these files ensures that your records will be preserved and will have worldwide circulation.

♦ Protecting priceless, irreplaceable family photographs can be difficult and costly; however, you can use certain preventive measures to minimize loss. One method is to make negatives and store them in a safe deposit box. In addition, organize, identify and label your photographs and share copies with family members.

"An additional benefit you will derive when pursuing some of these suggestions is the satisfaction you feel when you have transformed a genealogical 'pile' into something really worthwhile. The genealogical history that you can then share with family members makes lovely, treasured gifts that only you can give."

"Organizing and sharing is your genealogical insurance and your legacy to future generations. It's not difficult, just do it."

TODAY'S LAUGH: To a foreigner, a Yankee is an American. To a Southerner in the United States, a Yankee is a Northerner. To a Northerner, a Yankee lives in New England. To a New Englander, a Yankee is someone from Vermont. To a Vermonter, a Yankee is someone who still uses an outhouse!

INDEX INVALUABLE FOR SCOTTISH RESEARCH

New indexes to christenings and marriages in the Old Parochial Registers of the Established Church of Scotland (Presbyterian) are available at the Family History Library in Salt Lake City, and all the Family History Centers. The OPR Index is probably the most valuable resource ever offered to those who have ancestors in Scotland.

The OPR Index is of christenings and marriages extracted from microfilms as found in the Old Parochial Registers (parish registers) of the Church of Scotland (Presbyterian), and miscellaneous records kept by the Registrar General for Scotland at Edinburgh. It does not contain birth and marriage information from the records of other denominations. It also does not contain death or burial records. This index for each county is subdivided into christenings and marriages, with each index arranged by surname. All the counties including those that used the patronymic naming system also have a given name index. Within the given name index the entries are arranged chronologically.

The new indexes contain entries to over 6,000,000 births and more than 2,200,000 marriages from the OPRs. Covering all counties of Scotland, for all years prior to 1855 for which registers have survived, the earliest entry is dated 1553. So if you are looking for a Scottish ancestor, who was a member of the established church and in Scotland prior to 1855, do check the OPR Index.

The entries for christenings give the child's name, the parents' names, date of the christening or birth, and the parish where the record was found. Those for marriages give names of the bride and groom and the date and place of the marriage. The actual spelling as found in the records is used in the OPR Index. If the name is not found under the modern spelling, all possible spelling variations should be checked.

The indexes were produced by the Genealogical Society of Utah with cooperation from the General Register Office for Scotland. To use the OPR Index, go to the Family History Center, and access the library card catalog in the FamilySearch program. They are listed under "Scotland-(county name)-Church Records, Indexes."

Closer to home, here's some information for those seeking ancestors in San Francisco, CA. While all birth records for this city prior to April 18, 1906, were destroyed in the earthquake (except those that had been sent to the State Registrar of Vital Statistics between July 1, 1905, and March 31, 1906), most early death records are still available. The San Francisco Department of Public Health has these records; microfilm copies are available through the Family History Centers. These records are in the form of eight "books." Here are the years they cover:

Book 1 -- 8 Nov 1865 to 30 Sep 1869 (index missing)

Book 2 -- 1 Oct 1869 to 30 Apr 1873 (index missing)

Book 3 -- 1 Apr 1873 to 30 Jun 1889 (index missing, coroner's cases only)

Book M -- 1 Aug 1894 to 30 Jun 1896 (indexed)

Book O -- 1 Jul 1898 to 16 Mar 1900 (index only)

Book P -- 17 Mar 1900 to 22 Oct 1901 (indexed)

Book Q -- 23 Oct 1901 to 30 June 1903 (indexed)

Book R -- 1 Jul 1903 to 30 Jun 1904 (indexed)

Since July 1, 1905, all original birth and death certificates have been filed monthly with the State Registrar of Vital Statistics in Sacramento.

To check for film numbers for these records, look under "California--Vital Records, Indexes" in the FamilySearch Library Card Catalog. The nice folks at the Centers will assist you in ordering the correct film.

TODAY'S TIPS: Here are some German-Dutch words to help understand your family's records: a "morgen" was equal to 2 1/10 acres of land and a German-Dutch measurement derived from "morning," hence the area which can be plowed in one morning. A "guilder" is a Dutch coin equal to 1/12th of a pound. A "stiver" is a Dutch coin which equals 1/20th of a guilder.

VIDEOS CAN TELL STORY OF YOUR FAMILY

Many folks these days have camcorders. Genealogists who have camcorders have umpteen videos of the grandchildren, and think that these efforts at recording the family are genealogy enough. But there is something much more exciting that genealogists can do with their camcorders than just "doing" the three-year-old's birthday party and endless Christmases.

Mary Lou Peterson of Minneapolis, MN. has produced a video titled "Gift of Heritage." This video shows how to use your camcorder to create your own family documentary: Peterson uses her own efforts in this area to tell us her story and teach us her methods, and the results are striking.

"Gift of Heritage" begins with her ancestors Nils and Marie Aasen (depicted in a formal family portrait), a young couple with one child and another on the way, who emigrated to America from Norway. The second child was actually born in the mid-Atlantic. At this point in the video story, you see a drawing of the kind of ship they sailed on, hear the sea wind blowing and the sound a ship makes when plowing through the waves. You have already been shown a photo of their Norwegian homeland. Now you see a map of Wisconsin, where the family settled. In those first few minutes, I was hooked!

Peterson explained that the project began in a small way, with a simple desire to commit her family's genealogical tree, history, stories and old photographs to video. The project mushroomed and soon she was incorporating titles to identify the photographs, and dubbing in background music and sound effects to help tell her family's story. The end result was a family documentary that brought the family tree to life. It was shared and appreciated at a large family reunion, and several family members told her that after seeing the video they felt like they'd taken a journey into the past and met their ancestors face to face.

If you would like a copy of this video to help you through the steps of organizing and planning a family documentary video, send a check for $25.00 to Mary Lou Productions, P.O. Box 17233, Minneapolis, MN 55417. You could never give your family a better rendition of all the "stuff" you've collected on your family than to turn it into a story and tell that story as a family movie.

TODAY'S TIP: *The Royal Descents of 500 Immigrants to the American Colonies or the United States,* by Gary Boyd Roberts, published in 1993, is just the book to document your royal lineage. Most Americans with sizable New England, Yankee, mid-Atlantic Quaker, or Southern planter ancestry are descended from the kings and queens of England, Scotland and France. This book shows how they are descended, and so shows you how you can trace your family back to royalty. Roberts tells of nearly 500 people who came to the American colonies and left descendants, in some cases now numbering over a million — probably some of your ancestors! If you would like your own copy of this fascinating book, it may be ordered for $45.00 from Genealogical

Publishing Co., at 800-296-6687. This would be a dandy way to spend a rainy day, or a snowbound day, next winter.

TODAY'S TRIVIA: Before about 1800, the "Old Northwest Territory" didn't mean what it does today. At that time the "Northwest" was the area south of the Great Lakes, and between the Mississippi and Ohio Rivers. An ordinance passed on July 13, 1787 reads in part, "...there shall be formed in said territory not less than three nor more than five states...." Thus this area was formed into Ohio (1803), Indiana (1816), Illinois (1818), Michigan (1837) and Wisconsin (1848). Minnesota was added in 1858.

ENJOY THE LIGHTER SIDE OF GENEALOGY

Did you know that there were Inevitable Laws of Genealogy? Trying to "lighten up" this column a bit, I present the following list of such "laws" for your reading pleasure.

♦ The records you need for your family history are in the courthouse that burned.

♦ John, son of Thomas, the immigrant whom your relatives claim as immigrant ancestor, died on board ship at the age of twelve.

♦ The public ceremony in which your distinguished ancestor participated when the platform under him collapsed turned out to be a hanging.

♦ Records show that the grandfather, whom the family boasted, "He read the Bible at four years and graduated from college at sixteen," was really at the foot of his class.

♦ Your grandmother's maiden name, for which you've searched for years, was on an old letter in a box in the attic all the time.

♦ When at last you have solved the mystery of the skeleton in the closet, your tight-lipped spinster aunt claims, "I could have told you that all the time."

♦ You never asked your father about his family because you weren't interested in genealogy while he was alive.

♦ The family story your grandmother wrote for the family never got past the typist. She packed it away "somewhere" and promised to send a copy, but never did.

- The relative who had all the family photographs gave them to her daughter who had no interest in genealogy and no inclination to share.
- A great-uncle changed his surname because he was teased in school. He moved away, left no address, and was never heard from again.
- Brittle old newspapers containing the info you desired have fallen apart on the names and dates and places that you need.
- The only record you find for your great-grandfather is that his property was sol at a sheriff's sale for insolvency.
- The portior   index you need is continued in the next issue, on'   her died prior to publication.
- When   obituary for your grandmother, the inform   '. Her name is exchanged with her daugh   'uts of her sons is unknown, the date for he   ates that he was younger than she.
- The o   ot found among the three billion in the Famil   Library archives is yours.
- The v   records director sends you a negative reply, having just been insulted by a creep calling himself a genealogist.
- The 4-volume, 4,800 page history of the county where your great-grandfather lived is not indexed.
- The spelling of your European ancestor's name bears no relationship to its current spelling or pronunciation.
- Ink fades and paper deteriorates at a rate inversely proportional to the value of the data recorded.
- Your paternal grandfather's name was John Smith, and your maternal grandfather's name was John Brown.

TRACING ORIGINAL SOURCES PAYS OFF

These days, almost every genealogist has used the IGI (International Genealogical Index), one of the databases in the FamilySearch computer program which we're all using at the Family History Centers. But while almost all of us have used the IGI, how many have taken the time to track down the source of the information we find there? (And we must realize that the information in the IGI is just secondary information, and it's very desirable to go to the original source whenever possible.)

Information in the IGI comes from three major sources: (1) Extracted Records – volunteers who have copied out civil and church christenings, birth and marriage records from microfilmed records; (2) records submitted by any genealogist but particularly LDS members; and (3) membership records – deceased members of the LDS church.

The source of the information is important because it can help you to verify and understand the genealogical information that you find in the IGI, and it can help you find more information. Records vary in their content, depending on the record-keeping practices of a particular area, time or person doing the writing. And tracking down the source can help you find a "cousin," or the person who submitted the information.

To find a source, you need the Batch Number, and sometimes the sheet number and other information that is found in the next-to-last right-side column of the IGI. The first letter of the Batch Number indicates whether the source is an extracted record, a submitted form, or a membership record. If the word "film" appears in the column, the number refers to a microfilm number, which will lead to the microfilmed record from which the extractions were taken.

The resource guide, "Finding An IGI Source," published by the Family History Library, contains all the abbreviations which will help you "translate" and understand the IGI sources. A copy of this guide can be accessed at the Family History Centers or ordered from the Family History Library in Salt Lake. The volunteers at the various centers will help you to use and understand the IGI, just ask.

Once you have identified the source, you can order the microfilmed record containing the information on your ancestor. View the film at the center, and copy the information found in that source pertaining to your ancestor. And then you can say, "Yeah, I understand how to use the IGI!"

TODAY'S TRIVIA: If you discover that you have an ancestor who participated in the Alaska Gold Rush, consult the Dawson City Museum and Historical Society, P.O. Box 303, Dawson City, Yukon Territory, Canada, YOB 160. Be sure to include an IRC (postal reply coupon available from U.S. post offices) to cover return postage.

If you have an ancestor who passed through the Port of Galveston, Texas, you may obtain immigration information from a database set up by the Galveston Historical Foundation. If the ancestor is found, some of the information could be age, sex, occupation, ship's name, date of arrival and port of departure. Send SASE with $10.00 for each surname search requested to Texas Seaport, 2016 Strand, Galveston, TX 77550.

The Klamath Basin Genealogical Society has recorded all the known cemetery burials in Klamath County, OR. You may order the two volumes for $24.00, postpaid, from Louise Moultron, 1555 Hope St., Klamath Falls, OR 97603.

Tennessee has the greatest density of cemeteries in the U.S. at 30 per 100 square miles, Alaska has only 16 cemeteries, fewer than .1 per 100 square miles. It's been said that population density is often correlated with cemetery density and that recently settled areas tend to have fewer cemeteries because they have bigger, commercial ones. (But what about the tiny burial sites, that seem to be everywhere???)

TODAY'S LAUGH: Proverbs for busy genealogists: "I'm just catching up with yesterday — by tomorrow I should be ready for today!" "God put me on this earth to accomplish a certain number of things. Right now I'm so far behind that I'll never die!" "In the middle of every difficulty lies opportunity." And finally, a little poem: "We have two ends with a common link; with one we sit and with one we think. Success depends on what we use, heads we win and tails we lose."

WITCHCRAFT, OR JUST A BATCH OF BAD BREAD?

About a year ago, I did a column devoted to the Salem witchcraft trials. For American history buffs, and especially those with New England ancestry, this subject is of endless fascination.

A reader recently sent me an article that perhaps sheds new light on this subject and may help explain why our ancestors did what they did.

Titled, "Rotten Rye Bread Blamed for Salem Witch Trials," the article begins, "An unusual basis for the 1692 Salem witchcraft trials may lie buried in the November 1992 issue of *MD,* a medical magazine containing excerpts from a 1989 book by Marian K. Matossian (Yale University Press). Perhaps due to medical science we can now begin to understand more clearly the reasons for this tragic misapplication of colonial justice by which people were put to the stake or hanged solely on the strength of testimony given by several young women who claimed to have been "bewitched." The book is titled, *Poisons of the Past: Molds, Epidemics and History.*

"Investigators have long been curious about the geography of the Salem madness. Why 1692? Why Salem, MA, and the surrounding communities of Essex County, MA, and Fairfield County, CN? Historical documents indicate that 24 of the 30 victims suffered from "fits." Rather than convulsions; which in modern parlance involves loss of consciousness, the young women may well have exhibited spastic movements without fainting. They also complained of being bitten and pricked. In addition, they experienced temporary blindness, deafness and speechlessness. They had hallucinations and out-of-body experiences, such as flying through the air. They were nauseated and weak. Some died, as did several cows. All these symptoms were blamed on witchcraft when, in fact, they were probably the results of epidemic ergot poisoning from tainted rye bread and contaminated wild rye grass.

"Ergot is natural alkaloid with effects similar to those of the hallucinogen LSD. Produced by a fungus in rye, ergot colors the flour cherry red. Baking, unlike boiling, does not diminish the toxicity.

"In Salem, and similar communities, rye harvested in August usually lay unthreshed in barns until winter. Because of the bad weather, there was a food scarcity in Salem during the summer of 1692. Residents may have been forced unknowingly to rely on contaminated grain harvested more than a year before.

"Other facts confirm the ergot poisoning theory. By measuring the tree rings in New England, investigators have determined that 1691 was an unusually cold year, thereby facilitating the growth of ergot mold. The increasing population caused many farmers to plant crops on marginal swampy land, which was more suitable for growing rye, but also made the grain more susceptible to fungal contamination. Finally, court records show that at least some of the bread consumed at an alleged 'witch sacrament' in Essex County was red.

"The victims' symptoms were textbook typical for what modern scientists now know to be ergot poisoning. How sad, then, that the Salem witches were probably killed because of an epidemic over which they had no control and about which they hadn't a clue."

I need to add here that my own personal research does not bear out Matossian's claim that the witches were put to the stake. But if you would like to do more reading on the subject of the Salem witchcraft trials, I refer you to *1692 Witchhunt, The Layman's Guide to the Salem Witchcraft Trials,* by George M. Yool, published in 1992 by Heritage Books, Inc., 800-398-7709.

TODAY'S TIP: From the time of colonial America there have been numerous fraternal, beneficial, protective and ethnic societies active in this country. The basis of these organizations was varied: traditions, secret rituals, moral enhancement, service, employment, common origin, religion and insurance. Among the largest were the Masonic Order, the Knights of Columbus, the Independent Order of Odd Fellows, the Benevolent and Protective Order of Elks, the Fraternal Order of Eagles, the Modern Woodman of the World, and the Loyal Order of Moose. These and many others are listed in the *Encyclopedia of Associations,* by N. Yates and D. Akey, Gale Research Co., 1979, Volume 1 Section 10. If you know or suspect that your ancestor belonged to one of these organizations, send an SASE to the national society address (obtained from the above book) and ask for the address of the local chapter in your ancestor's location. Then send a self-addressed, stamped envelope to the local chapter, requesting biographical data on your ancestor. You'll find this book at your public library.

TEACHERS TREK ACROSS COUNTRY TO SEEK PAST

Today's column is the first of a series of reports on the nearly five-week trip that Susan Dechant and I took in April 1993 to learn more about American history and geography as it relates to genealogy. Susan teaches genealogy for the Northeast Washington Genealogical Society in Colville, and I teach the same subject in the Spokane area.

Just after Easter, we piled into Susan's red Toyota and began a 7,500-mile journey into America's past. Our goal was to increase our own appreciation of this country and to mold ourselves into better teachers because of this new understanding.

Our first stop was the Big Horn Battlefield, just east of Billings, Mont. There history smacks you right in the face as you walk up the slight rise to see the scattered white stones that mark where Custer and his men fell.

The next stop was Devil's Tower in northeastern Wyoming. We learned there is a movement to change the name of this landmark. It seems the name was given to the rocky tower by early white settlers who observed the "red devils" (American Indians) gathering there to hold religious services.

West of Laramie, WY, we stood in deep ruts carved by wagons following the Oregon Trail. We tried to imagine how many wagons it must have taken to carve these three-foot deep scars in the rock.

Standing on the overlook high above the Cumberland Gap, we could identify three states and observed that this was indeed a "gap" in the Appalachian Mountains through which settlers poured into Kentucky and then Ohio. The mountains didn't seem very forbidding to us Westerners, but history tells that they were a formidable barrier to our forebears.

It's no wonder our German immigrant ancestors were eager to make their homes in the Shenandoah Valley. The valleys between the mountains are fertile and flat, and are still green and inviting today. Dotted throughout Virginia are homes that were clearly built more than a hundred years ago and are still in use today. The visual proof of their age are the multiple chimneys rising from the rooftops.

Of course we visited Monticello, Mt. Vernon and Washington, DC. The National Park Service has done a wonderful job placing road signs to make sure you find the historical sites, and with interpretive centers to help you understand them.

At Monticello, we sat on the porch where Thomas Jefferson would have gathered with his family and friends. And at Mt. Vernon we stood near the tomb where Gen. and Mrs. George Washington are buried, along with more than 25 of their relatives. Susan and I wondered if our colonial ancestors (or yours?) ever came to visit with these two famous men.

We took an open-air tour bus through Arlington National Cemetery and learned that over 225,000 servicemen and women, along with their family members, rest here. The Custis-Lee Mansion, or Arlington House, crowns the hill and, in what was once the rose garden of Mary Custis Lee, is an imposing block monument to 2,111 unknown Confederate dead.

How many genealogists are seeking in vain to find the final resting place of their Civil War ancestors who lie in unmarked graves?

Many of us have ancestors who fought and died on Civil War battlefields. Susan and I began in Virginia with Appomattox, site of Lee's surrender, and worked our way backwards in time through Petersburg, Richmond, New Market, Fredericksburg, Manassas and then Gettysburg.

We crossed a tiny bit of beautiful West Virginia into Ohio, and could understand why there was such fierce competition for the rich farmlands that lie north of the Ohio River. The flat acres are divided by rows of deciduous trees supporting large populations of colorful birds like the cardinal and blue jay. We understood why our ancestral mothers resented being torn away from their homes in this lush area to move onto the dry a desolate new lands of Nebraska and Kansas.

There was more history than we could absorb in the Mackinaw Bridge area of northern Michigan, and in the Bismarck area of North Dakota. The Straits of Mackinaw have been a watery highway for American Indians, French Canadian fur trappers, explorers and shippers for hundreds of years.

On a clear, windy day we took the ferry to Mackinaw Island to view the Grand Hotel and long rows of "rich men's houses," built in the 1880s. We learned that people had inhabited this island for centuries, and that there was a large cemetery scattered with very old headstones.

Along the Missouri River near Bismarck, ND, is a site where so much history happened. American Indians have lived there since the dawn of time; Lewis and Clark wintered there and met Sacajawea at the Knife River village nearby. Gen. George Custer marched west from Ft. Abraham Lincoln to his destiny, and Norwegians by the thousands settled there.

Seeing the United States while learning more about American history was exciting for us, and served to reinforce how much the geographical environment dictated events involving our ancestors. We wish we could have taken everybody in our classes with us.

CAPITAL CITY
IS A TREASURE TROVE OF INFORMATION

Today's column is the second in a series on the American history, geography and genealogy trip that Susan Dechant and I took in the spring of 1993.

While in Washington, DC, we hoped to see all the archives, libraries and museums - and in five days that's not possible. We chose two of the Smithsonian museums: the building that houses the American History collection and the new Postal Museum.

In the Museum of American History, we saw the actual flag that was flying over Fort McHenry in Maryland, inspiring Francis Scott Key to write the "Star-Spangled Banner." The flag is about one fourth shorter than it was originally, and it has a ragged edge because so many of our ancestors snipped off souvenir pieces over the years!

An audio-visual presentation in the Postal Museum made us feel like we were in a swaying railway car, standing with the men sorting the mail. All of these museums have super gift shops which feature books explaining more about that particular part of history.

We also had an opportunity to take the walking tour down the inside of the Washington Monument. While descending the stairway of the 555-foot tower, the park ranger told us about the memorial stones studding the inside walls. These stones came from all 50 states and from religious and fraternal organizations, and each has a story.

Of course, we toured the Library of Congress, the National Archives, and the DAR building and library. We sat at the access computer in the Library of Congress, and smiled as we found our donated books are listed there. The main reading room, with its high painted dome and circular-desk work stations, was huge, and the book shelves and stacks supporting that room looked endless.

We stood at the rail looking down into the DAR library and heard the guide explain that this library had the best state-books collection east of Salt Lake City, and we itched to get to work!

Our tour of the National Archives took us into the barred and musty passages where we could peer through the wire and see the actual old records. We saw shelves full of hospital ledgers from the Civil War, just lying there. We could understand why armed guards and metal detectors stand by the entrance and exit to the archives. These pieces of American history, containing the names of our ancestors, are precious beyond measure.

The tour guide also explained that this main building was one of three that comprise the National Archives. Even though the storage facilities bulge with files, the government actually keeps only 1 to 2 percent of its records. And she said that yes, there are boxes of records from the Civil War era that have never been opened since they were moved from the original archives building into this newer one, and that was decades ago!

Because of the immense quantity of records, it is important that a genealogist who wants to access National Archives information do his homework and know what record group he wants to see.

We realized that it takes more than just a casual visit to do any serious genealogical research in these places.

Susan came to the Daughters of the American Revolution headquarters prepared with a list of three numbers to look up. These were three different applications from women joining the DAR, which showed descent from Adam Fisher, Susan's ancestor.

The papers have all been microfilmed, and within a short time she was looking at the three applications.

Two of the documents cited earlier applications, thereby giving Susan six more numbers (or papers) to look up. One of the applications, dated 1901 was too faint to read in the microfilm copy so Susan requested that a photocopy be sent to her.

I had come prepared to hold in my hands and look at an actual Civil War pension file. Although I teach my classes how to access these unmicrofilmed records from a distance, I had never been to Washington, DC, to access and use an entire original file in the National Archives. With the help of Bill Donahoe, a local area researcher who's helped me by mail in the past, I made arrangements to look at the pension record for Daniel Correll. Bill submitted the request slip on Friday, and on Monday morning Bill, Susan and I went to the appointed desk, and I was casually handed a packet of papers over 100 years old. I sat at a table and went through the papers showing that Daniel, and then his wife, had applied and documented their need for a pension for his service in the Civil War.

The papers looked so bright and fresh that one might guess they couldn't be so very old. I stepped to the copy machine and made copies of every document in the file so I could study them later at home. The problem with requesting these records by mail is that the National Archives will copy and send them to you for a fee, but for various reasons, they might not copy ALL the papers in the file. It was exciting to me to know that I had the entire file on Daniel.

If you would like some on-site help in Washington, DC, Bill would be delighted to hear from you. His address is RR1, Box 35-A, VA 601, Paris, VA 20130-8802. Send the outline of your problem to him, along with a self-addressed, stamped envelope, and you'll soon be benefiting from his years of experience.

TODAY'S TRIVIA: The word "newspaper" is said not to have been derived from the word "news" as you might think, but from North, East, West and South, indicating that the information is derived from the four corners of the globe. Comments anyone?

EASTERN CEMETERIES RAPIDLY DETERIORATING

Today's column is the third in a mini-series about a five-week genealogy trip I took around the country with Susan Dechant.

One thing we learned from our trip is that if you plan to go searching for the cemeteries and tombstones of your ancestors, particularly those buried "back east," then we suggest you do it soon! Those cemeteries are disappearing! And the ones that survive may appear quaint and idyllic, but a look around the edges will reveal a different story.

In Madison County, OH, for instance, there is a beautiful little rural cemetery near Plain City. The Darby Township Cemetery lies just outside of this small town along a bend in the narrow road. The name is prominently displayed in a black wrought-iron arched gateway. The cemetery itself looked lovely when we got there and fairly well tended. The grass was cut, there were no gopher holes, and only a few dandelions smiled about the grounds. If we had been looking at the Darby cemetery as a final resting place for our ancestors, we would have been pleased as we viewed it from the car.

Once out of the car, however, the reality of the situation quickly set in. We were there with some local friends to take photos of a typical old Ohio cemetery. So, camera in hand, we started walking and looking. But, instead of finding names carved on upright tombstones, we were finding empty spaces where tombstones had been! To be fair, there were still plenty of upright stones, and probably two-thirds of the cemetery was still in proper shape. It was the broken ones, the faded ones and the missing ones that really tugged at our hearts. These were the markers for somebody's family, markers that were expected to memorialize a person forever.

Too many stones were broken in half, propped next to the base. Many had ornaments (like lambs or urns) broken off and were weathered beyond reading or crusted with lichens. In some cases, stones had fallen and were covered over by grass. And too many stones were represented by little nubs — the broken stone was removed entirely.

But the real horror story unfolded just behind the Darby Township Cemetery. A little gully, channeling a small stream, lay at the farthest edge of the cemetery property. Here we found tombstones — broken ones and whole ones — in the weeds or pushed over the edge into the gully. In one back corner we discovered a stack of tombstones the size of a cord of wood that had been removed from the cemetery grounds. Susan and I nearly cried at the sight.

Our friends, Orville and Jane Russell, life-long genealogists and residents of the area, explained that there were 88 county cemeteries listed in a 1941 inventory. Recently, another survey was taken, and only 50 were found. What happened to them?

Orville explained that most of those missing cemeteries had been small private or family plots on private land. Over the years, they had fallen into disrepair or disuse, and slowly became overgrown. Or they ended up in an enlarged cow pasture where the Guernseys knocked over the stones and the cemetery gradually disappeared. Or possibly, when the land changed hands and the fences altered, the new farmers weren't of the same family as those buried in the "back corner by the pasture;" then it was easy to take the place lightly and allow the cows in.

Eventually, most of these little family cemeteries became farmland. In years past, there were no laws to protect family cemeteries; now there are. Thank goodness, say all genealogists.

If you're planning a trip to find and photograph your ancestor's tombstone in a cemetery east of the Mississippi, then, in my opinion, you'd better be doing it. Today's cemeteries may be protected by law from cows, but not from vandals or benign neglect. If you can't journey in person to Ohio or Virginia, perhaps a friend or relative can take pictures. If that's not possible, contact a local historical or genealogical society and ask if one of their members will do the honors for you.

You'll find guidebooks listing historical and genealogical societies in most public libraries, or any Family History Center. Do it today, and good luck!

CREATIVE FAMILY PROJECT: Would you like a new kind of genealogy project for the rest of the summer? How about one that combines genealogy with quilting? Ami Simms of Flint, MI, has written *Creating Scrapbook Quilts*, an exciting new way to preserve genealogy and family memories while creating an heirloom piece for the whole family to enjoy.

With this how-to book as a guide, old family photos, mementos and even letters can be turned into a quilt. Images are transferred to fabric, and pieces assembled to make a family photo album quilt, a travel diary, a mother's birthday or a hometown celebration piece.

The images can be photos, postcards from trips, letters from family, announcements, diplomas — anything you want. Flint's book tells how to transfer the images to fabric, where to order supplies, and even provides an address for commercial companies who will do the work if you don't want to. Several color photos of finished quilts complement the text. If compiling memories in fabric form sounds like a great summer project, you can order *Creating Scrapbook Quilts* for $14.45 from Mallery Press, 4206 Sheraton Dr., Flint, MI 48532, or call 800-A-STITCH. Why not make it a family project?

LIBRARIES ESSENTIAL TO TRAVELING

Today's column is the fourth in a series about travels throughout the country with my friend Susan Dechant to learn more about genealogy, history and geography.

After spending a delightful morning at the Columbus Zoo in central Ohio, we turned north to Toledo, heading for Michigan. Susan was driving and as I studied the map (we did a lot of map studying), I noticed the little town of Galion was just an inch or so off our route. Did we want detour and stop there?

Susan's maiden name was Gallyon, and she's found that this name is fairly uncommon. Her family immigrated in colonial times to Maryland, remaining there until her father broke the mold and moved to southern California. Since we have learned in doing genealogy that all possible spellings of a surname must be considered, we wondered what connection Galion, OH, might have to her Gallyon family?

Galion lies in the southeast corner of Crawford County, and having driven through about twenty miles of beautiful farmland, we assumed our destination would be a sleepy little farm village. Not so! Galion is a bustling, progressive-looking town where everybody seems to know the local history. We stopped at the first gas station to ask directions to the public library. A couple of old timers were at the counter, and so I told them we were looking for the reason why the town was named Galion. Their answer was short: "Don't think anybody knows." I thanked them, thinking they surely must be wrong.

The Galion Public Library is a fully restored Carnegie Library. The gold-embossed sign sits inside a beautiful wrought-iron fence, which was edged with daffodils. We found a parking place in front and eagerly ran up the stairs into the building. In response to our question, "We're here to learn how the town of Galion got its name and to see if my family is related to your founding fathers," the receptionist directed us downstairs to the Ohio Room. A young woman with a huge ring of keys cheerfully unlocked the door and pointed out where we should begin our search. We had our answer in about 30 minutes.

Here's where our story applies to almost any research situation. Most public libraries have a local history section with books about the area. There might also be a vertical file, a filing cabinet full of what I call tidbits — newspaper clippings, pamphlets, photographs and old letters, etc. Frequently this section is kept under lock and key because the information is so specialized and often old and rare. But there will usually be library personnel assigned to help patrons, as was the case in the Galion Public Library.

Susan began looking through the dozen or so huge history books about Crawford County while I dove into the vertical file. Because the material was so well organized, it took practically no time for the answer to appear. It seems the town of Galion was founded in 1825, and the name was assigned by the U.S. Postal Service. Several of the articles we found stated that fact quite clearly: "nobody knows exactly why the Postal Service chose the name." Seems the old timers in the gas station were right!

We hadn't been working in the Ohio Room very long when the nice lady assigned as curator and helper for those records offered assistance. Susan and I showed her what we'd found, and she agreed that we had the answer, such as it was.

She then suggested that we go around the corner to the Galion Chamber of Commerce to see what information they might have. The young woman with the keys called to see if the Chamber was still open, and the Ohio Room curator said she would make copies of our information and have them ready upon our return.

The Galion Chamber of Commerce had all sorts of maps and brochures of Crawford County and Galion. They even gave Susan a copy of a 1975 sesquicentennial celebration booklet. She was delighted.

Back at the library, we gathered our photocopies and were refused our offer to pay for them. The curator took Susan's name and address with the assurance that she'd send more information soon. The library personnel had really gone the extra mile to help two traveling genealogists, so we thanked them heartily all around and were soon back on the road again. The stop took less than one hour.

What can you learn from this experience? When you travel to ancestral places, take time to visit the public library. Even the smallest towns have a library, thanks to millionaire Andrew

Carnegie who, in the early 1900's, spent part of his fortune building libraries across America. The wonderful staff is there to help you, and no question is too difficult! Remember, libraries are places where miracles happen, so don't ever pass up a library when you're a traveling genealogist.

TODAY'S TIPS: My friend Martin Rosander gave me a suggestion to share with all of you. "Put family Bibles, or any old and special books, in plastic boxes — like Tupperware boxes — to keep them away from sticky fingers, chewing dogs, dust and light. This makes 'em safer to sit on the shelf, and these boxes are available in most any store." Thanks, Martin.

Another Spokane reader mailed my column to a friend in San Jose, CA, who, in turn, sent me a flyer about her book, *Beginner's Guide to Hispanic Genealogy*. Authors Patsy Ludwig and Norma Flores describe this 11-chapter book as a "cheat sheet for learning your history," and stress that their book is geared for the beginner having Mexican or Spanish background. Order this $11.50, postpaid, book from Ludwig at 3345 Jarvis Ave., San Jose, CA, 95118.

MATERIAL AVAILABLE ON MICHIGAN ANCESTORS

Today's column is the fifth in a miniseries about the "genealogy good stuff" that Susan Dechant and I learned during our 7,500-mile trip around the country.

We had several good reasons to visit Michigan, and planned to drive north through the entire state, across the Mackinaw Bridge and then westward through the Upper Peninsula.

I was born in Kalamazoo and had not been back to my birthplace for thirty years. My cousins and I did rendezvous, took pictures of family cemeteries, and had a great visit over dinner.

Also, Susan and I wanted to visit Mackinaw Island. Remember the movie, "Somewhere In Time," with Christopher Reeve and Jane Seymour? We fell in love with that movie long ago, and so going to the Grand Hotel was high on our list. Luckily, I had old friends in Mackinaw City so we stayed with them and rode the ferry out to Mackinaw Island on a bright windy day. It was just as beautiful as in the movie!

The ancestor-history of that little island goes back several hundred years, spanning American Indians, Indians, French Canadian fur trappers, Yankee boat captains and immigrants pouring through be Great Lakes towards the heartland of America. I lugged home several books to learn more about this area of ancestor hunting, and can't wait to dig into them.

The story I want to relate with this column is that Sharon Russell, my friend in Mackinaw City, is also a staunch member of the Cheboygan County Genealogical Society, and we talked genealogy for half the night. I was impressed with the amount of Michigan material available to researchers, and the varied activities of this small but dedicated group.

Sharon told us that the Cheboygan County Genealogical Society had about 75 members, and held two meetings a month year round. That alone was impressive! The Day Meeting is held the second Wednesday of the month, and the Night Meeting is on the third Tuesday, and often two different programs are presented. The society has recorded all 32 cemeteries in the county, and published them, too.

They have several annual seminars and workshops, and regularly make trips down to the Allen County Public Library in Ft. Wayne, IN. Several of these addicted genealogists have made repeated trips to Salt Lake, all this when they have to drive 200 miles just to get to a feeder airport.

The neatest thing that the Cheboygan County Genealogical Society does is to prepare family history packets to hand out to each new mother in the Cheboygan Hospital. About 200 babies are born there each year, and each family goes home with how-to instructions for recording the baby's genealogy. Susan and I thought that was the best idea we'd ever heard.

Sharon also explained that Michigan became a state in 1837, but people had been coming to settle the area for the previous 120 years. Her family had been in the Cheboygan area for several generations, and she said that this was quite typical. Because of this long-term settlement, there are many records available.

If you need genealogy information on Michigan, I would suggest that you write for a free information packet from the Library of Michigan, P.O. Box 30007, Lansing, MI 48909. Write also to the Detroit Public Library, Burton Historical Collection, 5201 Woodward Ave., Detroit, MI 48202.

The Burton Historical Collection is the largest genealogical collection in Michigan. If you will be traveling to Detroit, and plan to use this collection, you should know that Ancestry, Inc., has published *A Genealogical Guide to the Burton Historical Collection, Detroit Public Library.* Joseph Oldenburg is the author of this book, which can be ordered from Ancestry at 800-262-3787, or N. 1001 Calvert Ave., Baltimore, MD 21202.

Ancestors have lived in Michigan for centuries; white ancestry dates back to 1618, two years before the Pilgrims arrived at Plymouth. Federal census records help to tell the story. In 1800, there were 3100 white people in Michigan (American Indians were not enumerated until 1860). By 1820, the white population had grown to 8900, and by 1830 the population had zoomed to 29,000. These are somebody's ancestors — are they yours?

Susan and I went back and forth over the magnificent Straits of Mackinaw several times, and were in awe of the beauty of the enormous suspension bridge (200 feet off the water in midspan). But we were excited to cross to the north one last time, point our noses into the west wind and "head for the barn," happy to arrive safely after 7,500 miles.

TODAY'S LAUGH: Cartoon, bank teller to man cashing check: "Aside from your family coat of arms, do you have any other identification?"

NATIONAL GENEALOGICAL SOCIETY IS WORTH A SECOND LOOK

This is the last of a mini-series featuring genealogy tidbits and information I gathered during a month-long trip around the country with my friend Susan Dechant. With this column I want to tell you about the National Genealogical Society.

Susan and I have been members of this organization for several years. We have benefited from their publications and have enjoyed going to their annual national conferences.

Because Susan and I had been members of the National Genealogical Society for some time, we really wanted to visit NGS headquarters on our trip to Washington, DC. The NGS offices and library are actually in Arlington, VA, across the Potomac River from the Capitol.

Our hotel was also in Arlington and one day, as we walked to the Ballston Metro station to take the subway into Washington, we ran into Suzanne Murray, an NGS staffer.

It was a fun chance meeting, and she remembered both of us because we were enrolled with the NGS home-study course.

I have completed the course and Susan is nearly finished with the 16 lessons. We chatted right there on the street corner and told her we were coming to NGS headquarters at Glebe House the next day.

At the last minute, we found out the library was closed on Tuesday afternoons when we'd programmed our visit.

We were disappointed, but drove up anyway to have a look around. To the great credit of Dereka Smith, newly-appointed main librarian, she welcomed us right in when we said we'd come from Washington, the state.

The library is housed in a new building constructed on the "footprint," or foundation, of the original carriage house. Glebe House was the residence of the rector of the Episcopal Church in colonial times, and his "glebe" was like his parish.

So the first thing we learned was that NGS had its home in a stately old residence, one that is on the National Register of Historic Places.

The new library was designed to resemble the old carriage house, and we were fooled at first until we stepped inside this ultra-modern structure.

The NGS library is bulging with books and other reference materials. The only saving grace, Dereka explained, is that NGS has a home-loan program, and about half the collection is out on loan at any given time. There were hardly any work tables; researchers squeeze the aisles and often have to sit on the floor. But it's a busy and popular place. ("If you build it, they will come," is certainly a phrase that applies to genealogical libraries.) We felt like visiting VIPs as Dereka showed us the facility from top to bottom.

Then she took us over to the Glebe House itself. Even in April, this unairconditioned building was too warm. Yet, all the work of the 10,000-member society, established in 1903, is carried on here by a very small staff. It is here that the newsletter and quarterly are compiled and edited, national conferences are planned, the library is maintained, legislation relating to genealogy is monitored, international projects are arranged, and microfilming endeavors are coordinated. All this in about 1000 square feet with a staff of eight! Susan and I were impressed.

The most interesting area to us was the domain of Suzanne Murray and Bob Nailor, the Education Committee. It was to them that we sent our lessons for the home-study course, and it was their smiling faces we'd seen at the NGS booth in Jacksonville — and again at the Metro corner. They explained that at any given time, they are assisting several hundred folks who are working on that program. Genealogy education is a priority with the National Genealogical Society.

Suzanne took us around the various rooms in Glebe House and explained what went on. She pointed out the old wooden eagle that had been removed by crane from the top of the house and was sitting on the living room carpet awaiting restoration. (Editor's Note: The eagle assumed his rightful perch in 1996.)

Last of all, Suzanne showed us the newly revised NGS beginner's kit. Available for only $9.00, postpaid, this packet contains a 44-page instruction book outlining every step necessary to get started in genealogy, plus 20 pedigree charts and family group sheets. The instruction book is reprinted often and kept up to date. This is especially important to beginners as they are often lost when their letter goes to an old, incorrect address. The book details the how-tos of keeping records, correctly citing sources, accessing family records, and using libraries. Lists of local, state and federal sources are included.

A membership brochure for the National Genealogical Society is included in the beginner's kit. Their address is N. 4527 17th St., Arlington, VA 22207-2399. Membership is $40.00 annually, and for that amount you receive four issues of the newsletter and four of the quarterly, both of which teach and keep you up to date on genealogical "doings." And you also become eligible for the home-study course and to borrow books from their library. A working genealogist who really wants to succeed will learn genealogy and better understand sources with help from the National Genealogical Society.

At the very least, send the $9.00 and get their beginner's kit. Introduce yourself to the really wonderful world of genealogy and family history.

Susan and I spent only a couple of hours at NGS headquarters in Arlington, but when we next see Suzanne we'll greet each other like old friends. And that's exciting.

TODAY'S TIP: Was your ancestor a minister with the Methodist Church? The United Methodist Church will do an initial search in their files at no cost if your ancestor was a minister and will charge for copies only if information is found. Contact the General Commission on Archives and History, P.O. Box 127, Madison, NJ 07940.

QUESTIONS COME UP ABOUT 1920 CENSUS

Genealogists have been able to use the 1920 census for two years now, yet many questions continue to arise. So perhaps this is a good time to review some of the facts regarding this latest available federal decennial census.

When did the 1920 census officially begin? January 2, 1920.

The date of enumeration appears on the heading of each page of the census schedule. All responses were to reflect the individual's status as of January 1, 1920, even if the status had changed between January 1 and the day the enumerator arrived.

Children born between January 1 and the day of enumeration were not to be listed, while individuals alive on January 1, but deceased when the enumerator arrived, were to be counted. (Now is that what happened? Your guess!)

When did the census end? The law allowed 30 days for enumeration in rural areas and two weeks in places with populations of 2,500 or more. Influenza epidemics and severe winter weather caused many delays.

How does the 1920 census differ from the 1910 census? The 1920 census did not have questions regarding unemployment, Union or Confederate military service, number of children, or duration of marriage. It did include new questions: the year of arrival (if an immigrant), the year of naturalization and the mother tongue.

The 1920 census covered Guam, American Samoa and the Panama Canal Zone for the first time. Another important difference is that the 1920 census is completely Soundexed, but the 1910 census is so indexed for only 21 states.

The 1920 census was taken soon after World War I. Did the war affect the gathering of census information in any way? Yes.

Due to boundary modifications in Europe as a result of the war, individuals were uncertain about how to identify their national origin. Enumerators were instructed to spell out the name of the city, state, province or region of respondents who declared that they or their parents had been born in Germany, Austria-Hungary, Russia or Turkey.

Do the 1920 farm schedules exist? By authority of Congress, the non-population schedules, including farm schedules, were destroyed.

Do the original 1920 schedules still exist? No. Disposal of the original 1920 census schedules was authorized by the 83rd Congress.

Is there an index for each state? Yes. There is a Soundex index on microfilm for each state and territory.

What is Soundex? Soundex is a coded surname index to the census schedules. It was prepared by the Works Progress Administration between 1938 and 1940. The code is formed from the first letter of the last name, followed by a three-number code representing the remaining consonants in the name. The Soundex coding system was developed to find a surname even though it may have been recorded under various spellings.

Is it possible that my family was missed in the indexing? Yes!

There are no statistics on the rate of error in the index. With almost 106 million individuals on the 1920 census, it is highly probable that some names were overlooked.

What about servicemen? Enumerators were instructed not to report servicemen in the family enumerations but to treat them as residents of their duty posts.

The 1920 census includes schedules and a Soundex index for overseas military and naval forces. The same is true for institutions such as hospitals or prisons.

How can I use the naturalization information I find on the census? Designations in the "Citizenship" column should serve as a guide: NA stood for naturalized; PA for first papers (declaration of intention); AL for alien; and NR for citizenship not reported.

Why are census records closed for 72 years? In 1952, the Director of the Census and the Archivist of the United States agreed that population schedules were to be transferred to the

National Archives "with the provision that they remain closed for 72 years after the enumeration date for each census" for privacy reasons. At that time, 72 was considered the average life span for an American male.

Figuring out the Soundex code for names may be easy for some, confusing for others. For this latter group, there is a book that will help.

The Soundex Reference Guide, second edition, contains over 500,000 names, already Soundexed. This guide is available in a two-volume set for $99.95, or on disk for $49.95, from American Genealogical Lending Library, P.O. Box 329, Bountiful, UT 84011-0329. Call them at 800-760 AGLL to check availability.

By using this index, the researcher doesn't need to go through the procedure of coding names letter by letter or impatiently wait for help from busy librarians. Surname entries are filed alphabetically for easy reference. (This would be a wonderful gift from you to your genealogical library!)

TODAY'S TRIVIA: The Russian government's historical archives in St. Petersburg are now open to American researchers. Records include those from the 18th century through the 1917 Bolshevik Revolution. Records are of Russian nobility and heraldry; family history records of ethnic groups such as Cossack, Ukrainian, German, Balt, Finn, Jewish, etc.; histories of German colonies in Russia, including lists of colonists; and much more.

A Russian-American joint venture has been formed to make information more accessible to Americans. The nearest office is the Baltic-Russian Information Center, 907 Mission Ave., San Rafael, CA 94901.

TODAY'S LAUGH: Oops! Should you find "DPS" or "Decessit Sine Prole" on your ancestor's tombstone, you have a real problem, for that is Latin for "died without issue."

COMPUTERS OPEN WINDOWS FOR GENEALOGISTS

Nationally known genealogy columnist Myra Gormley said it best in 1994: "As computer technology opens doors — or windows, as the case may be — the genealogist-consumer is faced with an array of new research opportunities via modem."

For certain, the 21st-century technology has entered the field of genealogy, making it easier than ever to find information on your ancestors.

With the new on-line services, some say all you genealogists will never have to leave your chair to search critical databases and download information from home computers using a modem and the telephone lines. This is really good news for the homebound, or for those in care-giving situations. And it's just plain great news for any working genealogist.

People interested in signing up to use these services should take time to study details such as cost factors and the quality of the data available. Currently, commercial companies offering this on-line service have proven reputations of reliability and that is encouraging to anyone wanting to access these services.

The basic cost of these on-line services will average $15.00 to $20.00 per month. But for your money, you can access dozens of databases which could cost much more if you had to travel to the Family History Library in Salt Lake, or to purchase in book or disk form.

To jump into this new world of high-tech genealogy, talk to your friends and members of your local genealogical society who are already using this new technology. Ask their advice and opinions. Visit computer stores and ask questions about hardware and software. Stay tuned to genealogy periodicals for what's developing in computer genealogy.

A computer cannot "do" your genealogy for your, but will open doors — and windows — to all kinds of new sources.

Instructional videos

A boon of a very different sort to homebound genealogists, or any family historian (especially fledgling ones), is Ron Cook's new series of instructional videos. Have you ever sat at home and wondered, "Where do I begin?" If it isn't easy for you to attend genealogical society meetings and workshops, and you still need answers to the questions about how to get started in genealogy, then these videos will be of great interest to you.

The first tape covers home sources (how to use family mementos to learn about your forebears), published histories (how to find and use published county and family histories), and how to use the Ancestral File and International Genealogical Index. The last portion of this tape tells how to organize your research materials. Tape two teaches about census records and probate records. The third video instructs on land records, military records and vital records.

These are high-quality videos using a step-by-step approach. It shows a concept being taught in the classroom and then both instructor and student go into the Family History Library to demonstrate precisely how to use each concept and source presented.

Cook told me these three tapes are only the beginning. He envisions a complete library of video genealogy tapes.

These videos would be an excellent visual review for any seasoned genealogist and a definite boon for the entry-level genealogist. The set of three tapes may be ordered for $59.95, plus $7.95 shipping and handling fee, from Video Knowledge, 32 North 200 East, Suite 1, Spanish Fork, UT 84660, or by calling 800-34-ROOTS. These tapes are really like having a professional genealogist and teacher all to yourself!

TODAY'S TRIVIA: Did you know that the term "orphan" in old documents and court records frequently referred to someone under legal age whose father had died, but whose mother might be still alive? Often the mother was appointed guardian of children under the age of 14. But in most jurisdictions, if the child was over 14, he could name his own guardian and many times it was not the mother.

CIVIL WAR RECORDS UNLOCK MYSTERIES

Few records so rich with biographical information are overlooked more often than the "Tennessee Civil War Veterans Questionnaires."

The first set of questionnaires was sent in 1914 and 1915 to all known living Tennessee Civil War veterans by the state archivist. A second revised questionnaire was sent by the Director of the Tennessee Historical Commission in 1920. The number of forms distributed is not known, but a total of 1650 veterans responded by 1922, and their biographies now comprise one of the major genealogical record sources from that era.

Tennessee, like Pennsylvania, was a "keystone" state during the period of westward expansion. Millions of Americans living today have more than one ancestor who was born or lived in Tennessee before 1900. And while that ancestor may not have served in the Civil War, his brothers, cousins, or uncles could have been in the Union or Confederate armies. Perhaps one of them returned this questionnaire, which could help trace your family during a period when people were on the move and records are scant.

Most of the original questionnaires are handwritten, but some are typescripts. Two new questions were added to the revised form and others are arranged in a different order from the original. These records are filled with valuable genealogical information, including the veteran's name, residence, age, place of birth, occupation, the unit he served in during the war, parents' names and birthplaces, the names of maternal and paternal grandparents, and great-grandparents and their residences. Many veterans provided more than four generations of ancestry in addendum sheets. They include details about their family's arrival in America, property owned by the veteran and his parents, education and the general quality of his life.

The information from these questionnaires has been published in a book, *The Tennessee Civil War Veterans Questionnaires*, edited by Colleen Morse Elliott and Louise Armstrong Moxley, and available from Southern Historical Press, P.O. Box 1267, Greenville, SC 29602-1267.

Or you may order a surname search of this book for $9.50 from Lineages Inc., P.O. Box 417, Salt Lake City, UT 84110. (This professional search also includes two other Tennessee databases.) Thanks to *Lineages Club News*, article by Elliott West, for this information.

Readers Have Questions

A reader has asked: "What was the effect of the railroad on the distribution of population in eastern Washington, Oregon and Idaho?" In the last half of the 19th century, as the railroads expanded across the country, they hit upon some imaginative financing policies.

One scheme was to acquire a much wider swath of land than was actually needed for the railroad and then sell off the remaining parcels to immigrant settlers. The railroads not only offered the land at a good price, but they also offered the means to buy it and a way to get produce and products to market. They had little problem selling the land.

Thus, people settled along the railroad route and towns and cities quickly sprang up. Find an old state map and look for the cross-hatch lines indicating railroads. You'll notice that most of the population lived along this corridor.

Another reader's question is: "What is collateral research?" When you've been concentrating on your direct pedigree line (father to grandfather to great-grandfather, etc.) and you're just not finding the answers to your questions, then it might be time for collateral research.

When you do this type of research, you look into the lives of your ancestors' siblings and children — where did those aunts and uncles live? Where did they die? Were they written about in any family or county histories?

Sometimes you'll find things like this example: Suppose that you can't push past your great-grandfather, John Applebee, who was born in Tennessee in 1804. Suppose that he had a sister, Cicely Applebee, who married into the very old Byrd family of Virginia.

There are many books written about the Byrd families, and quite possibly there might be a biography of one Thomas Jefferson Byrd who married a Tennessee girl named Applebee and here perhaps you'll discover a reference to a biography on Cicely's family! Try it, it works.

TODAY'S LAUGH: Every family tree has its squirrels, nuts and knotheads.

CENTER AIDS SEARCH FOR SWEDISH ANCESTRY

Today's column will be another potpourri of information that I have gathered from my genealogical reading and from "sharings" sent by readers.

Swedish research center: Those of Swedish descent who are working on family history might want to consider writing to the Swenson Swedish Center in Illinois for information and help. This center aspires to be a national archive and research institute providing resources for study of the impact of Swedish immigrants on American life and culture.

The center became a reality when a Swedish immigrant named Birger Swenson, together with his wife Lyal, decided they wanted to do something meaningful to preserve the heritage which had become so important to them. In 1980, the Swensons established an endowment at Augustana College in support of the Swenson Swedish Immigration Research Center. Now, more than a decade later, the center has collected a vast library of books, periodicals, newspapers and original manuscripts concerning Swedish immigrants into America.

One important collection which recently became available through the center is the Lutheran Church records. In 1686, a law was passed in Sweden directing that detailed records be kept of all people living in that country. As all Swedes then belonged to the Lutheran Church, the task of record-keeping was assigned to the Lutheran State Church.

These Swedish church records are unique in the world. Extending back into the early 17th century, they contain a variety of detailed information on individual Swedes. Besides names, dates and places of birth and death, you can find records of the movement of families as they grew and changed. For information on this special collection, write to The Swenson Center, Box 175, Augustana College, Rock Island, IL 61202-2296.

Among other unique records are the Registers of Emigration from Sweden. As the idea of emigration fired the minds of landless Swedes and the populace began leaving in droves in the 19th century, the government ordered the Lutheran churches to keep track of who was leaving. These registers have recently been microfilmed in Sweden and made available through the Swenson Center.

Plan that reunion: Enid Potter Tronsen called in August to tell me about her Potter family reunion being held in Spokane. Since I'm a Potter too, I was all ears, and besides, Enid and I are very distant cousins from a colonial New England ancestor named Potter.

The reunion was of more recent cousins, all grandchildren of Myron and Mary (Laughlin) Potter, who homesteaded in Dooley, MT. The town has been plowed into wheatfields now (except for the Lutheran Church), so the cousins take turns hosting the reunion. There were 50 folks at the Spokane reunion, but only one still carries the Potter name (Enid's brother).

The cousins are getting older and feel it is vitally important that reunions of the second and third cousins continue into the next century. How many readers have a flock of cousins living close by and are thinking, "We should do that." Well, time's afleeting, and I recommend you just do it. Local parks host reunions all summer long. Why not yours? For some great ideas, consult Kathy Smith Anthenat's book, *Fantastic Family Reunions*, available from Heritage Books at 800-398-7709.

Irish newsletter: *The Irish at Home and Abroad* is a fantastic newsletter for those of Irish descent who are struggling with research in the "auld sod." I've seen the first few issues, and they make me wish I had Irish ancestors and could benefit from all the information and tips! Subscriptions are $15.00 annually, and you can contact the editors at P.O. Box 521806, Salt Lake City, UT 84152. Or call (801) 596-9314 to request a sample issue.

Maine research: For those of you researching in Maine, Heritage Books, Inc. has re-issued editions of books written in 1880 and 1925. The *History of Cumberland County, Maine,* by W.W. Clayton, is a two-volume set providing general history of the county, the city of Portland and other area towns, and includes over 300 biographical sketches. If you have Cumberland County ancestry, you'll be happy to know you can get your hands on this book. Call Heritage Books at 800-398-7709 to order or inquire about this set of books.

The other book is *Stackpole's History of Winthrop, Maine,* by David and Elizabeth Young. The authors have taken Stackpole's original 1925 book and added 110 family biographical sketches to the original 143. Would your Maine ancestor have lived in Winthrop? It is great to have access again to these classic old books.

TODAY'S LAUGHS: Nationally syndicated trivia columnist L.M. Boyd says, "Genetically, you only differ from your mother-in-law by 0.1 percent. So why don't you get along?"

Also, did you hear about the man who changed his name from Peter Eastman Jr. to Trout Fishing In America. Honest! I heard it on the news.

And from the Norwegian Medical Dictionary: "Barium" - what doctors do when treatment fails. "Coma" - a punctuation mark. "Fester" - quicker! "Hangnail" - coat hook. "Impotent" - distinguished; well known."

CIVIL WAR RECORDS ARE RECEIVING PROPER CARE

Recently there has been some anxiety regarding rumors that various Civil War records in the National Archives were in jeopardy of being destroyed.

I conveyed a message from concerned genealogists that we need to write letters in an attempt to stop this action. I have received updates on these situations, and share this new information with you. Thanks to Lillian Forster for her bird-dogging diligence regarding the matter of the Civil War records.

Forster sent me a letter she received in August from Texas senator, Phil Gramm. Gramm's letter was a copy of one he received from Michael Kurtz, acting assistant to the Archivist of the United States.

Here's what Kurtz had to say: "The National Archives has made considerable efforts to preserve Confederate records. The Confederate records in the National Archives amount to 5832 cubic feet. At approximately 2500 pages per cubic foot, the Confederate records contain over 14 million pages. We have thus far conserved and published over 10 million pages of the most heavily used of the Confederate records. All told, there are 63 microfilm publications (9739 rolls of microfilm) of Confederate records.

"Some 35 publications (7409 rolls of microfilm) reproduce all of the name indexes and individually compiled Confederate service records in the custody of the National Archives. Twenty-eight additional publications reproduce other types of records relating to the Confederate government. Much of this preservation microfilming and subsequent publication of the Confederate records was funded in part by a gift from the United Daughters of the Confederacy. Comparable records documenting Union service are not yet microfilmed.

"We also have undertaken other projects for conservation of paper records that are not being microfilmed immediately. For example, we have completed holdings maintenance on a series of records concerning Confederate notables, such as leading Confederate military officers, and laboratory conservation has been completed on a volume of designs for the Confederate flag.

"Recent press accounts of the condition of the Civil War records leave the wrong impression that the records are stored in poor environments. The Civil War records are housed in accordance with the basic standards of the archives profession for the storage of all historical records. They are kept in the stack areas of the National Archives Building in Washington, DC, and the temperature and humidity levels in these stacks are regulated to set a proper storage environment.

"We hope this information provides some perspective on the treatment of Confederate records. Let me add that the National Archives recently conducted a pilot project to train unpaid volunteers to perform basic preservation work for Civil War records. There were 28 people in the first group of volunteers. The pilot project was successful and we now hope to increase the size of this Civil War Volunteer Conservation Corps to as many as 45 to 60 volunteers working to preserve Civil War records.

"I hope this information contains answers to the questions your constituent has raised. If there are any further questions, please do not hesitate to call me. The telephone number is (202) 501-5300."

Many Irish Took The Long Route To America

Chattaroy reader Dian Crego Miller recently sent me a wonderful article that first appeared in the periodical "Quoddy Tides," published in Eastport, ME, in March, 1992.

The article was written by Marie Jones Holmes, and I'm delighted to be able to share parts of it, somewhat paraphrased, with you.

Titled *The Irish Came by the Thousands,* the article explains that many Americans, including those of Irish extraction, think of Boston and New York as the major ports of entry for the Irish. But, in fact, for many Irish immigrants, those cities were actually the second or third port of call in their journey to the United States.

For many Irish, the first port of call was Saint John or Saint Andrews, New Brunswick, Canada. A large proportion of the Irish immigrants who arrived in New Brunswick during the first half of the 1800s, including those who came as a result of the potato famine, did not stay there. It simply was more economical to enter through New Brunswick, with America as the ultimate destination. At that time, it was easy to get cheap passage to Eastport or Portland, ME, from New Brunswick.

In July 1832, it was reported that over 4000 immigrants had arrived so far that year in Saint John, with nearly 1000 carried to Eastport by the steamer *Henrietta* on her three trips. Others stayed a year or two in New Brunswick to earn some money before moving on to their final destination. Regular runs by steamer from Bangor and Portland, ME, to Boston were operating by the early 1840s.

People of smaller means sometimes started their journey south on foot. One route was the military road from Calais to Bangor, a dirt path through the wilderness which opened in 1830 and was enlarged to a regular state service in 1836. There was also a more westerly route known as the inside route. This consisted of taking a steamer from Saint John to Eastport, a mail stage to Bucksport or Bangor, and another steamer to Portland or Boston.

The Irish began coming to New Brunswick in the 1700s. In 1779 and 1780, there were proposals to change the name of the present Prince Edward Island and New Brunswick to New Ireland. Most of the Irish who arrived in the years immediately following the Napoleonic Wars came from Northern Ireland.

Records show that nearly 19,000 immigrants had reached New Brunswick ports in the years 1816 to 1826 and most came from Londonderry and were Protestant. Other records indicate that at least 35,000 immigrants, almost all of whom were Irish, reached New Brunswick in the years 1818 to 1826.

By the mid-1840s, Catholics numbered as large as any Protestant group in Saint John. The 1861 census, the first to include religious affiliation, showed Saint John's population was almost 40 percent Catholic.

It is widely believed that most of those who claim Irish ancestry in New Brunswick today are descendants of the famine Irish. This is not true. The majority are actually descendants of the prefamine Irish. The possession of land has historically been regarded by the Irish as the measure of both wealth and of independence. The vast expanse of land in North America had lured the Irish away from Ireland long before the famine.

The desire of many people in Great Britain to emigrate after the end of the Napoleonic Wars in 1815 came at a good time for New Brunswick. The closing of the Baltic ports to British shipping had forced timber merchants to turn to the British North American colonies for their supplies. The growth of the Atlantic timber trade made it easier for immigrants to get to New Brunswick. It was far more profitable for ships carrying timber to Britain to return full of immigrants rather than empty. With the increased demand for cheap passages, ship owners found they could make quick profits by putting in temporary decks and filling the holds with passengers. In 1818, the fare from Londonderry, Northern Ireland, to Saint Andrews, New Brunswick, was five guineas. To Saint John it was about three and a half guineas. Ships bound for American ports charged ten guineas.

Ships for Saint John and Saint Andrews were advertised as being convenient for immigrants going to Boston, New York and Philadelphia, and this route was taken whenever possible by poor immigrants. Sometimes advertisements for ship passage were purposely misleading.

Small-scale maps were used to lead the immigrants to believe that Boston was next to British North American ports. In addition, vessels bound for New Brunswick ports could, by law, carry ten passengers for every three carried in ships to U.S. ports.

As a result, ships to Canada and New Brunswick carried most of the immigrants bound for Boston, New York and Philadelphia. An import head tax charged to ships' masters or owners at U.S. ports was often passed on to the passenger. This gave New Brunswick-bound ships another advantage.

In some years, immigrants were welcomed in both New Brunswick and Maine. In other years, they were not. Immigrants were especially welcomed when times were good and when there was a shortage of labor.

Economic history from 1846 to 1851 directly correlates with the number of Irish immigrants passing through Maine ports, according to the Boston Federal Court naturalization records. Most Irish immigrants then came through the port of Eastport and settled nearby. They were laborers, bricklayers, blacksmiths and teamsters. In the late 1800s, Eastport town records show a large area known as "Irish Hollow." Massachusetts towns show similar settlement patterns of early Irish communities.

Not all Irish families coming to New Brunswick pushed on to America. The 1850 census of Charlotte County, New Brunswick, indicates many Irish families stayed right there. Most Irish who were to settle the Atlantic region of Canada had arrived by the time of Ireland's potato famine. During the famine years, ships bearing Irish passengers docked less often in Canada and more often in New York. One reason was economics: cheap fares were offered into New York and on the Erie Canal to entice Irish laborers "west" to work on the railroads.

Irish immigrants who did settle in New Brunswick often named their settlements after places they left in Ireland. There was St. Patrick's Lake, settled in 1786, and Kerr Lake settled in 1817. Cork, settled in 1842, was first called Teetotal settlement as many immigrants, before leaving for America, took the pledge to abstain from intoxicating liquor. Other New Brunswick names include Ballyshannon, New Ireland, Galway, Kerry, Donegal, Londonderry, Waterford, Hibernia, St. George and many more.

Conditions aboard immigrant ships varied from ship to ship. In the years prior to the 1840s, the death rate on ships and in quarantine was not very high. A check of ship returns for the early 1840s shows a death rate of less than 1 percent. It appears that regardless of conditions aboard ship, healthy immigrants could survive the voyage. High death rates came only when weak, starving immigrants were crowded into vessels, as happened during the famine. That's when the death rate often soared: it reached 15 percent in 1847, the worst year.

On Partridge Island in Saint John Harbor, the receiving station for immigrants, Irish passengers arrived under appalling circumstances. In 1847, nearly 15,000 people arrived at Saint John, fleeing famine and eviction at home; nearly 1,200 of those people died on the island and at the city's alms house.

Genealogists researching Irish immigrant ancestors, especially those arriving in Massachusetts in the 1700s, might do well to take another look at the situation — especially if the researchers can't seem to push any further back than the port of arrival. Perhaps your 18th century Irish ancestor sailed to New Brunswick, or other Atlantic Canadian ports. Or, perhaps before he moved south to America, he left family members buried in Canadian soil.

Thanks to Dian for sharing such an interesting article.

MILITARY TIES I am always recommending books in this column since I'm a book lover at heart and recognize that the answer to most every question can be found by looking in the right book. This is especially true for folks wanting to know more about their ancestor's involvement with the U.S. military.

Ancestry Publishing's newest offering, *U.S. Military Records, A Guide to Federal and State Sources, Colonial America to the Present,* will answer nearly every question about U.S. military records, what they are and where they are. Compiled by James C. Neagles, this hardbound, 455-page book is the most exciting new research aid that I've seen in a good, long while.

Chapter titles tell the story: "Records Created During Military Service," "Post-Service Records and Records Relating to Civilian Affairs" (such as pensions), "Resources in the National Archives in Washington, DC, and in the Reference Branches," "Resources for History and Research In and Outside of Washington, DC." Nearly 200 pages are devoted to "State Resources."

There is a chapter on "Published Sources," and a brief history of all American military conflicts, is included. This $39.95 book would make a wonderful Christmas present. Call 800-531-1790 to order Neagles' brand new book on U.S. Military Records.

TODAY'S LAUGH: None but a mule denies his family. (Anonymous.)

WELL-KNOWN FAMILIES GOOD FOR LAUGHS

Since today is Christmas Day – and not a day for heavy genealogical reading – allow me to share a couple cute stories about two favorite families of mine: the Bean family and the Tate family.

The Bean family is quite well known. Perhaps you've heard of them? Have you heard of the Bean family that fled to Peru to avoid persecution by the British back in 1780? They're the LIMA BEAN family. And how about John Paul Bean who commanded a ship in the War of 1812? His male descendants have all been Annapolis graduates. A patriotic bunch, those NAVY BEANS.

Speaking of military men, have you heard about the men in the family who became paratroopers during the war? JUMPING BEANS they were called. And, McTavish Bean? He was a mercenary for the Polish count in 1774. He lived out his life in Warsaw, and founded a line that exists to this day. Perhaps you've heard of them — the POLE BEANS?

Then, of course, there was the German branch of family, industrialists, famed for their elegant automobiles, the MERCEDES BEANS. And the famous, old, very large Irish family, the ones who always loudly celebrate St. Patrick's Day: the GREEN BEANS.

Then, there's the family branch that became large landowners, principally having orchards and running a home-canning business, the JELLY BEANS. Surely you've heard that Lady Flora Dora and was immortalized in Madame Tussaud's Wax Museum in London where she's known as the WAX BEAN.

One branch of the family migrated to Mexico, where they perfected the recipe for a soup known around the world — the CHILI BEANS. (Or did that family branch live in Alaska?)

The Bean family has always gotten along with their neighbors. One branch intermarried with a fine Cuban family and became the famed GARBANZO BEANS.

There's a family line in China, the SOY BEANS, and of course, the BLACK BEANS in Swaziland, and the Sioux line descending directly from Chief Crazy Horse, the RED BEANS. And some were great horsemen on the Great Plains of America, the PINTO BEANS.

Of course, there was Machine Gun Bean, the gangster. He got the electric chair. Odd thing, though. The power failed just as they threw the switch. They had to make repairs before electrocuting him, which developed into a little joke in the family about him: the REFRIED BEAN.

And, it seems that every Bean family has a lazy brother — the BEAN DIP; his ugly wife — the BEAN BAG; and their maddening children, the BEAN SPROUTS. They have an annual family affair, the BEAN BALL.

Lastly, there is the very important, but little-known, French side of the Bean family. No not the common FRENCH BEANS! This is a high-class family. In the 17th century, they changed their name to LEGUME.

Now let me introduce you to the Tate family.

First, there is old man DIC TATE who wants to run everything, while his son RO TATE tries to change everything. His wife, AGI TATE, stirs up plenty of trouble with the help of her sister, IRRI TATE. Whenever there are new projects, uncle HESI TATE and his wife VEGI TATE want to wait until next year.

Then there is cousin IMI TATE who wishes her family were like all her friends' families. Cousin DEVAS TATE provides the voice of doom, while POTEN TATE has cut himself off completely from the rest of the family.

Cousin COGI TATE and his wife MEDI TATE always think things over and are usually very positive in their ideas. And, of course, cousin LEVI TATE always keeps things up in the air! Last of all are Mr. and Mrs. FACILI TATE and their children who always seem to pick up the pieces, keep the schedule, and run the show.

Today's column ends with a genealogy poem penned by Willis Corbitt:

I think that I shall never see the finish of my family tree
As it forever seems to grow from roots that started very low,
Way back in ancient history times in foreign lands and distant climes.
From them grew trunk and branching limb that dated back to time so dim
One seldom knows exactly when the parents met and married then.
Though a verse like this is made by me, and the end's in sight as you can see
'Tis not the same with Family Trees that grow and grow through centuries.

1995

POPE GREGORY XIII CORRECTED CAESAR'S ERROR, BUT MADE ONE OF HIS OWN

Tomorrow begins a new year and people around the world will simply start the calendar year of 1996 with little thought. It wasn't always that easy. Today's column will discuss how different calendars have influenced genealogy over the years.

In September 1752, England and her colonies switched from the "old style" Julian calendar to the "new style" Gregorian calendar.

The Julian calendar, introduced by Julius Caesar in 46 B.C., had been adding a 29th day to February every four years, with no exception. Compared with the true astronomical year of 365.2422 days, that was three days too many every 400 years. The result was that the calendar was slowly getting out of step with the natural seasons.

In 1582, Pope Gregory XIII corrected the error by dropping three leap years every four centuries, making the new Gregorian calendar accurate to about one day in 3,000 years. But Gregory also decided — unwisely, in retrospect — to remove, at one stroke, every erroneous Feb. 29th that had occurred since 200 A.D.

He did this by deleting 10 days from October 1582. In countries that followed the papal decree, there were only 21 days in October that year.

This is where the first and worst source of confusion happens.

Not all of Europe followed the pope in those days. Protestant countries saw no reason to shake up their calendar just because the pope decreed it. And so, by the end of 1582, and for years afterward, Catholic countries had dates that were 10 days ahead of those in Protestant countries.

June 11 in England was June 21 in France and Spain. And the difference carried over to America, between the English colonies on the one hand and those of France and Spain on the other.

The difference increased to 11 days in 1700 because that was another erroneous Julian leap year.

England finally made the switch in 1752, the last major Protestant country to do so. And, of course, the English colonies switched at the same time. The only important holdouts were the Greek and Russian Orthodox areas of Eastern Europe. Every other country used the same calendar again, just as they had done before 1582.

Dates between 1582 and 1752 cause genealogists most of the headaches, as different countries switched at different times.

A second difference in the calendars was that, until 1752, the English began their year on March 25th. January, February and most of March belonged to the old year, not the new.

That was tradition dating back even before Julius Caesar, to the very early calendars that began the year on or about the vernal equinox.

March was called the first month, April the second month, and so on to February, which was the 12th month. The reason February is a strange month, even now, is that it was originally the last month of the year.

A date like February 20, 1711, when it appears in an original document of the time, was two months after December 20, 1711, and two months before April 20, 1712. The same data might be written February 20, 1711/1712, but not always. It might also be written as 20 12th month 1711, or 20 12th month 1711/1712. They are all the same date, exactly 100 years before February 20, 1812. And that particular February had 29 days, because that's how leap years were done in the "old style."

A modern writer, referring to an old-style date like that, might put it down in one of three ways: 1711, 1712, or 1711/1712. It's up to the writer to inform the reader how he is handling the dates, but not all do.

Thus enters confusion of a far worse degree than the first kind: not just a question of 10 or 11 days, but a question of a whole year. It's not uncommon to find errors of two months arising from the difference between the old and new ways of counting months.

All of this, of course, applies only to the years before 1752. From that date onward, the English and American calendars have been as they are now.

For the genealogy researcher, knowing the days of the week can sometimes help checking doubtful dates and spotting errors.

Baptisms, for example, were usually done on Sundays in most churches.

James Savage, a leading New England genealogist in the mid-1800s, always checked the day of the week on baptisms. If it was a Puritan church and the day was not Sunday, he knew there was something wrong with the date. Not all churches followed the Sunday rule that rigidly, but if there are two possible interpretations of a baptismal date, and one is a Sunday, that's usually the correct date.

As an example of how this affects genealogy, consider that Abraham Gourden and Sarah Hodder were married in Boston on 12 May 1698, by the well-known minister, Cotton Mather. The Gourden's first child, Elizabeth, was born 27 Feb 1698. As every genealogist should know, but may forget, there was no cause for embarrassment in the Gourden and Hodder families. Baby Elizabeth was born precisely 9 1/2 months after the wedding. The two dates are in the Julian calendar, or Old Style. In the Gregorian Calendar, or New Style, the February date would be 1699.

If you would like to study more about this confusing topic, read Leo H. Garman's article, "Genealogists and the Gregorian Calendar," in the April 1898 issue of *Nexus*, the New England Historic Genealogical Society's newsletter. Also, look under Calendars and Calendar History in any genealogy textbook or in most encyclopedias.

TODAY'S TRIVIA: *Milling Around: A Guide to Old Mills Open to the Public,* is a new brochure from the Society for the Preservation of Old Mills, listing the location and telephone number of more than 100 mills in America, Canada and the United Kingdom. It includes grist mills, windmills and even a sugar mill. For a copy send a self-addressed, stamped enveloped to SPOOM, Attn: Fred Beals, 1431 Folkstone Ct., Mishasaka, IN 46544.

START AT YOUR DOWNTOWN LIBRARY
FOR HERITAGE RESEARCH

Author Alex Haley said there is a hunger in all of us to know our roots. If that is true — and I believe it is — then genealogy is a hobby that can be enjoyed by anyone willing to dig deep to discover those roots.

In past columns, I have discussed dozens of resource items for folks with English, Irish, Scottish, Welsh, Italian, Spanish, Greek or Native American ancestry. Today I have good resources for those with African-American roots.

No matter where your family lived 100 or more years ago, all genealogists begin in an identical way.

"First the Family," is genealogy rule No. 1 for everyone. Talk to your family, ask questions, ask about old photos and family stories — then begin to dig into your ancestor's official records.

Those with African-American ancestry are caught in a dilemma different from most researchers. If they are "lucky," their Southern roots-searching will lead them to a white plantation owner whose records could be quite easy to trace for at least one side of their lineage.

In mid-October, 1994, a short article ran in the newspaper on Gen. Colin Powell, a fifth-generation Jamaican. Seems that Sir Eyre Coote (1762-1823), while Lt. Gov. of Jamaica, had a child by one of his slaves who became Powell's ancestor. Sir Eyre's lineage is well documented by Burke's Peerage in England.

The genealogy section of most public libraries has items of specific interest to those tracing African-American history, including Charles L. Blockson's *Black Genealogy*; there are also magazine articles on beginning black genealogy in the vertical file.

The African American Genealogical Research Institute (AAGRI) was founded in 1993 to help blacks trace their ancestry. This group, which is building a research library, has the National Surname Registry and Index and a helpful newsletter which publishes queries and lists new research guides in its "Book Shelf" section. Write to AAGRI, P.O. Box 637, Matteson, IL 60443-6370, for more information.

A parallel organization is the AfroAmerican Historical and Genealogical Society, Inc. Headed by Barbara D. Walker, this organization publishes *AAHGS News*, a first-class, multi-page newsletter. Membership in AAHGS ($25.00 per year at this writing) includes the newsletter. Send your check to AAHGS, Inc., P.O. Box 73086, Washington, DC 20056-3086.

A recent issue carried announcements of upcoming conferences of specific interest to African Americans, snips of history involving African Americans, opportunities for historical archaeology, archival records of specific interest, queries and how-to articles.

The best feature is its new resources section, highlighting new records collections being cataloged and new, available books.

One cited source was a new CD-ROM, *Index to Black Periodicals,* compiled by G.K. Hall, and available at the New York Public Library. (It costs $895.00, so I doubt many will want to purchase it, but isn't it nice to realize somebody has done such an index?) More than 100,000 citations provide complete bibliographic information on books, films, manuscript collections, artwork and much more — all by and about people of African origin.

The California African American Genealogical Society (CAAGS), P.O. Box 8442, Los Angeles, CA 90008, was founded to encourage and support the use of genealogy as a tool for African-Americans to become aware of their history, encourage the collection and preservation of African-American genealogical materials and stimulate members to study, research and record their family histories.

For $11.00 they offer a CAAGS *Society Surname Directory*, a listing of surnames being researched by members and a *Beginning Black Genealogy* how-to book for $7.00.

A super starting place for African-American research is Cyndi's List on the Internet (www.oz.net/cyndihow/sites.htm). Also, check your library catalog; new books and resources are appearing all the time on the topic of ethnic research.

TODAY'S LAUGH: Two new classes for genealogists might just be (according to Desmond Walls Allen, nationally known genealogical author and lecturer), "How to Write the Stories to Go Along with the Facts," and "How to Write the Facts to Go Along with the Stories."

LEARN MORE ABOUT YOUR FAMILY
BY INVESTIGATING EVERYONE LISTED
ON A GIVEN CHART

How often have you heard a fellow genealogist say, "We never spelled our surname that way!" Or perhaps this: "I'm only interested in doing genealogy on my direct line." Sometimes you might even hear, "Our family has always lived in Missouri." Once I even heard, "Why bother to find out about all those brothers and sisters — that could take forever!"

Family historians who say and believe these things are like work horses wearing blinders limiting their vision to see only straight ahead. My advice is to take off those restrictive blinders, increase your peripheral vision and take another long look at the information you've already gathered onto your charts.

The timely topic of researching collateral relatives has been presented at many genealogy conferences in recent years. Only beginning genealogists fail to realize the importance of gathering all possible information about every name on the family group chart that they've collected from the very beginning of their research.

With experience comes the realization that not only can we learn more about our family by looking into the lives of everyone listed on a given chart, but that this is sometimes the only way to solve the next-generation-back problem.

Pamela Cook Spanogle, in a December 1980 article in *Journal*, a publication of the Western New York Genealogical Society, wrote that there are two types of relationships between any two related individuals.

The first is the lineal relationship: parent-child, parent-grandparent, etc. These people are called direct-line relatives. The direct line is divided into ancestors and descendants.

The other type of kinship is the collateral relationship, in which people are related because they share a common ancestor. A collateral relationship can be as close as brothers and sisters or as distant as 13th cousins.

It quickly becomes apparent that any individual has potentially far more collateral relatives than direct-line relatives.

Research should always begin with the direct line. But after the easy, direct and obvious sources have been exhausted, researchers should not give up. Other clues must be looked for and the most obvious next sources utilized and studied. Usually, it is easy to find are records on collateral ancestors. Brothers and sisters share certain common properties — the same parents, the same cousins, the same ancestors, often the same birthplaces and the same religion.

It was not uncommon for families who lived in the same area to migrate together to new counties, states or countries.

Spanogle urged genealogists to stop regarding collateral lines as just some extra names filling in the spaces on otherwise blank charts.

Collateral relatives are targets of opportunity and are every bit as important a resource as wills, deeds and the vital records we look for every day.

FOREIGN BIRTH, DEATH RECORDS

Do you need to obtain birth or death records of a person who lived outside the United States? Most, but not all, foreign countries record births and deaths and most countries will provide certification of vital events occurring within their boundaries.

To receive a copy of a foreign birth or death record, contact the American embassy or consulate of the country in question. Addresses and telephone numbers for these offices are listed in the U.S. Department of State Publication 7846, "Foreign Consular Offices in the United States," available in many local libraries. Copies may also be ordered from the U.S. Government Printing Office, Washington, DC 20402.

If the embassy or consulate is unable to help, American citizens may obtain assistance by writing to the Office of Overseas Citizens Services, U.S. Department of State, Washington, DC 20520.

RUSSIAN IMMIGRATION

Between 1871 and 1910, more than 2.3 million people from the Russian Empire emigrated to the United States; some 600,000 between 1871 and 1898; and 1.7 million between 1899 and 1910. Several nationalities or ethnic groups were represented in this migration: Poles, Ukrainians, Jews, Finns, Lithuanians, Latvians, Estonians and Germans (the so-called Volga Germans).

While this extraordinary migration has been documented, there has never been an account, by name, of those who were swept along in this floodtide of immigration. However, with the expertise and resources of the Balch Center for Immigration Research in Philadelphia, such documentation is now possible — and available in printed form.

Genealogical Publishing Co. recently published the first two volumes of a series of books that lists passengers arriving at the port of New York from the Russian Empire.

Volume 1 spans the time period January 1875 to September 1882, and Volume 2 covers October 1882 to April 1886. Together, these two volumes contain data on 105,000 persons of Russian nationality who emigrated to the U.S. from Russian territories. More volumes in this series are promised.

Both customs passengers lists and immigrations passengers lists are represented in the books, and information on each person can include name, age, occupation, country of origin, place of residence and destination.

The books ($60.00 each) may be ordered from GPC at 800-296-6687. They would be a dandy addition to any Pacific Northwest genealogy library since this area became home to thousands of Volga Germans.

If you have Russian ancestry, Jonathan D. Shea's book will be of interest. *Russian Language Documents from Russian Poland: A Translation Manual for Genealogists,* is a 73-page book covering several subjects in depth: Polish Provinces of the Russian Empire; the Russian alphabet; structure of Polish and Russian languages; expressions of time, date and age; birth, death and marriage records; and translating miscellaneous Russian government documents.

Shea's book is currently out of print; look for a copy in your nearest genealogical library.

RECORDS INFLUENCED BY GOVERNMENT POLICIES AS WELL AS THE TRIBAL HISTORY

In September, I joined nearly 1,600 genealogists at the Federation of Genealogical Societies conference in Seattle. As it was a national conference, a wide range of topics was presented, making it difficult to choose which session to attend of the five or six that were offered each hour.

One especially enjoyable presentation was "Federal Native American Sources: Starting Your Search for Native American Ancestors," by Susan H. Karren, assistant director at the National Archives, Pacific Northwest Region, 6125 Sand Point Way NE, Seattle, WA 98115.

Karren said searching for Native American ancestors may be one of the more difficult — but most rewarding — research problems facing a family historian. All too often, the information needed to begin your search may well be the very information you are seeking.

In addition, as with all federal searches, today's records are dependent on government policies that were in place when the records were created, as well as the tribal history. Records that may exist for one tribe may not for another, and records that exist for one specific time period may not exist for another.

In order to ensure the most successful search possible, it's necessary to broaden your search to include general government policies towards Native Americans and what this means in terms of records created.

Once you have identified the tribe or tribes to which your ancestor belonged, it will be necessary to do general tribal research.

Karren said two basic reference books "live" on her desk: "Indian Tribes of North America" by John Swanton, and "Guide to Records in the National Archives Relating to American Indians," published by the National Archives. She also said any guide book for Native American research should be considered for use, as each one can cover a separate piece to fit into the whole puzzle of this kind of research.

Karren said the "Treaty Period" was 1774 to 1870. Up until 1774, representatives of the Crown dealt with tribal representatives to purchase land, and the only records they created were tribal treaties. From 1774 to 1789, departments of the young government were established to deal with the tribes, to keep the peace and to regulate trade. Indian agents were named.

Beginning in 1780, education for Native Americans was considered important. Dartmouth College received $5,000 for Native American education, but no individual records exist from this period. Some education records from this period, however, may exist in private, state or local repositories.

From 1789 to 1834, Indian affairs were placed under the Secretary of War. Treaties were negotiated over settlement, trade and purchase of land. From 1802 on, the major thrust of the Indian policy was to push Native Americans westward, culminating in the wholesale removal of tribes to west of the Mississippi. During this time there were still no individual records created, and those that were created were primarily between the government and the tribe.

The "Removal Period" was from 1830 to 1870, when tribes east of the Mississippi were relocated west of the Mississippi, primarily to the Indian Territory of Oklahoma, Kansas and Missouri. Best known of the relocated tribes were the so-called Five Civilized Tribes — Cherokee, Choctaw, Creek, Chickasaw and Seminole — but other tribes were also removed.

Some census rolls and muster lists were created during this time period, but they are not alphabetized nor indexed. Some of these early records are available on microfilm.

Karren went on to explain that the period of the 1850s to 1887 was known as the "Reservation Period."

Indians were put on to specific land areas, almost always totally different from their ancestral homelands. They were issued rations in an attempt to "keep them quiet," but it didn't always work.

Records created during this period include annuity rolls which kept track of who got what rations — usually listing only the heads of families. And, these records are neither alphabetized nor indexed.

Indian schools were developed both on and off the reservations. By 1887, some 227 schools existed, 163 operated by the government and 64 by private organizations, usually missionaries.

School records generally list the student's name, age, where he or she was born, parents, tribal affiliation and degree of blood.

The National Archives has school records for both reservation and federal non-reservation schools, some of which have been microfilmed. Records of private schools are with churches or local and state historical societies.

If you would like a copy of Susan Karren's taped presentation, order it for $7.50, plus $2.00 postage, from Repeat Performance, 2911 Crabapple Lane, Hobart, IN 46342. Request tape No. F-67, FGS-95 followed by the title and name.

A bit of trivia Karren shared was to explain that a "full-blooded Native American" ancestor could have been half of one tribe, a quarter of another and a quarter of yet another, due to tribal mixing.

TODAY'S TIPS: Clark H. Flint, 1615 Seward St., Evanston, IL 60202-2023, is looking for information on the Knights of the Golden Circle, a secret society labeled as an "outlawed, pro-Southern, paramilitary organization" which aided Union Army deserters.

And, the Sons of Confederate Veterans was founded in 1896 to preserve and defend the history and principles of the Old

South. It serves today as a means for a gentleman to honor his Southern ancestry with memorial, historical and educational activities.

If you are a male descendant of a Confederate ancestor, "claim your heritage now with pride" (so reads their ad). Contact Lt. CIC Peter W. Orlebeke, 3411 St. Cloud Circle, Dallas, TX 75229.

TODAY'S LAUGH: My favorite Pilgrim cartoon shows a woman knitting a tiny baby garment, and her surprised-looking husband says, "You mean I'm going to be a forefather?"

A MULTITUDE OF ERRORS HAS CREPT INTO RECORDS; CENSUS INDEXES ARE HELPFUL, BUT HARDLY PERFECT

The U.S. Federal census is the best, most widely used tool we have for researching our American ancestors, according to Arlene Eakle, a nationally known genealogical author and lecturer.

Census indexes are a wonderful guide to the original records, but genealogists should know that indexes are fraught with errors.

Efforts to create error-free indexes began under a cloud of handicaps. No indexer, regardless of skill, could make up for deficiencies in the census records they had to use.

People known to be alive at the time of the census, but omitted by the census taker, won't be added to an index. Neither will someone enumerated on a page skipped by the microfilm camera operator.

An entry obscured by illegible penmanship, faded ink or misspelling may also not appear in an index in the place where a researcher first looks.

Misspelled surnames are the most significant problem created by census takers.

Given that most enumerators were political appointees — selected for whom they knew, not what they knew — one should not be surprised that both spelling and penmanship were, in many instances, atrocious.

Today, the phonetic rendering of those names, even some with familiar spellings, has befuddled those who have attempted to decipher them. Misreading the original record can banish that person to historical oblivion. Sadly, it has happened all too often.

Over the last few years, several groups have contributed to published census indexes, including members of local genealogical or historical societies who transcribed pages for the community where they live.

Their efforts were usually published locally in limited quantities. But some indexing projects have been very ambitious. For example, the Indiana Historical Society recently published a statewide index to Indiana's 1870 census.

The production of census indexes is dominated by commercial firms. The largest was Accelerated Indexing Systems Inc. (Ever noticed the "AIS" stamped on the spine of the indexes at the library?) This company began indexing census records in 1967 and compiled some 600 titles.

The firm published census indexes for every state and territory through 1860 for which the population schedules exist, and for some states in 1870. All AIS indexes published through December 1983 are available on microfiche, organized in seven "searches," or groups of states and time periods.

This collection of some 40 million names may be used at any Family History Center as the "AIS Census Indexes."

A second indexing firm was Index Publishing, which did 30-plus indexes in the 1980s. Then Precision Indexing, a subsidiary of the American Genealogical Lending Library (AGLL), took on the task of census indexing.

AGLL is one of the most established and reputable companies providing services to genealogists. Precision Indexing offers more columns of information than its predecessors. This company is now working on 1870 indexes.

No index is guaranteed perfect, and this was never more true than with census indexes. Beginning genealogists are taught to run right to census indexes before they use the microfilms. But beginners must also learn that, with an error rate approaching 20 percent in some instances, not finding your ancestor in the census index does not mean that you will not find him in the actual census.

Genealogists must always view the original county or town census and not just stop with the index.

Most of the information for this column was gleaned from an article in the *Illinois State Genealogical Society Quarterly,* Vol. 23, No. 3, Fall 1991, titled "Census Indexes: A Primer," by David Paul Davenport.

I recommend the nine-page article, with dozens of examples of how errors crept into the census indexes, as a homework assignment for any serious genealogist.

Another useful guide on this subject is Richard H. Saldana's "A Practical Guide To The 'Misteaks' Made In Census Indexes." Published in 1987, Saldana gives 63 pages of examples of census index "misteaks." This book can be ordered through AGLL at 800-760-AGLL, or write P.O. Box 329 Bountiful, UT, 84011-0329.

TODAY'S TRIVIA: Have you ever wondered exactly how census takers in those early days wrote those names? What sort of writing instrument did they use?

Quill pens, made from bird wing feathers, were used from the time of Christ to about 1800. The first steel-point pen was patented in England in 1803. The first fountain pen was patented in New York in 1884 and was the chief writing instrument in the western world until World War II. The ballpoint pen didn't appear until 1938, and it took years to perfect.

Pencil history is a bit different. The first "lead crayon" appeared in 1795. The year 1812 saw the first appearance of cedar-wood-encased-lead pencil. The first mechanical pencil appeared in 1877.

So, you guess what sort of writing instrument those early census takers used.

TODAY'S LAUGH: Remember: Pruning family trees is NOT allowed.

LDS SOFTWARE UPDATED, CORRECTED AND ENHANCED

Whenever I teach a beginner's class, the following question is always asked: "Do I need a computer to do genealogy?" The answer is no, because the computer is only a tool to store and manipulate the data that you use your eyes, brain and fingers to compile.

But, if you do use a computer, you really do need a genealogy program.

"What's the best program?" is the next question that arises.

I think all genealogy computer programs are 80 percent alike — you type names into all of them and they arrange the data into pedigrees and family groups. The remaining 20 percent is the "whistles and bells" that make one program different from another. This is where personal preferences come into play.

If you have a real grasp of the essentials of a genealogy program and know what you really want, then I say investigate to see which one you like best.

If, however, you are just beginning or just want a "standard, simple workhorse," then PAF is a good bet. PAF is Personal Ancestral File, designed by the LDS Church folks to compliment their in-house computer program, Ancestral File. PAF is a standard family-linking program that allows you to type in information on an individual and then link that person into his or her family. Other programs cost from $60 to $300. PAF comes fully documented and fully supported with a Salt Lake City telephone number you can call for help.

If you'd like to try PAF, take your charts and forms to any Family History Center and they will let you use the program there for free. You can input some information, print it out, and see what you think. You also might be able to purchase the program at the center (it's not available in stores). You can also order it by calling 800-537-5950.

Good luck and happy "PAF-fing."

TODAYS TRIVIA: Here's a story I think you'll like. There are millions of tombstones in the world, and each is important to the families they represent. But some tombstones are interesting to everyone simply because they are unique. The stone for Siamese twins Chang and Eng Bunker is an example.

Chang and Eng Bunker were born near Bangkok, capital of Siam, in 1811. The twins, once known as "double monsters," were joined at the breastbone by cartilage and ligaments. With today's medical technology, they probably could have been successfully separated. But the brothers lived face to face until their deaths.

They each married — in a double ceremony — two daughters of a minister. Chang and his wife, Adelaide, had 10 children; and Eng and his wife, Sarah Ann, had 12.

The sisters did not get along, so the twins maintained two separate households. They spent three days with Adelaide followed by three days with Sarah Ann.

They were brought from Siam to Britain in 1829 to go on tour as a novelty. By 1833, they had saved $60,000 from exhibition fees, migrated to America and bought a plantation in North Carolina. They became U.S. citizens, joined the Baptist Church, and spent the rest of their lives in Surry County.

It's not known how they came to take the surname Bunker, but the name was passed on to descendants.

In 1874, Chang died, probably from arrhythmia. Eng died a few hours later — some said from fright at being attached to his dead brother. They are buried in the cemetery at White Plains Baptist Church near Mount Airy, NC. The single headstone, divided into halves, gives the birth and death dates for Chang, Eng and both of their wives.

On your next trip to North Carolina, you might want to visit the grave site for Chang and Eng and see their single-yet-double tombstone.

TODAY'S TRIVIA: Did your ancestor, born before 1765, provide military service during the eight years of the Revolutionary War? Would you like to find him the easy way? Would you like to pay $15.00 to a research team to check 53 volumes of records and provide you with a full report on the search, including up to 25 copies of pertinent record pages?

The Southern California Research Team, P.O. Box 4377, Burbank, CA 91503, will provide this service to you. Write to them for forms and information on other search services.

MORE TIPS ON AN ARRAY OF GENEALOGICAL TOPICS

Today's column is a continuation of genealogical bits and pieces I've collected that might be of use to you.

Antonia Mattheou has written *Tracing Your Greek Ancestry,* a small, 50-page book with large amounts of information on all areas of basic concern to students of Greek family history.

It covers research in both America and Greece, sources and services available in the two countries, addresses of the Bishops' offices in Greece and Cyprus, maps and a discussion of research difficulties unique to family history searching in this Mediterranean country.

Those with ancestry in this little country will no doubt be delighted to find a published guide written especially for them.

Tracing Your Greek Ancestry is available for $10.00, postpaid, from the author at 7S-21 177th Street, Flushing, NY 11366-1522.

CIVIL WAR CONSCRIPTION

As the Civil War progressed, volunteers for both armies waned and cash bounties were no longer effective. On April 16, 1862, the Confederacy passed its first conscription act to draft all white males between the ages of 18 and 35 for a three-year term. Six months later, the age limit was raised to 45 years. In February 1864, the draft age was again changed to include all men between 17 and 50 years old. In desperation, on March 13, 1865, the Confederacy passed a law offering freedom to slaves if they would enlist.

The Union draft, passed March 3, 1863, included men between the ages of 20 and 45. It was used only if a given district failed to produce its quota of volunteer troops.

Both the North and South allowed draftees to pay a commutation fee and avoid the draft. For the draftee in the South, the fee was $500; in the North, it was $300.

Draftees could also avoid military service by supplying an able-bodied substitute. Fees paid to the substitute to take a draftee's place varied according to supply and demand. A son could voluntarily replace a father or brother. Those who could afford the fee could hire a substitute and avoid the draft altogether.

Both subscription and the substitution were introduced as a means of freeing skilled labor, such as gunsmiths, for crucial war industries. But the privilege was used and abused until, near the end of the war, army morale was devastated. To the poor and draftee soldiers, it became apparent that it was a rich man's war and a poor man's fight.

I learned about this in an article by Irene Griffey, C.G., in a 1993 issue of *Bluegrass Roots*.

DIRECTORY AVAILABLE

The Association of Professional Genealogists' recently published directory of its members is available for $15.00, postpaid.

This directory can be helpful in a variety of ways: finding a researcher in a distant area; finding speakers for seminars and reunions; help for authors needing specific geographic background, consultation on specific research problems.

The 1995 directory is cross-indexed by research specialties, geographic specialties, related services and member residence. Helpful information is given on hiring a professional genealogist.

If you want to hire a researcher in a specific area and you'd like some "insurance" about getting a "good one" then the APG Directory is a good place to start. Send your cheek to APG Directory, 3421 M St. NW, Ste. 236, Washington, DC 20007.

GERMAN GENEALOGY

Interest in family history and genealogy is booming in Germany, according to the March 1995 issue of *This Week in Germany*, a publication of the German Information Center in New York City.

One organization feeling the effects of this revival is the Deutsche Zentralstelle fur Genealogie (German Center for Genealogy) in Leipzig (Saxony). Last year, it fielded some 3,000 inquiries from around the world.

The letters came because the center has an unrivaled collection of materials for research in Eastern Germany and the parts of Pomerania, Prussia and Silesia that were once German.

The collection includes an extensive library of publications on family history, covering the entire German-speaking world, a collection of 100,000 personal documents and a genealogical card index begun in 1921 which provides basic information on 1.4 million people.

Perhaps the most important of the center's holdings is the collection of 16,000 church registers dating back to the 16th century — some original and some microfilmed copies — that once belonged to the Third Reich's Office of Family Relations.

The center does not do individual research, but it will tell you if it has useful materials for your search. You will then have to hire a professional. You must furnish the specific place where your ancestors lived.

The center's address is Schongauer Strasse 1, Postfach 274 D-04002, Leipzig, Germany.

My advice would be to first check what is available via the National Archives and Family History Center in Salt Lake City before hiring help in the Leipzig Center.

FAMILY REUNIONS

It's estimated that 350,000 reunions are held annually in the United States: family, class, church and military.

Reunions magazine has articles on how to plan, organize and conduct a successful reunion. Subscription to this periodical is $15.00 per year. Write to P.O. Box 11727, Milwaukee, WI, 53211-0727, or call 414-263-4567. Their advertising cheerfully says to call with any specific reunion questions and they will happily supply you with information.

A wonderful guide for planning family reunions is *Fantastic Family Reunions,* by Kathy Smith Anthenat. This 8.5x11 book is full of photographs, patterns, games and ideas that have been used by other families in their successful reunions. *Fantastic Family Reunions* is available from Heritage Books, Inc., 800-398-7709.

TODAY'S LAUGH: Unpunctuated words chiseled on a tombstone can sometimes cause great merriment. Consider: "Here lies Peter Montgomery who was accidently shot in his thirtieth year." Or, "Erected to the Memory of John Phillips Accidently Shot as a Mark of Affection by his Brother." Also, how to explain the cryptic message on a stone in Edgartown, MA: "...death was caused by bathing..."

SEVERAL SOURCES RECOMMENDED TO ASSIST IN SEARCHES NORTH OF THE BORDER

Like the United States, Canada is largely a nation of immigrants. If you are searching for your Canadian roots or tracing your family tree in any Canadian province, a bit of background information will help make the next steps easier.

During the 18th century, some 110,000 immigrants fled to Canada from the Highlands of Scotland. During the same period, about 100,000 came from Ireland. The government in power pushed the emigration of these groups with little regard to the dangers of unbelievable overcrowding, death by drowning, cholera, dysentery or running out of food and water while crossing the Atlantic, despite advertisements that described the voyage in glowing prose.

By 1850, some 12,000 German-speaking people settled in mainly four areas: Nova Scotia, the Niagara Peninsula, and the Kitchener and Pembroke area townships of Ontario.

Descendants of United Empire Loyalists, those British citizens who remained loyal to England during the Revolutionary War, numbered 30,000 in the Maritimes and 10,000 in the colony of Quebec by 1850.

Immigrants from the Ukraine numbered 200,000 by 1914, some 70,000 more by 1930, and 30,000 more by 1946. These folks settled largely in Manitoba.

By 1931, about 150,000 Jews were welcomed into Canada; numerous other ethnic groups arrived in groups or families during this same time period.

Folks beginning their Canadian genealogy need to know they might work in Canada for only a few generations before "going across the ocean" to the Old Country. Then the research becomes specialized to that country and applies to immigrants worldwide.

But where to start in Canada? Begin researching your Canadian roots by talking to family members and gathering all the bits and pieces of information that you already know about your family.

Write the information down on proper pedigree and family group forms. Write to long distance family members or call them to jog their memories. Ask them to look in old trunks, behind old photos, in old Bibles, anywhere family information might have been tucked.

Like researching in other places, you need to know the province and the town. Can you really research in "America" or "New Jersey"? You need to know that it was Trenton in Mercer County in New Jersey, right? It's the same for Canada.

When you're ready, I suggest a good, basic research guide: *In Search of Your Canadian Roots*, by Angus Baxter, updated in 1994 by Genealogical Publishing Co. (1001 N. Calvert St., Baltimore, MD 21202; 800-296-6687). This $16.95, 350-page book covers all the basics for Canada with chapters on each province.

The Family History Library in Salt Lake has compiled a research outline for Canada and a smaller one for each province. In a very few pages, these guides list the steps necessary to begin your Canadian research; they suggest film numbers of specific items in the library, and they give pertinent addresses.

The research outlines are available at any Family History Center or from the Family History Library, 35 N. West Temple, Salt Lake City, UT 84150.

The National Archives of Canada has prepared a 45-page booklet that fits nicely into a stamped, self-addressed envelope. Titled *Tracing Your Ancestors In Canada*, the booklet is a guide to what is available at the Canadian National Archives and how to access that material.

The last paragraph in the introduction reads: "Genealogical services of the National Archives of Canada are confined to the identification of potential source material in response to specific inquiries, within the limitations of available staff. Persons unable to undertake their own research at the Archives, or through microfilm loans, are referred to professional researchers."

If you'd like a free copy of this guide, write to the National Archives of Canada, 395 Wellington Street, Ottawa, Canada, K1A ON3, or call (613) 995-5138. The brochure is available in English or French. Then write to the province you need for information about publications it offers (both for cost and for free) that would be of use to you.

The Alberta Family History Society, P.O. Box 30270, Station B, Calgary, T2M 4P1, AB, is a thriving group of genealogists. It sponsors an annual conference with most classes centering on Canadian research topics. It also can advise you of the several area libraries with good Canadian genealogy collections. If you are researching Canadian roots, perhaps you should check it out.

The Interlink Bookshop in Victoria, British Columbia, is another Canadian resource that can be of help. Sherry Irvine's inventory includes much more than just Canadian books and maps. The Interlink Bookshop carries a huge array of books and maps of England, Scotland and Ireland. I was impressed with the free, 13-page catalog she sent me. It's a free call to ask about a specific item or to request a catalog: 800 747-4877. Irvine has written *Your English Ancestry: A Guide for North Americans*, published by Ancestry Publishers (800-262-3787), which is available for workshops and seminars.

She offered another tip: The Cloverdale Branch of the Surrey Public Library has an extensive collection of Canadian materials. It sells a guide to its holdings for about $10.00. Write to it at Cloverdale Branch, Surrey Public Library, 5642 - 172A Street, Cloverdale, B.C. V3S 4G9. (Surrey is just south of Vancouver.)

Irvine also reminds researchers of the excellent resources for researching Canada West in Victoria at the British Columbia Provincial Archives, "as they were for a long time the archives for all of Western Canada."

So next time you plan a getaway to one of our favorite places, Victoria, British Columbia, plan to stay an extra day or two and take your genealogy notebook with you.

TODAY'S LAUGH: Be kind to your relatives; without them you would be an orphan.

FINDING THE INFORMATION IS ONE STEP; KEEPING IT ALL IN PROPER ORDER IS THE NEXT

Odds are your genealogy papers, charts, forms and notes are not in totally shipshape order.

I'd also lay odds that you wish they were, that you plan to get to working on the problem, and that you hope you aren't hit by a train anytime soon before you get all that stuff in order for your kids and grandkids.

Perhaps you just haven't been pricked (or punched) by the right motivation. Well, folks, help is on the way. Excuses begone!

Lynne Farmer, owner of the Skeleton Closet System of Record Keeping, has designed a terrific and 100-percent thorough method of keeping all our genealogical data.

She offers a complete system of keeping track of the notes, copies, photos and charts that comprise our family genealogies.

A good record-keeping system should be just as important to every genealogist as the gathering of all those wonderful records. How disappointing to spend hours looking for a certain piece of information that you know you filed somewhere, but you just can't find it.

The Skeleton Closet System of Record Keeping will help you properly store your records in such a way that you can find the information you're looking for at a moment's touch.

The basis of the system is the pedigree charts and family group sheets. All Skeleton Closet forms are printed (printed, not Xeroxed) on acid-free paper, and come three-hole punched. Numbered forms are offered, as well as unnumbered ones used to extend the lines. (Why would you want Person No. 16 on Chart No. 1 to become Person No. 1 on Chart No. 2? He should be Person No. 32, right?)

Group sheets come plain or with space for photos. These family forms are organized into surname files, with small binders used to keep together one family's forms along with all that family's documentation.

They are so easy to pick up and take to the library when you want to work on that particular family — everything you already know about that family is in that one binder.

The Skeleton Closet Offers specialized forms to abstract information from census records, military records (service and pension), land records and several others.

The cemetery record form has space for a picture of the tombstone and suggests that you include a map of the cemetery on the reverse side of the form.

Other special forms include a Person Possession form — do you have Grandma's doll? Or Grandpa's tool? Or piece of jewelry or crystal? Why not take a photo of the item and attach it to a form describing what it is, who owned it and how you came to have it — all of this to hopefully forestall the kids from chucking your mementos in the dump because they did not realize what they were.

Other helpful organizers developed by the Skeleton Closet include Surname Directory, Genie Organizer and Personal Library. These are small binders for 5.5 x 8.5 specialized sheets.

In the Surname Directory, you list a summary of all you know about a family on one page — and then you can easily take your whole genealogy library with you.

The Genie Organizer is a genealogist's address book. With this binder you keep track of all your genealogy correspondents, plus library addresses, reunion addresses and addresses for organizations, publications and newspaper columns.

The Personal Library directory helps you keep track of your reference books, the geographical and surname books on your shelves, the periodicals you subscribe to and a Wish Book list.

To show that Lynne Farmer has thought of everything, each binder comes with a bookplate inside the front cover for your name, address and phone number— in case you leave it at the library.

You can request a complete catalog from the Skeleton Closet by sending $2.50 to 636 Magnolia Dr., Maitland, FL 32751.

Don't be wasting any more time — start today to really get organized.

TODAY'S TIPS: Some helpful ideas from the readers:

Betty Driscoll Ratzman of Spokane wrote to heap praise on Al and Betty Shane of the Kootenai County (Idaho) Genealogical Society. The Shanes have spent more than 10 years compiling almost all available records of Kootenai County and gladly share that information. Their books may be used in the genealogy section of the Hayden Lake Public Library, or write to them at 2315 Hastings Ave., Coeur d'Alene, ID 83814, 208-667-7818.

Reader Marie Larson of Liberty Lake warns of a new genealogy scam. Her mail brought a postcard, postmarked Australia, announcing by "royal proclamation issued by Prince Kevin of Hutt" that a book on her family surname is available for only $5.00. We checked with an Australian research specialist at the Family History Library, who says it is "bunk."

TODAY'S LAUGH: A tombstone inscription reads, "On the twenty-second of June, Jonathan Fiddle went out of tune."

CHURCH DEPENDS ENTIRELY ON VOLUNTEERS TO PROVIDE HELP FOR INQUIRING GENEALOGISTS

Today's column is a follow-up to two recent columns about Presbyterian church records and the Swenson Swedish Immigration Research Center.

In March, 1995, I wrote to the Presbyterian Church (U.S.A.) Department of History, 125 Lombard St., Philadelphia, PA 19147-1516. My letter was answered promptly by Susan J. Sullivan, information service librarian, who replied, "We receive many letters from genealogists, and many of them have no concept of what we can and cannot provide."

She enclosed three fliers explaining what the library can provide regarding genealogy.

The first sheet was a standard Genealogical Inquiry Reply Form stating that its Department of History has more than 20,000 volumes of manuscript records of American Presbyterian congregations, and the library and archives have other pertinent materials.

Unfortunately, the material is not circulated, but visiting genealogists can use the collection Monday through Friday. Some restrictions are imposed on material that is less than 50 years old.

"Our staff is fully occupied with work for the church, and we are entirely dependent on volunteers to respond to genealogical inquiries," the form reads. "We receive so many genealogical inquiries that the most our volunteers can do is check to see if we hold the records of particular churches."

If they do have the records, either you or a representative of yours will have to do the actual search. Those who research for a fee include: Owen T. Robbins, 514 Woodland Terrace, Philadelphia, PA 19104, and Milton Botwinick, P.O. Box 13464, Philadelphia, PA 19101.

On the reply form is a list of routine answers with boxes to be checked off by staff members:

❑ We are returning your check since we cannot provide the services you expected.

❑ The enclosed copies from our catalogs show records which belong to the church(es) which you specified.

❑ We cannot identify records of genealogical interest in our catalogs from the church(es) which you specified.

❑ Your letter did not provide enough information for a search of our catalog for our holdings of records. If you can provide us with sufficient information, we will add your letter to those awaiting reply.

A large note on the bottom of the reply form states, "There is no comprehensive index to the thousands of family names included in records in our library and archives. There is no comprehensive index of churches by county. Local church records are cataloged solely under the name of the city or town which served as the church's post office location.

"Therefore, to conduct a family name search, it is essential to know the location (town or city) and the correct name of the person's congregation."

A flier detailing the "Presbyterian Ministerial Biographical Sketch Search Service" was included in my letter. For a fee of $10.00, the library will search its indexes on Presbyterian ministers and provide sketches from ready-reference sources.

If you want genealogical help from the Presbyterian Church's history department, write first for these informational fliers — and then follow the good advice they offer.

♦Jill Seaholm, a research staff member at the Swenson Swedish Immigration Research Center, wrote to me after a reader sent her a copy of a column I wrote about the center. It seems I shared some misinformation with all of you.

The center does not have the Swedish church records, but rather has the Swedish-American church records. The center is the North American distributing agent for the purchase of the Swedish parish records in microfiche, which must be ordered from Sweden.

The Svensk Arkivinformation, or Swedish Archive information (SVAR), was established in 1977 as a government-owned project to make archival materials accessible to researchers.

These materials are previously microfilmed Swedish parish registers, including records of births, baptisms, marriages, deaths, funerals and household examinations from the 1600s to about 1900. However, according to the flier, few records date back that far; the birth-marriage-death records date to 1860.

Again, according to the SVAR flier, first send them a request listing what parish/county/province you need and the types of records you want. Their reply will tell you what they offer and the number of microfiche it takes to cover the records in question. The microfiche are $4.00 each.

The center also publishes an annual newsletter, *The Swenson Center News* — free for the asking. The 1995 issue had several articles of interest to Swedish researchers, listed several other publications of the center (some in paper, some on microfiche), and told of the annual October Swedish-American Genealogy tour to Salt Lake.

If you're interested in this publication, ask to be placed on the center's mailing list.

The address is Swenson Center, Augustana College, 639 - 38th St., Rock Island, IL 61201-2273; phone (309) 794-7204; and fax (309) 794-7443.

TODAY'S LAUGH: You know you're a genealogist's spouse when:
• You're the only person in the bridge club who knows what a Soundex is.
• Your house has more pictures of tombstones than of the kids.
• The mailman can't believe that you get this much mail from folks you don't know.

- You have to explain to your mother why you can't go 25 miles for Sunday dinner but you can go 300 miles to check out another cemetery.
- Your neighbors think you're crazy, your friends wonder and you know you are.

GENEALOGY CAN BE A LAUGHING MATTER

The end of summer is fast approaching and since we want to wring every lovely flower-, sun- and water-drenched moment we can from these shortening days and not think about anything "heavy," how about some genealogy humor?

In 1915, the Cabell County, West Virginia Board of Education published a list of Rules for Conduct of Teachers:

1. You will not marry during the term of your contract.

2. You are not to keep company with men.

3. You must be home between the hours of 8 p.m. and 6 a.m. unless attending a school function.

4. You may not loiter downtown in ice cream stores.

5. You may not travel beyond the city limits unless you have the permission of the chairman of the board.

6. You may not ride in a carriage or automobile with any man unless he is your father or brother.

7. You may not smoke cigarettes.

8. You may not dress in bright colors.

9. You may under no circumstances dye your hair.

10. You must wear at least two petticoats.

11. Your dresses must not be any shorter than two inches above the ankle.

12. To keep the schoolroom neat and clean, you must sweep the floor at least once daily, scrub the floor at least once a week with hot, soapy water; clean the black boards at least once a day; and start the fire at 7 a.m. so the room will be warm by 8 a.m.

From the *Quincy (IL) Daily Whig,* May 12, 1882, comes this article:

"SHOT TO DEATH, A TRAGEDY IN LIBERTY TOWNSHIP, A WOMAN IN THE CASE"

We present the facts as reported by the trustworthy citizens of Liberty township, where the killing took place.

It seems that Dan Swartz, a man about 35 years of age, had gotten Mary Malone with child.

Mary's virtue was frequently called into question by her neighbors — meaning they did not regard her virtue as stalwart or untainted.

Mary Malone had two brothers, John and Taylor, who wanted Dan Swartz to marry her and become the legal as well as the actual, father of her soon-expected child.

Dan objected.

Dan owned a blacksmith shop in the village, and Joe, his brother, ran a store near by.

On a Wednesday, morning, Mary's brothers, John and Taylor Malone — young men between 23 and 25 years old, who lived about a mile from the Swartzes — went to see Dan to convince him to marry Mary.

However, it seems there was no attempt at convincing. The Malone brothers opened fire on the reluctant Dan with their revolvers as soon as they saw him.

The Swartz brothers — Dan and Joe — responded to the Malones: Dan with a shotgun and Joe with a revolver; both aimed at John. The shot from Joe Schwartz's gun hit John Malone's left breast near or in the heart, and Dan's bullet ended in John's forehead just above the left eye. The two fatal shots were fired simultaneously.

When John Malone fell, his brother, Taylor, turned and ran as fast as his feet would carry him.

Directly after the killing, Andrew Swartz — brother to the reluctant Dan and Joe — rode to Liberty to have Esquire Buttz hold an inquest into the shooting of John

Malone. The killing took place between 10 and 11 in the morning, and the inquest was held that afternoon.

Dan and Joe Swartz posted bail and were ordered to appear at their preliminary examination, but Taylor Malone could not give bail and was held in arrest.

Unfortunately, there's no final conclusion we can report of this Malone/Swartz melodrama. But, if a reader has a Baby Malone or a Baby Swartz on their family charts who was born in 1882 in Illinois to a mother named Mary, this might be the story of that child's beginning.

Dee Hepworth of Spokane shared this next story with me. Seems the children of a prominent family decided to give their father a book of his family history. They interviewed a biographer to write the book, confiding to him that there was one major family problem — Uncle Willie.

Uncle Willie, they explained, was the black sheep of their father's family. Uncle Willie, they continued, had been found guilty of murder and was confined to Sing Sing Prison before he ultimately paid the price for his crime in the electric chair.

Feeling greatly challenged, the biographer paused, then said, "I'd simply say that Uncle Willie occupied a chair of applied electronics at one of the nation's leading institutions; that he was attached to his position by the strongest ties; and that he had a very electrifying personality."

He was hired on the spot.

Grandchildren are a continuing source of pleasure and funny stories for genealogists, and mine are no exception. While visiting with 4-year old Aleena, the conversation turned to where babies come from. "I was in Mommy's tummy," she said. I agreed and added that her daddy was once in my tummy and that someday maybe she would have a baby in her tummy. "And they'll drive me crazy!" she promptly said with a big smile.

Having lunch with 5-year old Justin, his mom and his great-grandmother (my daughter and her grandmother), my daughter said they might need to trade in their van for a new one next year. Justin paused between bites and, looking surprised, asked, "Does Daddy know about this?"

Three-year old Trevor, upon encountering a round of kiwi fruit for the first time, states his opinion: "It tastes sour wet."

As Art Linkletter said, kids say the darnedest things. Too bad more moms don't keep a notebook handy to jot down these pearls of family wisdom.

FAMILY HISTORY CENTERS
PROVIDE A VAST ARRAY OF INFORMATION

If you consider yourself a working genealogist but aren't taking advantage of the Family History Center in your area, you are missing a for-sure good bet.

The Genealogical Society of Utah was organized in 1894 with a total library of 11 books. At its centennial mark last year, the Family History Library in Salt Lake City had 258,000 books. New book acquisitions number more than 1,000 each month. And, the library has a microfilm collection of nearly 2 million rolls; about 5,000 rolls are cataloged every month.

To ensure these resources are available to genealogists everywhere, hundreds of Family History Centers are located across America and throughout the world. It is almost a fact that wherever you find a Latter-day Saints church, you will find that special kind of public library — the Family History Center.

What are these books and what's on these rolls of microfilm? The books fall into three categories:

1. How-to
2. Family and area histories
3. Local and area records

New books on how to access such-and-such records pop up regularly and are a real boon to working genealogists. Need to know more about how to find Church of the Brethren records? Vital statistics form the Ukraine? Or even how to use Iowa state censuses? Chances are the center has something published to help you.

Two larger resources are family histories and local or area works. More and more people are writing their family's stories, and many donate a copy of their work to the Family History Library.   Checking the card catalog reveals family histories for names from Abastine to Zumwaltis (I'm just guessing on those two!). The point is, don't think your surname is so unusual that there has never been a book written about it, because you'd probably be wrong. These books can vary from a pamphlet of a few pages to a multi-page, hard-bound tome — and they are certainly worth a look.

The other group of books is local or area records. Genealogical societies around the world are gathering and publishing their local records — cemetery transcriptions, vital courthouse records, newspaper abstracts, county histories.... No matter where your ancestral family lived, you can almost certainly find a published reference on that area in Salt Lake's library. And of course, most of these books are available through your local Family History Center.

If you have visited a center, you have undoubtedly used the FamilySearch computer and its library card catalog, plus its huge databases of information. Chances are nearly 99 percent that you can find at least one of your ancestors' names in one of these databases. The IGI (International Genealogical Index) and the Ancestral File are the two main databases on the FamilySearch program.

Ever wonder how the information gets into these databases?

Family information is shared into the Ancestral File by working genealogists everywhere, folks like you and me, which means documentation of that information is only as good as the submitter has found and listed. But with millions of family-linked names, it is a source worth checking. ("Family-linked" means the information is in pedigree lines.)

IGI information comes largely from the Home Records Extraction program. Anyone of any faith may volunteer to work on this project. The Family History Center makes paper copies from microfilmed vital or church records that are sent to a local coordinator. These coordinators work in their own homes, on their own computers, reading the records and entering the extracted names into the computer. I recently worked on a batch of 1906 marriages in Johnson County, Kansas. This volunteer work ultimately benefits everybody.

CHINESE CONNECTION

I have previously written about new how-to books and ethnic guides; another case in point is a very special resource guide that just came to my attention.

China Connection: Finding Ancestral Roots for Chinese in America, by Jeanie W. Chooey Low, is a compact guide for doing Chinese-American family history research. Low included background information on historical and economic factors that influenced early Chinese immigration to America. Her emphasis is the period of the Chinese Exclusion Acts from 1882 to 1943 which affected Chinese immigration to the United States and the creation of "paper names" for some Chinese-American families.

Paper names were created by immigrant Chinese to help them stay in America when fear of deportation and low immigration quotas were hindering immigration. After the San Francisco earthquake and fire of 1906, when most official birth records were destroyed, these paper names helped U.S.-born Chinese remain in the states. Hassles over these alternate names continued into the 1960s.

Low's research was carefully done from public and private sources. With this book you will learn how and where to obtain records, such as Angel Island immigration interviews and Chinese mortuary records. Hints on how to translate Chinese gravestones and how to recognize Chinese numbers are included. Resources, addresses, charts and illustrations, plus a bibliography for more reading, make this 65-page book a must for those with Chinese-American heritage. Order the book, $13.95, postpaid, from the JWC Low Co., P.O. Box 472012, San Francisco, CA 94147.

TODAY'S TRIVIA: Even the Wall Street Journal carries genealogy stories. Alice Sprow of Spokane sent a clipping about a father-and-son team in Sunbury, OH, who collect information on Ohio's 6,000 ghost towns. The men figure they have another 2,000 to find. Who would have guessed?

RECORDS FROM WORLD WAR I
CAN PROVIDE A WEALTH OF INFORMATION

In 1917, a national project was begun to honor the Americans who served in World War I. A group of historians volunteered to government officials to help document the war — and thus was born the collecting and completing of memorial registers to those who served in "the war to end all wars."

Although this was a nationally sponsored project, it was up to each state — more particularly each county — to collect records of its soldiers and also write up what had happened on the home front. Forms were sent to each veteran or his survivors asking for information and a photo.

According to Nancy Compau, librarian in the Northwest Room at the Spokane Public Library, it seems that while this project was well-intentioned and well-begun, individual efforts were rarely completed and published. The only two completed projects she knows of in Washington state were for Whitman and Snohomish counties. The Northwest Room also has information from Yellowstone County, Montana.

In Spokane County, G.W. Fuller, head librarian in 1919, and W.S. Lewis, founder of the Eastern Washington Historical Society, began collecting information on local soldiers. They mailed questionnaires, contacted school boards and clipped newspaper items, gluing the material to cards for files labeled with each man's name.

But in these files the information languished until 1991! That's when the Spokane library moved across the street from its old building into the empty department store. While preparing for the transfer, Nancy Compau found some very dusty, unidentified boxes high on a shelf in a forgotten part of the basement. Looking into them, she found the World War I veterans' files.

These files have since been cleaned up and organized and now reside safely in the Northwest Room.

Compau would be delighted to help genealogists use this wonderful resource. She recently corresponded with a Florida man in his 70s who had never known his father. He wrote to her saying he'd just discovered that his father had died in World War I and that he was from Spokane. Although his mother had remarried and never told him anything about his father, a family member finally told him that much.

After reading the soldier's file, Compau sent the son in Florida a picture of his father and news that he'd been a hero, cited for "outstanding courage."

That's the kind of success story all genealogists want to hear.

Incidentally, some of the artwork in the three books I looked at in the Northwest Room are truly beautiful.

Here's an example of why you'd want to be looking to find these old records. The Spokane County files contain the record of 1st Lt. Louis Hampden Pinkham Jr. He was 29 when he entered the service on Aug. 23, 1917, and was deployed for training at the Presidio in San Francisco. He was shipped to France, where he died of pneumonia in 1919. His mother furnished the information for his file, which includes a newspaper article and personal accounts of his war experience:

"We have seen heavy fighting, desperate at times. My battery has fired more shots than any battery in the brigade.... and I have never failed on any mission given me though my men and I have gone days and nights without sleep."

I strongly urge you to write letters to county and state archives to look for memorial registers or unpublished collected files of your World War I ancestor.

Most World War I men were drafted. Nearly 24 million men, 18 to 45 years old, registered for the draft. There were a dozen questions for them to answer on the registration card, including name, date and place of birth, nationality and citizenship, occupation and personal description.

I teach in my classes that if your ancestor was between 18 and 45 in 1917, then he had to register for the draft regardless if he ever served.

These registrations have been microfilmed and are available at the Family History Library in Salt Lake City and the local Family History Centers. That's the "good news."

The "bad news" is that you must know the county where your ancestor registered, for they are filmed by county. You will not likely find him if all you know is the state. To find the film numbers, using Family Search at the computer, look under United States - Military Records - World War I 1914-1918.

There are other resources to find information on your World War I ancestor: The National Personnel Records Center, 9700 Page Blvd., St. Louis, MO 63132-5100, has service and pension papers. Write first for form R6-7231 to access the records. Many states have lists of veterans' names, such as *The Official Roster of Ohio Soldiers, Sailors and Marines, World War 1917-1918*, published by the state of Ohio in 1928.

Publishing lists of veterans' names is a continuing project of genealogical societies. The Northeast Washington Genealogical Society in Colville, in its Pioneer Branches magazine, carried a list of World War I draft registrations from Stevens County, as first printed in *The Colville Examiner* on June 16, 1917. (A total of 1,597 men from Stevens County registered.)

Don't forget to check your home and family sources. In a recent class, a student brought a postcard his ancestor had sent to his family in Cheney. It was a military, preprinted postcard, sent for free stating the man's name and organization and the phrase, "The ship on which I sailed has arrived safely overseas."

VETERANS ORGANIZATION FLOURISHED
AFTER CIVIL WAR,
BUT MEMBERSHIP DWINDLED IN THIS CENTURY

I've received two letters recently asking about the "GAR" initials carved on ancestors' tombstones: What do the letters mean, and do they lead to further genealogical information?

I was happy to do a bit of digging for all of us.

The Grand Army of the Republic was founded in 1866 by Benjamin F. Stephenson and a small group of his friends as an association for Union Veterans of the Civil War.

Stephenson was a physician in Springfield, IL, who had served as surgeon in the 14th Illinois Infantry. On April 6, 1866, the first post was established at Decatur, IL. By July 12 of that year, during a state convention, 39 posts had been chartered. And, at the first national encampment on November 20, 1866, at Indianapolis, ten states and the District of Columbia were represented.

The GAR quickly attained a preeminent place among veterans organizations formed at the close of the Civil War. Between 1881 and '82, membership rose from 87,718 to 131,900 — and during the next eight years, the increase was just as rapid. The peak was reached in 1890, when 409,489 members were reported. At the last encampment in 1949, however, only six members attended and it was decided to disband the organization when they had all died. The last member, Albert Woolman, died Aug. 6, 1956.

One purpose of the GAR, as set forth in its constitution, was the "defense of the last soldiery of the United States, morally, socially and politically."

At an early date in its history, partisan purposes were forbidden, but for many years the organization was a powerful political force. Its unremitting efforts for pension increases and other benefits for veterans and their dependents led both major political parties to bid for its support by favoring such measures. Its members were generally disposed to vote for the higher bidder. But by 1900, the GAR ceased to be dominant force in politics.

The GAR gave rise to or attracted auxiliary societies: The Woman's Relief Corps was organized in the 1883, the Ladies of the Grand Army of the Republic in 1886, and the Sons of Union Veterans of the Civil War in 1881. For several years these three groups, along with the Daughters of the Union Veterans of the Civil War (DUV) and Auxiliary to the Sons of Union Veterans of the Civil War, carried on the work begun by the GAR in establishing and improving veterans facilities.

In a related article by Robert S. Davis Jr., in the most recent *Heritage Quest* magazine (No. 57), I found this information:

"The major veterans' organizations were the Grand Army of the Republic and the United Confederate Veterans. Records of these organizations survive only in collections in individual state archives and other manuscript repositories. There is no nationwide inventory of what has survived.

"For the GAR, no complete collection of even the printed annual proceedings of its state departments, a rich source of genealogically valuable death notices, are known to survive, although the GAR did not officially disband until 1955. The Daughters of Union Veterans of the Civil War still exists," Davis wrote. "For the United Confederate Veterans, copies of their magazine, *Confederate Veteran*, survive and have been reprinted with an index."

Some fragmented Spokane-area GAR records are housed in the Eastern Washington Historical Society archives in the Cheney Cowles Museum.

If you think your ancestor was a member, contact the historical society for the place in which he lived. You will need to know the approximate dates of your forebear's membership when you write. These addresses may be found in Elizabeth Petty Bently's book, *The Genealogists' Address Book*, available at most genealogical libraries, or from Genealogical Publishing Co. at 800-296-6687, for $34.95. (When writing to the archives, include a self-addressed, stamped envelope and a $5.00 donation for their help.)

So, now you know as much as I was able to ferret out about the GAR and its records.

Reader Kathleen Emerson in Poulson, Mont., sent me a brochure from the Butte-Silver Bow Public Archives. For those of us researching in the Butte area, sounds like this place is a gold mine of information (Ooops! Copper mine!).

Established in 1981, this repository archives includes many maps — mining claim maps and Sanborn Fire Insurance maps — a large collection of books on the area's history from 1890 to modern day, and a large collection of organizational records

(fraternal societies like the Oddfellows, Masons, Knights of Phythias....)

They also have an extensive area newspaper collection, a representative collection from the many international labor unions active in Butte dating back to 1900, and 65 personal collections, representing individuals and private business.

The archives also has the usual genealogical resources such as city directories, a cemetery index from 1880-1980, an obituary file, early marriage licenses (1877-1880s), birth books (1906-1920), high school annuals, coroner's registers, early telephone books, naturalization records and census records for 1880, 1900 and 1910.

Butte was home to a large number of ethnic groups: Swedish, Serbian, Croatian, Chinese, Welsh, Italian and Irish, to name a few.

Ellen Crain, archives director, and her staff "are very pleasant and nice to deal with," Emerson wrote. "They have done limited mail searches for me with very reasonable costs."

Adding a personal note, Emerson said she's been following advice learned last summer: "'Get out the old pick and shovel and dig.' I can't believe how much I've learned or how much fun I've had doing it!"

TODAY'S QUOTE: From Hank Jones, "Remember that the mark of a really great genealogist is the willingness to re-evaluate and revise his own work."

MANY FAMILY HISTORIANS
TURN TO THE DAR FOR HELP

It doesn't take long for a new genealogist to learn that the Daughters of the American Revolution has something to offer — but they don't always know what the DAR is nor what it offers.

A 1994 NSDAR Fact Sheet has all the answers.

The National Society of Daughters of the American Revolution was founded in 1890 and incorporated in 1896. While some 800,000 members have joined since 1890, today's membership numbers about 200,000.

There are chapters in all 50 states, the District of Columbia, Australia, Canada, France, Mexico and the United Kingdom.

The group's objectives are historic preservation, promotion of education and patriotic endeavor.

Its national headquarters is three huge adjoining structures within sight of the White House in Washington, DC, which houses the Americana Room (a repository of more than 5,000 documents of early American history), the DAR Museum (33 state rooms decorated and supported by the various state chapters), the Seimes Microfilm Center, Continental Hall and its respected library.

The DAR promotes American heritage through the arts and historic preservation and sponsors an annual American history writing contest for young students. Two American Indian schools and six Appalachian schools are supported by the DAR.

I could easily finish this column chronicling the good works of the DAR.

However, it is for genealogical information that many family historians turn to the DAR. Its library is open to the public (except during its Congress each April) and is itself worth a trip to Washington, DC.

The library has nearly 83,000 pages of unpublished source records, copied and bound, gathered by the various state chapters in their continuing efforts to preserve American history.

The Seimes Microfilm Center is the depository for NSDAR applications and supplements. The applications often lead to more information and further sources on our ancestors. You can personally look at these applications at the center if you know the name of your patriot ancestor. The records can also be accessed by mail using the appropriate form. (For a form, contact DAR headquarters directly.)

To genealogists, the group's best-known resource is its DAR Patriot Index. In the index's new edition, more than 3,330 pages of patriot names are listed.

These names, in these books, lead you to the application files held by the Seimes Microfilm Center. Whenever a woman fills out an application to join the DAR, she has not only listed her ancestry back to a Revolutionary War patriot, but (hopefully) has documented that lineage with notes on the fourth page of the application.

The application files are especially valuable when you consider that many patriot ancestors did not live to collect a pension for their service in the Revolutionary War and therefore will not be found in the National Archives military pension records.

But, if your ancestor provided a cart to haul supplies behind the Army, or a dozen leghorns for an Army supper, or in any way rendered a service that can be documented, then you are eligible to join the DAR.

The address for the National Society Daughters of the American Revolution is 1776 "D" Street, NW, Washington, DC 20006-5392. Write to them about accessing their material by mail, or to plan a visit.

Now you know what the organization has to offer, especially to the family historian.

TODAY'S TRIVIA: Marta Metcalf, 3915 Yorktown Rd., Chattanooga, TN 37416, is updating the book, *Kelloggs In the Old World and the New*. The Spokane Public Library's genealogy section has this three-volume set by Timothy Hopkins, first published in 1903, and many Inland Northwest genealogists trace their Kellogg line back into this book. If you are interested in Metcalf's project, contact her directly.

♦Do we always know the best methods to preserve and protect our family's important papers and photographs? Craig A. Tuttle's 111-page book, *An Ounce of Preservation,* is a complete guide to making sure precious documents and photographs are stored properly. In addition, the book covers proper storage of works of art on paper, greeting cards, sports cards, scrapbooks, magazines, comic books, stamps and posters. The cost of this informative book is $12.95, and may be ordered from Upper Access Inc., by telephoning 800-356-9315.

♦Sheila Benedict, a California genealogist, has begun an ambitious project of indexing the names of men who served in the American Civil War and are buried in California. She requests data on all who served, both Union and Confederate, and where they served. Her goal is to compile a set of reference books as comprehensive as possible. Write her at P.O. Box 1867, Santa Ynez, CA 93460-1867, or call (909) 928-9875.

♦In Welsh, surnames "ab" or "ap" is the prefix for "son of." Then the name gets shortened. Son of Evan becomes Ab Evan and winds up Bevans. Son of Rhys goes through Ap Rhys to Price. Son of Richard goes through Ap Richard to Pritchard.

Two Standard Ways To Document
An Ancestor's Death

The two best ways to document an ancestor's death are with death certificates and obituaries. Both are fairly easy to find, and while each yields personal information on the deceased, there are differences between the two records.

Newspaper obituaries often pre-date official death certificates. Even in the smallest frontier communities there was a hunger among folks to know the details of their neighbors' lives, and so small newspapers sprang up almost immediately. Funerals and wakes were often big social and community events and deemed newsworthy.

The mechanics of how to find a newspaper obituary will be left for another column. Today, let's just become more aware of the information they can provide to convince you that obituaries are worth the search.

Obituaries often contain date and place of birth, parents' names, date and place of marriage, in-law statistics, mention of previous marriages, names of all children, including those who may have preceded parents in death and in later times, even a photo of the deceased. The funeral home, funeral arrangements and cemetery are also usually mentioned.

Newspaper-clipped family obituaries can be found in odd places. Try searching through the old family Bible; obits are often tucked between the pages. Look behind the photos in old albums, in boxes of old family items such as school report cards, greeting cards, etc. Search the bottom of drawers in dressers, buffets and desks. Ask other relatives to search these same places.

Proving that "you just never know," I obtained a newspaper obituary on a great-grandfather from the descended relatives of his first wife. Our family came from the second wife, and I had never pursued the first wife's line. However, a descendant saw my query in a national magazine and wrote to me. She even had photos of him as a young man — when he was married to that first wife.

Obituaries are often accepted as proof of an ancestor's death when no other records are obtainable. Keep in mind, however, they can contain errors, so it's wise to cross-check the data whenever possible.

Death certificates provide much the same information as obituaries, but there are some differences.

Often, a death certificate gives the exact time of death, the specific cause of death and how long the person was ill. The form might also indicate if the person was to be buried where they died or if the remains were to be sent elsewhere. It gives the name of the attending physician and the informant — the person who gave the deceased's information to the authorities — both of which could lead to further records. The informant's name can be quite important, for it's often a close relative.

I have seen the places of birth for the parents listed on death certificates. However, the veracity of that information is only as good as the informant's knowledge. (Would you know the birthplaces for your mother-in-law's parents if you were asked?)

Death certificates issued after about 1905-15 were recorded and kept at the state level, usually the state capital's Bureau of Vital Statistics. Statewide recording of vital statistics varied from state to state. Ancestry's *Red Book*, and the government pamphlet *Where To Write For Vital Records* both give this exact date for each state. Forms to order certificates are available in Thomas J. Kemp's book, *International Vital Records Handbook*. Some states have excellent indexes to many of these records; Washington has a death index covering 1907 to 1973. Other states, such as New York, have laws prohibiting access to the records within a period of about 75 years.

Before states began recording death records, the statistics were kept at the county level, usually the county courthouse. The previously cited sources, plus *The Handy Book* from Everton Publishers, gives the address and phone number for each county courthouse. These sources will tell if the record exists or was lost, as in a fire.

I suggest researchers call to verify the correct fees. The booklet, *Where To Write For Vital Records,* available at any genealogical library, lists the telephone numbers for each state. A recorded message tells the correct amount. It would be a shame to have your letter sent back from Oklahoma (in your SASE!) saying that you need to send $1.00 more.

There's a small, ongoing controversy about whether it's worth the time, effort and money to collect more than one piece of documentation for any event in an ancestor's life. Why not obtain the cheapest and easiest and stop there?

My answer to that is, if you were to collect the death certificate, the funeral home record, the funeral program card, the cemetery record and both obituaries — want-ad and editorial — I'd bet each document would contain a tidbit or two of new information.

Prove it to yourself on your next ancestor hunt.

TODAY'S LAUGH: A recent rerun of "The Waltons" told the story of a neighbor who had searched out her family tree. At show's end, when the family all says good night, a child's voice asks "Gramps, when are we gonna get a family tree?" The gravelly voice comes back, "You're in one!"

CENSUS PROCEDURES AREN'T AS DETAILED AS THEY ONCE WERE

In the year 2044, doing genealogy as we know it today will be a nearly impossible pursuit because many of the types of records we're accustomed to using won't be as useful, as accessible or as complete.

So said renowned genealogist Robert Charles Anderson at the National Genealogical Society conference in 1995 in San Diego.

Anderson said genealogists usually first look for "survey records," the broadest avenue likely to find answers, like censuses and city directories. By 2044, what will be the survey records?

Quoting a government report, he said in future years, sample census-taking might replace the actual contacting-every-person census that has been the standard since 1790.

This might be good enough for government statistical purposes and congressional apportionment, but it will not be good enough for genealogists. Recent newspaper articles have hinted at changes like contacting one in five families, etc., which would save many government dollars.

Anderson gave some statistics of his own:

Census records from 1930 through 1990 have been microfilmed and the original schedules destroyed.

The filming quality is no better than the 1910 and 1920 censuses, but there is no going back to the originals.

Early schedules were taken on loose sheets arranged by township in rural areas and by street in urban areas before filming. So, while they are not indexed, they aren't too hard to use.

The 1990 schedules, however, were filmed as they came in, with no order at all, and will be impossible to use.

One last little-known fact: The amount of personal statistics gathered on every citizen in each census has been steadily decreasing the last few censuses.

A case in point: In 1960, only 25 percent of the people were asked about the birthplaces of their parents. In Anderson's opinion, the value of the U.S. censuses for genealogists has reached its peak and in the future will be of far less value.

Moving next to military records, Anderson said we might assume newer military records would be as complete, as saved and as accessible as were the records of old. Not so. A 1973 fire in the National Personnel Records Center in St. Louis, MO., destroyed more than 90 percent of the Army's 201 files — the main personnel files from 1912 to 1960. (Naval records survived.) He said Vietnam records are "a mess" due to the haste of the military pullout from that country, and the records being "dumped" and never organized.

"Where is the money and the time to organize all those records?" he asked.

City directories have been a great source for genealogists seeking urban ancestors. But, for the past decade, New York, Los Angeles and Chicago haven't published directories because they are too big and too costly.

Many second-tier cities publish directories only every couple of years for the same reasons. Telephone directories in the '90s list only about half the population because so many people opt for unlisted numbers. So, no documentation is left there.

Anderson said many government agencies now practice "selective retention" when it comes to saving records. These days, the Supreme Court generates more paperwork in two sessions than it did in the first 150 years of operation! This same sort of flooding is happening in all court levels. Which leads to the question, where is all this paperwork to be stored, not to mention being indexed and made accessible?

Fees for copies of records have skyrocketed in recent years. Barely 20 years ago, copies were free; then they were cheap. Now, the prices are double-digit. Anderson wonders if this is because the cost of doing business is rising, or is it to keep folks out of the records?

Rules for accessing records are becoming more restrictive. You must demonstrate "direct and tangible interest," which means you must be a direct descendant. There is a move in some states to limit records to licensed researchers and investigators.

The last point Anderson made was that the changing social values of Americans will greatly hinder future genealogists. Increasing illegitimacy, non-standard reproductive behavior, more irregular migration patterns and the increased number of illegal aliens will all make genealogy a much more frustrating hobby.

As an example, Anderson said, documenting an ancestor in early English records is fairly easy, and one can often trace ancestry into the 1700s — if you can get that far to begin with. By the 1800s, conditions in England were radically different from previous years. The industrial age arrived and the internal migration to the big cities to better jobs was so great that accurate records do not exist.

Many fledgling genealogists in England get frustrated at that 100-year back roadblock and so quit the hobby for easier things to do.

Are we in America heading for a similar impasse? Will future genealogists find that the years of 1960-2044 to be an impossible barrier to document their way through?

Anderson ended his presentation with these sobering thoughts: As of today, technology and great minds have no "for sure" answers to these many tentacled problems. It is fact that we are approaching major changes in records gathering, storage and access in the 21st century, and we can only wonder and hope that our descendants will have the pleasure we've known in learning about our forebears.

TODAY'S LAUGH: Susan Dechant of Kettle Falls shares this tidbit: On Dec. 20, 1820, Missouri imposed a $1.00 "Bachelor Tax" on unmarried men between the ages of 21 and 50.

WRITE CLEARLY AND BE SPECIFIC WHEN SENDING REQUESTS FOR INFORMATION ABOUT ANCESTORS

When was the last time you received an answer to a genealogical query? Surely, as good genealogists, you send out queries regularly. Genealogical queries are an underused resource, which is a shame. Queries can bring cartloads of information and should be used often.

Perhaps you are not sending out queries because you are discouraged. You're not sure where to send them, and you don't seem to get answers anyway. Let me help you solve this problem.

The first step in the proper use of genealogical queries is analyzing your charts and pinpointing your questions. What is it you need to know? You must be precise here; if there is a blank space on your pedigree chart, then that hole is the basis for a sound query.

For instance, perhaps you do not know where your great-grandfather died and is buried. Analyze your charts, and see what you do know about the family. Where did his wife die? Where did the children live and die? Was Dad with them, perhaps? Do you have a military or fraternal organization record on him? Those papers will yield clues as to where he lived in later life.

When did he die? Again, looking closely at your charts and research papers will give you an idea. If he was a member of the Grand Army of the Republic in 1889, then he didn't die before then. As he aged, did he possibly go to live with one of his children, especially if he was a widower?

Once you determine a time frame and a possible location, then you're ready to decide where to send that query. Let's say you've narrowed the hunt down to Jay County, IN. You think he might have died there. Is there a genealogical or historical society that has a publication that carries queries? What about a newspaper genealogy column that circulates in Jay County? Reference books in any genealogical library will give you those answers and addresses.

When you write and send that query, make sure to keep within the allowed number of words, and send the proper fee if there is one. Usually, the charge for queries is modest.

There are some definite tips for writing a successful query, and they all revolve around being clear, complete and concise. Make sure the reader of your query will know without a doubt what it is you need to know. To that end, type or print your query carefully, double-spacing the text. Keep it brief. Limit the use of pronouns. (Too many of these little rascals can leave the reader asking, "Who?") Avoid abbreviations; write out all the words and let the query editor make the abbreviations.

Capitalize all surnames. There is a big difference between Henry Joseph and Henry JOSEPH. In the first case, the reader might ask, "what was his surname?" And mention only one or two surnames per query, as in "seeking death date and place for Henry JOSEPH, believed to have lived the last years of his life with his daughter Anna Maria (JOSEPH) CLINTON and her husband Abraham CLINTON in Muncie, Jay County, IN, and dying after 1891."

Write the dates and the places out completely. The dates should be written as "26 Nov 1891," and the places should include three parts — town, county and state. Be sure to include your own name and address with your query. Type it right with the query and not just on the envelope, to make the editor's job easier.

When you're all finished writing your query, read it out loud. Does it make sense? Is your meaning clear? Then read it out loud to someone else. Does it make sense to them? Is it clear, concise, complete and to the point?

Which of these queries is best: "I am looking for information on my great-grandfather, Wallace William, who may have died in your county after the Civil War," or "I am seeking to learn the death date and death place for my great-grandfather, Wallace C. WILLIAM, who may have died in Jefferson County, IN, sometime near 1892, when his widow's probate papers were filed."

If you want to know when your query was published, or to have a copy of the published query, send a stamped, self-addressed envelope along with it. Keep a copy for your files. You may want to send the same query to the same place in a year or so.

When you receive an answer to your query, be prompt with a reply. A postcard of thanks will do (I love to send picture postcards of Spokane to Easterners). If the query has helped you find a "cousin," then be generous and offer to pay for copies and to share copies of your research with them.

Where else besides specific, regional places should you send your query? Anywhere you can think of! Send your query to state genealogical society publications and not just to the county addresses. Send your query to the national genealogical magazines like the *Genealogical Helper* and *Heritage Quest*. Send your query to surname publications. If your query is about a Baldwin ancestor, then send your query to the publisher of *Baldwin By-Lines*. Send your query to the fraternal organization or to the church your ancestor attended if they have publications and accept queries. Send it to the newspaper.

I would certainly think that if you have a bona-fide query about an ancestor that you could quickly come up with a dozen places to send that query, and with some study could find a dozen more. You could also toss a bottle in the ocean!

Make it your next homework project to write up that research problem into a good query, then figure out a dozen places to send it. Then sit back and wait for your mail carrier to bring those answers.

PENNSYLVANIA GROUP MIGHT BE ABLE TO HELP YOU

Kathleen O'Conner, genealogist and librarian at Gonzaga's Foley Library, has received a good deal of help from the Genealogical Research Society of Northeastern Pennsylvania and recommends the group to all of us. This group aims to collect and computerize all existing records within a six-county area of Northeastern Pennsylvania and to provide research services to all genealogists with an interest in this area.

The flier that O'Conner passed on to me stated the group's research policy: For a $10.00 (nonmember) donation, and a large SASE, it will do some research in its collection of resources. A balance sheet explaining how the $10.00 was used for research will be included with each reply. For more information, write to GRSNP, P.O. Box 175, Olyphant, PA 18447-0175.

NATIONAL YELLOW BOOK IS A GREAT RESOURCE FOR TRACKING DOWN BURIAL INFORMATION

In the Jan.-Feb. 1989 issue of *Heritage Quest* magazine, Mona Gee Wallace wrote the article, "Researching with the Yellow Book of Funeral Directors." This resource may be new to you, and is one you will be delighted to learn more about.

The National Yellow Book of Funeral Directors can be a big help to anyone looking for family information. This annually-published volume lists all the funeral homes in the United States and Canada. The listing is by state, town and lastly by county. The population of the town is given, as are the area and zip codes. The complete name and street address of any funeral homes in that town are listed in alphabetical order.

This book was compiled for the use of funeral directors, but is of great use to genealogists. If you know that your ancestor died in the little town of Adams, Nebraska, but that's about all you know about old Grandpa, then a letter to the funeral home there may bring you all sorts of good information. The employees of funeral homes also seem to be the nicest, most helpful folks.

For example, I have often wandered in Fairmount Cemetery in Spokane, past the tombstones of the Tannatt family. There are four family members buried there: Miriam Tannatt Merriam, Elizabeth Forster Tannatt, Elizabeth Tappon Tannatt and Gen. Thomas R. Tannatt, 1838-1913. It was the general that I often wondered about — what war would he have been general in?

A visit to Hennessey Funeral Home shed some light on this veteran. According to the 1913 record, he was Thomas Redding Tannatt, a retired Army officer, born in New York. His father was James Tannatt, born in England; and his mother Mary Gilmon, was born in Scotland. The funeral home record didn't answer all my questions about the good general, but did make more of him than just a name chiseled in stone. (Funeral homes are usually reluctant to release funeral information to non-family members, so do state the relationship when you write or visit.)

Use the *National Yellow Book for Funeral Directors* to locate more information on your ancestor via his or her funeral record. This book can be found at some area Family History Centers, and the genealogy section of many public libraries. All funeral homes have a copy, and if the staff is not too busy, they will let you use theirs. When you find the name of the town or county funeral home and when you are ready to write to them for information, be sure to state the name of your ancestor and the date of his or her death. Always include a stamped, self-addressed envelope, and a check for $5.00 for the copies you hope they'll find.

USE IGI AND ANCESTRAL FILE TO FIND CLUES

Doris Woodward, editor of the *Bulletin* of the Eastern Washington Genealogical Society, told me far too many genealogists take what they find in the International Genealogical Index and Ancestral File as "gospel," instead of as clues or partial answers.

The IGI is a computerized database of many millions of individual names, listed with parents or spouse and a specific date and place. The IGI was created for religious reasons by the

Church of Jesus Christ of Latter-day Saints, but has always been a public source of information to all genealogists. At the computer, you type in a name, select a location, and if that name is in the file you'll see the name highlighted on the screen. A couple of further keystrokes reveals to you the source of the information.

The Ancestral File is a newer computerized family-linked database. To use Ancestral File, you type in the name of an ancestor. When the name appears you can hit keys that will show you the person's pedigree or descendants. A further keystroke will lead you to the submitter of that information.

There are millions of names in these files, and surely some of your ancestral names will be there. But, you will just as surely not find every name in these databases. Beginners shouldn't give up just because they didn't find sought-after names in these databases. Those of you who do find names, don't stop there! A source citation of "IGI" or "Ancestral File" is not good enough.

The proper source citation is to list exactly where the information in these files was *originally* found; or in some cases, who submitted the information.

The information contained in the IGI generally comes from two major sources. Either the data is from submissions from genealogists sharing their information, or from folks doing records' extractions. The Family History Library has microfilmed an incredible amount of records, including millions of church records. These could be records from churches of any denomination, from most any country. Paper copies of the microfilms are given to volunteer extractors who carefully read them and type the information into a computer program. This information is then transferred to the IGI.

If you find your ancestor's name in the IGI, you will want to see which source applies to your record. If the name is there from an individual submission, then you have a cousin to contact! If the name is there from a church record, then you will want to scrutinize that entire record — perhaps other family members were active in that same congregation.

The information in the Ancestral File comes directly from genealogists like you and me. It is a newer compilation (usually within the last decade). Every genealogist is encouraged to submit their pedigree and family group information into Ancestral File because it is a well-known fact that by sharing genealogy, we all benefit. If you find your family in Ancestral

File, you can also find the name of the submitter, too — another cousin.

Make it a mid-year resolution: promise never again to accept "IGI" or "Ancestral File" as a source, for they really are not complete sources. These databases will direct you to the source.

TODAY'S LAUGH: You are the most important nut on your family tree.

HELPFUL DIRECTORY HAS ADDRESSES OF EVERY PRESBYTERIAN CHURCH IN THE NATION

Looking back several hundred years, we find many of our ancestors were Presbyterians. The earliest Presbyterian churches in the American colonies were planted on Long Island by New England Puritans in the last half of the 1600s.

Over the next two centuries, the church spread west and south, forming ten geographically diverse groups. By the mid-1960s, the Presbyterian churches in America had over three million members in over 10,000 congregations.

In pursuit of her Presbyterian ancestors, Susan Sunderman paid a visit to the First Presbyterian Church in downtown Spokane. She learned that the *Directory of the Presbyterian Church (USA)* is an annual listing of all the Presbyterian churches in the nation published by the Office of the General Assembly.

This directory is a valuable reference tool to use in searching for Presbyterian ancestors. Using this book, you could find the address for a particular church in a specific town. Then, you could write and inquire if that church has records that would document your ancestor's membership.

Also in that office, Sunderman found a blue three-ring notebook containing several interesting items. One paper lists the names of the Presbyterian Historical Society, 245 Lombard St., Philadelphia, PA 19147, and the Department of History, P.O. Box 849, Montreat, NC 28757.

These repositories include sermons, addresses, photos, and all non-current records of existing and dissolved churches, presbyteries and synods. They also contain copies of oral histories and baptism and marriage records. Through these repositories you could also access over 5,500 local histories, and a listing of church-related historical sites.

A listing of Presbyterian Church-related periodicals was included in that notebook. One flier listed *The Journal of Presbyterian History,* a quarterly published by the Presbyterian Historical Society and costing $10.00 annually. *The Presbyterian Key* is the newsletter published by the same society.

Sunderman found two books of interest in the library at the First Presbyterian Church in downtown Spokane. They were *Presbyterians in the South, Vols. I & II,* by Ernst Trice Thompson (John Knox Press, 1973) and *Presbyterian Women of America* by Lois Boyd and Douglas Brackenridge (Greenwood Press, 1983).

The staff at your local Presbyterian may be able to assist you in learning more about these resources. I suggest that you call for an appointment before you visit; all churches are busy places.

If your ancestor was a Canadian Presbyterian, write to the Archivist, 50 St. George St., Toronto, Canada MSS 2E6.

For more background on Presbyterian records and record keeping, you might order the taped lecture by Virginia R. Patton, "United States Church Records: The Presbyterians." This lecture was presented at the National Genealogical Society Conference held in Columbus, OH, in 1986. The tape, number S-7, can be ordered for about $7.00 from TRIAD, P.O. Box 120, Toulon, IL 61483, or by calling 309-286-3531.

Heritage Books offerings

♦The publishing firm of Heritage Books, Inc. is always finding new and old genealogy books to print and offer to genealogists. Some of their latest offerings include several volumes of a magazine anthology, *The Narragansett Historical Register,* edited by James N. Arnold.

The aim of this magazine, originally published starting in 1882, was to collect the history of the state of Rhode Island and Providence Plantations and preserve all information of historical value. Heritage Books intends to continue offering this series as long as interest lasts. Having these volumes at your fingertips would be like spending afternoons in the Rhode Island Historical Society.

♦*A Biographical Dictionary, Containing a Brief Account of the First Settlers, and Other Eminent Characters Among the*

Magistrates, Ministers, Literary and Worthy Men in New England, by John Eliot, was first published in 1809 and has long been out of print. This entertaining collection of biographies details the extraordinary incidents and qualities of the fathers of the 18th century in New England, described as "remarkable for their piety and moral worth, and also for their active virtues." This 517-page book is fully indexed.

♦ The last resource from Heritage Books I would like to mention is *The Mayflower Descendant: Index of Persons,* Volumes 1-34. *The Mayflower Descendant* was a lively magazine, but was never indexed. This new book from Heritage Books addresses that problem. Heritage also carries the complete set of magazine volumes in clothbound book form and also on CD-Rom.

Any of these books, and a free catalog, can be requested from Heritage Books, Inc., by calling 800-398-7709, 8:30 a.m. to 5:00 p.m. EST. Their catalog lists over 800 titles of genealogy and history, covering the U.S., Canada and the British Isles.

TODAY'S TIP: Do you know what an IRC is? An International Reply Coupon is a tiny piece of official-looking paper that you purchase for about $1.00 each at your main post office (not the grocery store ones). When you write to other countries an IRC can be exchanged for the proper postage, paying for a reply back to you. Think of it as an international SASE.

WEALTH OF RECORDS CAN BE A GENEALOGICAL GOLD MINE FOR PEOPLE WITH ANCESTRY TRACED TO THE PLAINS STATE

North Dakota offers more research help to those seeking to document their ancestors' past there than almost any other state.

Part of the reason is that North Dakota's history (genealogically speaking) goes back only to the 1850s, so the records are fairly recent.

Some of the credit goes to farsighted historians and archivists who collected and saved the records.

The State Historical Society of North Dakota is in partnership with the North Dakota Heritage Center, located near the state capitol at 612 East Boulevard Avenue, Bismarck, ND 58505-0830.

This center, built about 10 years ago, includes a wonderful museum of North Dakota's past from prehistory times to the 1990s. The state archives are in the Heritage Center and offer a wide range of resources the historian and genealogist can use in-house.

The Center has a generous by-mail research policy. Leaflets telling of the records and research policies and fees offered by the archives and historical society are free and are sent upon request.

The leaflets include titles to aid in researching land laws, lists of available research materials, tips for newspaper research, property and naturalization records, census and pioneer biography file data and photo archive information.

One important database for genealogists is the North Dakota Death Index. Located in the archives of the Heritage Center in Bismarck, this reference must be used in person or via mail request. It is not available on microfilm. The list is alphabetical by Soundex and spans the years 1915 to 1989. Plans are underway to stretch it back to the earlier 1900s and update it to the present. This index gives the full name, age, sex, date of birth, location of residence in North Dakota and the date and county of death.

There are dozens of books in the archives' library giving information on the thousands of immigrants who flooded into Dakota Territory in the last half of the 1800s. These records are well organized and indexed.

They are matched with naturalization records.

Census records for North Dakota include: 1850 Minnesota, which includes Pembina County in present-day North Dakota; 1860, 1870 and 1880 Dakota Territory (indexed); 1885 Northern Dakota Territory (unindexed); and 1915 and 1925 state censuses (unindexed).

There are also many Indian reservation censuses spanning 1885 to 1939. They also have the 1900 and 1920 federal censuses (indexed by Soundex) and the 1910 census (no index).

The Education and Interpretation Division of the North Dakota State Historical Society publishes a quarterly newsletter called *Plains Talk* and sponsors annual workshops and conferences. To be placed on its mailing list, write to it at the address above.

Another interesting research aid is the *Guide to Doing North Dakota Local History,* written by Dr. D. Jerome Tweton. The guide is published by the North Dakota Humanities Council.

This 40-page booklet tells how to get started in North Dakota research and where to find materials. It's a great beginner's tool for research in that state. It's free and may be requested by calling 800-338-6543.

The Germans from Russia Heritage Society is headquartered in Bismarck, ND. The group is for descendants of those born in Germany 200 years ago, who later migrated to Russia and then eventually to America.

The group's library features a 100,000-card obituary file, a 500-volume history library, and a collection of over 6,000 pedigree charts.

If you would like more information on this group, please write to GRHS, 1008 E. Central Ave., Bismarck, ND 58501, or call 701-223-6167.

The Prairie Heritage Chapter of the Germans from Russia Heritage Society offers a comprehensive research guide to all beginning genealogists. It's especially good for those working in North Dakota or having Germans-from-Russia ancestry.

The *Handbook for Researching Family Roots,* by Diane J. Wandler and other members of the Prairie Heritage Chapter, is a nearly 300-page book detailing the steps necessary for research success.

One whole chapter highlights the state historical societies of North and South Dakota, Nebraska, Iowa, Montana and Minnesota. Another chapter tells about the Germans from Russia group and how to research pertinent records. Detailed maps and a lengthy bibliography are included.

This book can be ordered for $25.00, postpaid, from the Prairie Heritage Chapter, P.O. Box 328, Bismarck, ND 58502-0328.

If your pedigree contains ancestors immigrating into and settling the prairie lands that came to be Dakota Territory and then North Dakota, I encourage you to write to the Heritage Center (address above) and request information to help you.

TODAY'S LAUGH: Today's not-so-funny laugh comes from a 1932 book that I found in the Garrison Public Library in North Dakota. Author Annie Abel Henderson transcribed the journal of F.A. Chardon, penned between 1834 and 1839 while he was stationed at Fort Clark, a post on the Missouri River about halfway between Minot and Bismarck.

The entry catching my eye read, "31 Mar 1838. Newman and his wife, after six days quarreling and pouting with each other, had a separation. He started down to the Ree (Arikara Indian) camp in quest of another. O may success attend him in the wife line; it is his third since his fall hunt."

IF THE SEARCH FOR YOUR ANCESTORS' RECORDS IS PROVING FRUITLESS, TRY LOOKING AT CANADIAN PASSENGER LISTS

In a previous two-part column last December, material was presented on Irish immigrants coming to America through Canadian ports. I have since learned that immigrants from all parts of Europe and the British Isles came through Canadian ports to many places in the U.S.

Passenger lists dating as early as 1865 can be found in Quebec City. More extensive lists covering a wider area of geography and beginning in 1895 are located in the St. Albans District, VT.

A passage from an article by Charles Addington in the Nov.-Dec. 1994 issue of *Genealogical Helper* explains this phenomenon:

"The flow of immigrants to the U.S. via Canada partly reflected settlement patterns. As the settlement of the U.S. continued its westward direction, there was a resulting stream of immigrants whose inland destination was far to the west of ports on the eastern coast of the U.S. Many immigrants were going to places that were nearer to the Canadian-United States border than they were to New York City, Philadelphia, Boston and so on. In this historic and geographic context, the regular passenger service to Canada from ports such as Liverpool and Glasgow became a reasonably convenient alternative route for some migrants to the U.S., because the U.S.-bound migrant could complete his or her journey to the U.S. by rail upon arrival in Canada."

The heartland of America was the ultimate destination for many of the immigrants in the last half of the 19th century. It cost less to come to the middle of the U.S. via Canada than it was to make the longer sea journey — arriving in American seaports then taking a 1,500-mile train ride west. Cheaper fares on ships going to Canada were a big factor in encouraging immigrants to take a Canadian route.

Michael Tepper, in his book, *American Passenger Arrival Records,* says that about 40 percent of all passengers arriving in Canada were actually bound for the United States.

Addington's article continues: "In this connection, the passenger lists for Quebec City, beginning in 1865, are worth noting in some details, they are the longest continuous set of lists for any Canadian port to survive."

His article then explains exactly what statistics can be learned from these early passenger lists. But, the main thing I want to mention here is that the lists from Quebec City after the 1860s increasingly state the final destination of each passenger.

Perhaps if you've been wanting to experience the thrill of finding your immigrant ancestor's name on a passenger list and haven't been so lucky, this bit of news will give you hope. Plan to check these Canadian passenger lists. If you know where your ancestor lived in the U.S., this geographic clue will help ensure that you'll pinpoint the right person on the lists.

Last January, while we were visiting the Family History Library in Salt Lake, Bruce Austin found a reference notebook giving this same information. It really fired his imagination. A handout on the immigration and passenger lists reference table reads:

"Anyone searching for information on an ancestor or relative who might have entered or attempted to enter the United States from Canada during the period 1895-1924 should consult the St. Albans District manifest records index, a set of 400 rolls of microfilm. These records include information on individuals who entered the U.S. not only in the St. Albans District of Vermont, but also in the states of Washington, Montana, North Dakota, Minnesota, Michigan, New York and other places along the U.S./Canadian border."

It was this last part that caught Austin's eye — would he finally find the passenger list for his Minnesota ancestor in these records? Who would have guessed to look for Washington or Minnesota information in records filed in St. Albans, Vermont?

This flier further explained the terminology found in these records, outlining the dozen or so points of information that can be found on the cards comprising these records.

Information on obtaining these passenger lists from the National Archives of Canada and a short bibliography of further references are also included in this handout. Please note that, with regards to the St. Albans District records, apparently only the index has been microfilmed. Once you find your ancestor's name in the index, then you must write to the National Archives of Canada for the record.

The *Helper* article explains that other surviving Canadian official passenger lists — including Quebec City, 1865-1919; Halifax, Nova Scotia, 1880-1919; St. John, New Brunswick, 1900-1918; and Vancouver, British Columbia, 1905-1919 — have been microfilmed and are available through both the National Archives of Canada and the Family History Library.

Another source of information on this topic is the article, "Manifest Destiny: Immigrants Arriving in the U.S. through Canada," by Joan Nichols, found in the Winter 1994 *Forum*, a newsletter of the Federation of Genealogical Societies. Included in this article are copied examples of what some of the records actually look like.

TODAY'S LAUGH: Always remember that ancestors, just like you, are absolutely unique — just like everyone else.

LISTS FROM GERMAN PORT CAN PROVIDE VALUABLE INFORMATION ABOUT EUROPEAN EMIGRANTS

The Hamburg passenger lists contain the names of millions of Europeans who emigrated through the port of Hamburg between 1850 and 1934 (except for 1915 through 1919, the World War I years). Nearly one-third of the people who emigrated from central and eastern Europe during this time are included on these lists.

If you have ancestors who emigrated from these areas, the Hamburg passenger lists could provide important genealogical information about them, including their hometowns. Extensive indexes make these records easier to use than most other passenger lists and emigration records.

You may not need to look at the Hamburg passenger lists if you already know where your European ancestors were born. Also, if they came through the ports of Bremen, LeHavre, Amsterdam, Rotterdam or Antwerp, you need to know that their emigration records were either destroyed or are not available at the Family History Library.

The lists are made up of two sections: The direct lists (with index) list passengers who left Hamburg, Germany, and sailed directly to their destination without stopping at other European ports. The indirect lists (with index) list passengers who stopped at other European ports before sailing to their final destination. About 20 percent of the immigrants leaving Europe took indirect routes.

The Hamburg passenger records are on 486 rolls of microfilm at the Family History Library. For film numbers, consult the library card catalog on the FamilySearch computer program.

Before using the index, you need to know the year an emigrant left Germany. The 1900 census is a good place to begin searching for this information. Again, try to find out whether the emigrant traveled directly to the intended country of destination or stopped at other ports along the way by thoroughly checking through all previously collected records.

Most of the lists have been indexed. The only ones not indexed are those from 1850 to 1854 (these are arranged alphabetically). There are two sets of indexes: the "Fifteen-year Index to the Direct Hamburg Passenger Lists, 1856-1871" and the regular indexes.

If your emigrant departed between 1850 and 1854, search the alphabetical passenger list for those years. If the departure is between 1856 and 1871, search the 15-year index first. If the person is not listed in the 15-year index, search the regular index.

Both the direct and indirect lists have regular indexes. They are divided into segments that cover one or part of a year. The direct indexes begin in 1854 and end in 1934. The indirect indexes begin in 1854 and end in 1910.

Using the indexes, use the Family History Library Catalog to find the film number. These films can then be ordered into your nearby Family History Center.

If you cannot find your ancestor in the index, there could be several reasons.

Your emigrant did not sail from Hamburg; they may have sailed from one of several other possible ports in Europe, most of which have few or no records available. Your emigrant could be listed on another page because the first was full; search the sections of other letters of the alphabet.

Your emigrant's name could be spelled differently than it appears in your records today; look for alternate spellings of the name. Your emigrant could have come at a different date than you thought. Try other years.

Using the Hamburg passenger lists to find your immigrant ancestor can be a confusing, many-step course of research. To learn more about this resource, ask about the four-page resource guide, *The Hamburg Passenger Lists, 1850-1934,* at the Family History Center. Also ask about the microfiche No. 6000034, which is a more thorough guide to the lists.

A parallel resource would be *German Immigration to America in the Nineteenth Century: A Genealogist's Guide,* by Marilyn A. Wellauer. This 90-page book offers insights into the conditions surrounding 19th century emigration. Page 48 reads, "In 1851 the city fathers of Bremen and Hamburg founded information bureaus for emigrants, marking the beginning of government control of the process of emigration. The purpose of both organizations was to render aid, assistance, and protection to the emigrants descending on the cities, to provide the travelers with guides, and to see that fair prices for transportation were levied.

"In April 1849, construction began on a large Emigrant House in Bremerhaven, near Bremen, and it was finished a year later. It was equipped to sleep 1,500-2,000 persons in nine sleeping halls. The kitchen could accommodate about 3,500 persons, and the hospital's capacity was 35 patients. There was a chapel with Protestant and Catholic facilities. By the middle of the century, Hamburg and Bremen were recommended for the good condition of their ships and lodgings."

This enjoyable little book can be ordered by $12.00 from the author at 3239 N. 58th St., Milwaukee, WI 53216.

Genealogy by video

If your circumstances don't allow you to attend a genealogy class, or if you would benefit from a slow, step-by-step review of genealogical procedures, then I've got good news for you. "The Genealogist's Video Research Guide" is a package of four genealogy lessons that you can view as often as you wish right in your own home. The first tape covers home sources, published histories, proper record keeping, and accessing the databases of the Family History Library. The second discusses census and probate records, and third highlights land, military and vital records. Beginners will find that these videos get them off to a good start, and more advanced researchers will appreciate the opportunity for repeated viewing. These videos carry a 30-day money-back guarantee, and can be ordered for $59.95 from Video Knowledge, 32 North 200 East, Suite No. 1, Spanish Fork, UT 84660, or call 800-34-ROOTS.

WHEN OFFICIAL RECORDS ARE LACKING, GENEALOGISTS CAN USE OTHER RESOURCES

Early immigrants to the area that would become Colorado mostly had one thing on their mind: gold.

Headlines in 1858 chronicled the discovery of gold at the foot of the Rocky Mountains in the region later named Colorado. Thousands of adventurous souls reacted to such headlines by crossing the plains in wagons inscribed "Pike's Peak or Bust!" But not all came for gold.

Consumption, or tuberculosis, was rampant in the 19th century, and many came to the "pure air" of the West, seeking a cure for their disease.

In 1858, the land of present-day Colorado was made up of parts of four territories: Kansas, Nebraska, New Mexico and Utah. The Territory of Colorado was established in 1861, and in 1876 it became the 38th state.

The transcontinental railroad was completed in 1869, and this spurred settlement of the area. The 1870 territorial population was nearly 40,000. By 1880, the number had swelled to nearly 200,000. It's quite likely that some member of your family ended up in Colorado in the last half of the 19th century.

Because of its recent settlement pattern, it would seem at first that research in Colorado would be difficult. Vital registration — the official keeping of births, deaths and marriages — began relatively late in Colorado. Some statistics are available back to 1900, but it was 1906 when death records really began to be kept, and 1928 when total registration of births was made mandatory.

Luckily for researchers, Colorado newspapers began appearing in 1859. The Colorado Historical Society has indexed most of Colorado's earliest newspapers, and many of these indexes have been published in their quarterly magazine. These indexes would be a substitute for official vital records, for notices of marriages, births and deaths were published in the newspaper. The *Heritage Quest* magazine, Jan-Feb 1990, has a name listing of the 337 papers being published in Colorado in 1909. Forty-seven of these were daily papers.

If you're looking for an ancestor who went West and need some help learning about Colorado records, here are some tips. *The National Genealogical Society Quarterly* back in June 1989 ran a 20-page article highlighting all major record collections for Colorado. Kathleen W. Hinckley, C.G.R.S., wrote the article and has come to be the recognized authority on Colorado research.

I wrote to Hinckley in 1994 with a question about the Colorado marriage index. Her answer explained that "the statewide Colorado marriage index is by groom only and also only covers the years 1900-1939. There is no index for the years 1940-1974, but a cataloging error in the Family History Library catalog would lead researchers to think there is. There is a bride-and-groom index beginning in 1975 to the present.

"Also, I've found that the 1900-1939 index is not 100 percent complete; I've found marriages in the counties that were not in the statewide index. There is a project under way to index the brides in that 1900-1939 index, but all that has been completed so far are the brides with grooms with surnames that begin with "A."

This index may be used via the Family History Centers, or by writing to the Colorado Genealogical Society (address below).

Hinckley welcomes questions from those needing research help in Colorado, and will send a brochure outlining her professional services upon request. Her address is P.O. Box 740637, Arvada, CO 80006-0637. You may also call her at (303) 422-9371.

Other sources to help you learn about the records of Colorado would be *The Genealogist's Address Book,* by Elizabeth Petty Bently; *The Red Book,* published by Ancestry, Inc.; and the *Research Outline: Colorado*, a small brochure published by the Family History Library. The books can be accessed at most genealogical libraries, and the brochure can be found in some Family History Centers.

Some helpful addresses would include: the Colorado Historical Society, Stephen H. Hart Library, 1300 Broadway, Denver, CO 80203; the Colorado State Library, 201 E. Colfax Ave., Denver, CO 80203; and the Colorado Genealogical Society, P.O. Box 9218, Denver, CO 80209. Be sure to include a stamped, self-addressed envelope with any requests for information.

Priscilla DeAngeles wrote an article on "Italians in Colorado," for the Nov-Dec 1992 issue of *Heritage Quest* magazine. She wrote that "life was not easy for the early Italian immigrant families in the West of the late 19th century. There were the usual hardships of a rugged country and climate with few creature comforts such as medical care. Added to these anxieties was open discrimination against Catholics and southern Europeans, and back-breaking labor in mines, railroads and farming."

But, the Italian presence in Colorado continued, and Denver today boasts a large Italian population.

CD-ROM resources available

Back in January, the American Genealogical Lending Library announced placement of its Census Index Databases on CD-ROM. Available now are CDs for New York City 1870, which includes Long Island; Georgia 1870; and Pennsylvania 1870, which includes Philadelphia.

All of AGLL's Precision Indexing databases are being converted to CD-ROM, and there will be technical support available on all products. As an added bonus, a full copy of the AGLL film/fiche catalog is included on each CD. This catalog is a great reference tool to over 250,000 titles. For more information, including current prices, please write AGLL, P.O. Box 329, Bountiful, UT 84011-0329, or call 800-760-AGLL.

TODAY'S LAUGH: "He that has no fools, knaves, or beggars in his family was begot by a flash of lightning." (Old English proverb).

BROAD REQUEST WON'T GET YOU MUCH

One of the first things we are eager to do as beginning genealogists is to write the county courthouse and ask for the marriage licenses of our ancestors.

All too often, we're disappointed with a negative reply. Perhaps I can help you understand why that happens.

It will really help to think about the procedure and the steps involved with completing the necessary paperwork.

Think back to when you prepared for your own marriage. First, you visited the courthouse. You paid the fee and filled out a marriage application. This helped you to obtain a license which was a piece of paper authorizing any person of proper authority to marry the two persons whose names appeared on it.

You took this license to your priest, minister or justice of the peace, and he recognized the legitimacy of the document and exercised his authority to marry you.

Remember having to sign something right after you were married? You both signed the license, acknowledging that you had used the license within the designated time period and did indeed get married.

The license was returned to the courthouse, becoming part of the marriage return. Then a marriage certificate was issued to you. Perhaps the clerk in the courthouse entered the information of your marriage in a marriage register book.

This same procedure took place for your ancestors. The actual physical paperwork might have been somewhat different, but basically the process was the same.

Sometimes the clerk had a big two-part license book. The skinny part on the left was like the application, and was filled out with all sorts of personal information about the bride and groom. The larger right-hand part was the actual license that was issued to the couple. This particular register is a gold mine if you can find one!

Another piece of paperwork was the marriage consent form. If the bride or groom was underage, a parent had to sign to give consent.

In Southern states, a marriage bond had to be posted. This was official notice of a sum of money posted by somebody knowing the bride (usually her father) which would go to her in the event of a divorce.

A similar link in this chain of paperwork, but one that isn't usually found in the courthouse, is the posting of intentions or banns. In some churches, the couple had to post banns for several weeks in a row to notify one and all of their intention to marry so that anyone opposing the marriage had time to speak up. This paperwork usually is found in the church records.

The paperwork changed as the years went by. During one period, the county may have kept very few records, and then years later (under a different clerk) may have kept everything. These documents are most certainly not side-by-side on the shelves in the courthouse! They could be in different rooms or even down in the basement, and sometimes different ones have been converted to microfilm.

Some records may never have ended up in the courthouse, such as the marriage certificates. Those may have stayed with the couple.

I have mentioned nearly a dozen different kinds of marriage-related documents. The marriage application is potentially the best source of family information. The marriage license just gives the names and ages of the bride and groom. The marriage certificate just says that he and she got married. The banns, bonds and consents all give family information tidbits, but never as much as does the application.

So after this review, what will you be asking for in the future? The marriage application! But if you write and ask specifically for the marriage application for such-and-such a year, and applications don't exist for that decade, then the clerk isn't fibbing to say "We don't have the record." But they may well have some other marriage documents, and that's the point. When you write in the future, do not just ask for one specific marriage document. Instead, phrase your question: "May I have a photocopy of any marriage documentation you might have showing the marriage of so and so?"

This question might cause clerks to groan, because they are being asking to check several different places to answer just one letter. The clerk may well be too busy to do this for you, and your letter might get shuffled to the bottom of the pile more than once.

A better avenue to success would really be to visit the courthouse yourself after you have done your homework and know exactly what the courthouse does and doesn't have, and for what years. You accomplish this by writing or calling the courthouse and asking specific questions, or by using any of several different reference books found in most genealogy libraries.

If a personal visit is impossible, then consider hiring somebody living in that county to go and do the work for you. The small fee you'd have to pay for an hour or two of somebody's time might save you money in the long run, and would certainly be worthwhile if it resulted in success. You can locate an agent by contacting the genealogy society in that county. You can find those addresses in reference books in any genealogical collection.

TODAY'S TIPS:
♦Ruth McMahon has indexed the death records of Detroit, Wayne Co., MI, for the years 1868-1897. She will check for a name for $2.00, plus an SASE. Write her at 8232 Beacon Lane, Northville, MI 48167-9418.

♦There is no charge to register for the *Surname Directory for Arkansas Ancestors*. The directory will sell for a small fee. Send a long SASE for more information and a registration form to Arkansas Genealogical Society, P.O. Box 908, Hot Springs, AR 71902-0908.

♦Those working on Hungarian ancestry might want to contact the Hungarian Genealogical Society, c/o Kathy Karocki, 124 Esther St., Toledo, OH 43605-1435. This group offers a newsletter, publications, and translation services.

PERHAPS YOUR ANCESTORS WERE "PLAIN PEOPLE" WHO PLAYED AN UNHERALDED ROLE DURING THE CIVIL WAR

I just finished reading a delightful little book titled, *The Plain People of the Confederacy*.

I picked this book up some time ago at a used book sale in the Holland Library, down on the Washington State University campus in Pullman, WA.

Author Bell Irvin Wiley wrote the book in 1943, when it was first published by Louisiana State University Press. It was reprinted in 1963 by Encounter Paperback of Chicago.

The preface to the small book is worth quoting:

"The common folk, white and black, constituted the bone and sinew of the Southern Confederacy. White yeomen comprised the bulk of the armies that followed Lee in Virginia, Joe Johnston in the central South, and Kirby Smith beyond the Mississippi.

"These rustics were not all exemplary soldiers by any means. Some of them were overly fond of liquor; others were impervious to discipline; thousands absented themselves without leave; many preferred filth to cleanliness; hundreds played the coward when the bullets whistled close.

"But on the whole, they were good fighters. It is not too much to say that the record of the Confederacy on the field of battle must stand or fall on the basis of their performance.

"The wives, children, parents, and other home connections of the plain soldiers composed the overwhelming majority of the South's civilian population. These people had many rough edges. Many could not write.

"Their speech was usually crude and their manners unpolished. But they had many virtues. For the most part they were sturdy, hard-working, respectable citizens.

"The colored folk constituted about a third of the Confederacy's populace. They were not the docile, 'Old Kentucky Home' type of subservients that romancers have depicted them to be. Most of them idealized freedom and grasped it with alacrity when Yankee soldiers brought it within convenient reach.

"While the slaves waited for emancipation, they raised foodstuffs for civilians and soldiers, ran spinning wheels and looms on the plantations, worked in factories and mines, built fortifications, and served as nurses, cooks, and personal servants in the Southern army. Their good humor buoyed the spirits of white associates both at home and on the firing line. Their contribution to the Southern cause was enormous."

This book really brightened one of our February gray days for me. As we've done our Southern genealogy, we are all too aware of the "big people" — the politicians, plantation owners and generals. Yet most of our ancestors were the plain people, the "little people."

Even in published sources, the "common taters" of the South are barely mentioned, and then only as a group. It was time for me to take another look.

Pages 10 and 11 of the book tell that "Confederate soldiers had many other woes besides hunger and raggedness. In summer, the flies, mosquitoes and gnats that swarmed about encampments made life utterly miserable. Body lice gnawed away without regard to season."

"There is not a man in the army, officer or private, that does not have from a battalion to a brigade of body lice on him," wrote one Reb in 1863. Others dubbed the pests with such military names as "graybacks," "Zouaves," "tigers," and "Bragg's bodyguard."

If you have Southern ancestry and have been pleased and proud to document Confederate service, please take time to think about all the family and friends involved with that "Johnnie Reb." That soldier had parents, siblings, children and cousins, and possibly a host of servants, who were the "plain people of the Confederacy." Take the time to learn about them, too.

While we're talking about the Civil War, did you know that of the 2.3 million men enlisted in the Union Army, 70 percent were under 23 years of age? Approximately 100,000 were 16.

There were 300 lads 13 or less, and records show there were 25 soldiers no older than 10.

Did you know that Union Army hospitals treated over 6 million cases during the war? There were twice as many deaths from disease as from hostile bullets. Diarrhea and dysentery alone took the lives of 44,558 Union soldiers.

You cannot really do genealogy without some understanding of history. To know that your ancestor died in a Southern prison camp is one thing, but to know the full circumstances of that camp, how, why, when and where it operated, is to know the full story.

All too many family historians eagerly and cheerfully gather skeletal information (the main facts: born when and where; married when and where; died when and where) and chase on to the next ancestor.

The discovery of a Southern or Confederate ancestor is a case in point. There is so much information at your fingertips about the Civil War that there is no excuse for not learning the complete story of your ancestor's life.

Visit the library. Get some books and start learning today about that history as it applies to your genealogy.

TODAY'S LAUGH: Notice in *The Settler*, a newspaper of Bradford County, PA, for Aug. 4, 1922: "At Burlington, Sunday, were married Eliphalet Gustin, bordering on 70 years of age, and Miss Sally Mills, aged about 16 years, after a courtship of full half an hour."

THOSE TRYING TO TRACK DOWN ANCESTORS IN THE 46TH STATE SHOULD DO THEIR HOMEWORK FIRST

Oklahoma became a designated U.S. territory in 1890 and a state in 1907. The name comes from two Choctaw words, "okla," (people) and "homa" (red), meaning the "land of the red people "

After the United States acquired the area that is now Oklahoma in the Louisiana Purchase of 1803, white settlers soon began arriving. The name for the state came about because the U.S. government in the 1820s began to move all the native tribes living east of the Mississippi River to the designated Indian territory in what would become Arkansas and Oklahoma. For many years, about half of what would become Oklahoma was one big tribal reservation.

The Indian Territories were in eastern Oklahoma; the official territory of Oklahoma was established in the western side of Oklahoma. White settlers heading west had to cross Indian lands which was a reason for constant strife. Eventually some of these white settlers preferred staying on tribal lands, causing a whole set of new problems. During the Civil War, many of the tribes sided with the Confederacy (after all, their ancestors were buried there), and because of their allegiance suffered horribly during the war as their lives and property were destroyed.

After the war, the discovery of oil on tribal lands enlarged the scope of the troubles between the white immigrants and the transplanted native tribes.

If you have ancestry in Oklahoma, then you had better do your homework regarding the geography, history of the state and its peoples before jumping in and writing letters. You need to answer such questions as: What records of whites exist? Of the many tribes? Who exactly lived where? Which censuses should include my ancestors? Where are the vital records? The census records? Where are these records kept?

The place to begin your homework assignment is to visit your local public library and check out a couple of general books on Oklahoma. Read, enjoy and learn the history of this, the 46th state. Some suggested reading would be *Oklahoma: A History of Five Centuries,* by Arrell M. Gibson, and *A Guide to the Indian Tribes of Oklahoma,* by Muriel H. Wright. Your library will have others.

The Family History Centers will have leaflet guides for researching in any of the 50 states. The guide for Oklahoma is 11 pages long and includes a great map showing where the tribes were settled, and dates the areas were opened up for white settlement.

The guide lists names and addresses for the major archives and libraries, lists books on Oklahoma history and biography, explains that the 1870 and 1880 censuses have been lost, gives addresses for the major religious denominations in Oklahoma, tells where to find city directories and lists books on

Oklahoma's peoples. This research guide is a dandy place to begin your homework assignment.

The Oklahoma Historical Society is located near the state capitol in Oklahoma City. It has 3.5 million documents representing 66 of the 67 tribes that resided in Indian Territory. The newspaper collection contains 28,000 reels of microfilm on state newspapers published from 1844 to the present.

Membership in the Oklahoma Historical Society is $15.00 annually, and with membership you will receive four issues of *The Chronicles of Oklahoma,* and twelve issues of *Mistletoe Leaves.* Both of these publications carry articles and features on the history, people and places of Oklahoma.

If you would like to request research help by mail, you must first write for the "Biographical Research Request Form." Send a self-addressed, stamped envelope to the OHS, Library Resources Division, 2100 N. Lincoln Blvd., Oklahoma City, OK 73105. This completed form must accompany all requests for research. A research fee of $15.00 will be charged to all out-of-state letter requests that involve research, as opposed to a request that is a simple look up and copy. Photocopies are 20 cents per page, 50 cents for microfilm copies, and $1.00 for faxed copies. Add $1.50 per request for postage.

The Tulsa Genealogical Society, P.O. Box 585, Tulsa, OK 74101, asks annual dues of $15.00. With membership comes *Tulsa Annals,* a periodical full of Oklahoma records and information. (Most public libraries have back-issues of this periodical.) Members can submit free queries to this publication; a fee of $5.00 is asked for non-members.

This society has also compiled and made available records of area cemeteries, funeral homes and voter registrations. I do not know if it does any research by mail, but if you write to inquire, don't forget to include a stamped, self-addressed envelope.

The Oklahoma Genealogical Society was organized in 1955 and has published material on Oklahoma for 39 years. All back issues, and a subject index to these issues, are available. Annual membership is $10.00. Send a long SASE for informational brochures to OGS, P.O. Box 12986, Oklahoma City, OK 73157.

The Oklahoma Genealogical Research Group, P.O. Box 171, Stigler, OK 74462, offers all kinds of research help, including a quarterly genealogy newsletter in Oklahoma and the funeral home and cemetery records for their respective counties. For a fee of $16.95 they will search these records for the surname of your choice. You may request a free copy of their newsletter.

TODAY'S TIP: I have recommended the newsletter, *The Irish, At Home and Abroad*, compiled by Dwight Radford and Kyle Betit in this column. The latest project of these authors is a 75-page "detailed overview of Irish record sources, written to help the North American be successful in Irish research." This guide can be ordered for $18.95 to *The Irish*, P.O. Box 521806, Salt Lake City, UT 84152.

AIDS TO RESEARCHING FAMILY HISTORY IN DEUTSCHLAND INCLUDE 300,000 MARRIAGE LISTINGS

The Winter 1994 issue of *The German Genealogical Digest* carried several articles of interest to genealogists.

One chronicles the Gerber family from Saxony and Switzerland to Pennsylvania and is a good case study for any genealogist.

Another explains guild records.

A guild was an association of men with similar interests or pursuits usually associated with medieval times. German guilds were active from the 1200s to the 19th century. Guild records can bridge the gaps in parish registers or cover time periods prior to parish registers.

They contain names of skilled laborers, craftsmen and apprentices and may also include some vital records-type information.

The article explained where German guild records can be accessed.

A small percentage of guild records has been microfilmed, and these are available through the Family History Centers.

Another article, "North German Marriage Records" by Laraine Ferguson, explains that "an ambitious project to identify sources and provide publications of the population history of Northern Germany has become a valuable resource for German family researchers. A significant organizational achievement has been accomplished by Franz Schubert of Gottingen, Germany, in coordinating the indexing and publishing marriage records from the beginning of parish registers in North Germany to the year 1750, and in some cases, to the year 1876."

Schubert and his associates indexed and published more than 300,000 marriage entries, and more are forthcoming.

These lists provide the genealogist with a book series that will save untold hours of research time. Many indexed parish records are available only in German archives, and parish records available on microfilm (through the Family History Library) are often difficult to read because of the language and script.

These records are now neatly typed and indexed. Names of the bride and groom, marriage date, and often names of their parents, are provided.

To subscribe, send $24.00 (for one year) to *GGD*, N. 245 Vine, No. 106, Salt Lake City, UT 84103. Individual issues can be ordered for $8.00; back issues are available. I highly recommend this publication to anyone researching German ancestry.

While we're on the subject of German research, my friend Charlotte Jacob-Hanson, who lives in Bad Soden, Germany, writes a newsletter column explaining old German language idioms.

One idiom you might encounter in a biographical sketch about your German ancestor would be "jemandem einen Korb geben," translated "to give someone a basket." This means to reject someone, to turn someone down, and goes back to the 12th and 13th centuries, the age of courtly romance.

It seems a maiden could choose how she wished to receive a suitor.

If he was a favored candidate for her hand, he would be received through the front door. If not, a basket, usually with a weak bottom, was let down over the wall to him. On being hoisted up to the maiden's window, he would likely fall through the basket.

In this way the basket evolved into a symbol of rejection.

The summer 1994 issue of *News of the Family History Library* tells of a new German acquisition that could prove to be a wonderful resource. Half a million German pedigrees, mostly dating from 1650 to 1850, are available on microfilm at the Family History Library and through the Family History Centers.

Many of these pedigrees are hundreds of pages long. Titled the German Pedigree Card Index, this database is more than 600 pedigree films (listed under the FHLC computer number 677728). The explanations will be written in German, but the flier says the catalog contains a brief explanation in English.

The flier also tells that the library has acquired 135 new microfilms about Germans in Russia. The German Protestant Church of Russia was organized into several consistories and headquartered in St. Petersburg.

The new microfilms contain 274 volumes of the consistories' church record transcripts stored at the Russian State Historical Archives. These records are from German settlements near St. Petersburg, the Black Sea, Bessarabia and the Crimea from 1833 to 1885.

CORNISH COUSINS AREN'T THAT HARD TO FIND

Cornwall is a peninsula of granite, ancient and unspoiled, uncoiling for the best part of 100 miles into the open Atlantic. It is the home of legendary King Arthur, and ancestral home to many in the United States today claiming Cornish ancestry.

When the mining industry dwindled in the 19th century, tens of thousands of men and women and their families left Cornwall, taking precious skills with them to develop famous mines all over the world.

If finding the background of a particular ancestor has you stumped, but you know that he was a miner, then perhaps you have a Cornish family.

Here are a few Cornish-related resources to help in your ancestral search and to help you understand your Cornish heritage:

Cornish World is a new publication calling itself "the international magazine for the Cornish." Regular features tell how our Cornish ancestors lived hundreds of years ago and how our cousins live there today. Articles tell how to trace and find those ancestors and present-day cousins plus articles on Cornish culture.

The magazine has access to Cornwall's local libraries, record offices and parish records and its researchers and contributors are Cornwall experts who will be pleased to answer readers' questions.

Cornish World also encourages individuals and group tours to visit Cornwall.

To subscribe, send £12 (about $20.00) to *Cornish World*, Institute of Cornish Studies, Trevithick Centre, Trevenson Road, Redruth, Cornwall TR15 3PL, United Kingdom.

The best way to send money overseas is to call Ruesch International, 800-424-2923. Tell them how much you need to send and to what country, and they will tell you how much to send to them. For a $2.00 fee, they will provide you with a proper draft to send to the country in question.

Tam Kernewek is a quarterly newsletter of the Cornish American Heritage Society and comes with membership of $10.00 to join the society. The newsletter, founded in 1982 for the Gathering of Cornish Cousins, carries queries, book reviews and a library list. It also has a non-circulation library, but librarian Jean Joltiffe will be glad to check their holdings for specific information.

Write to her at 2405 N. Brookfield Rd., Brookfield, WI 53045, and don't forget that self-addressed stamped envelope.

To subscribe to the newsletter, send your check to CAHS, c/o Tam Kernewek Editor, Richard Hay, 3618 Ligon Rd., Ellicott City, MD 21042-5239.

The newsletter also features Cornish gatherings around the country. The main annual reunion, sponsored by the Cornish American Heritage Society, features folk dancing, Cornish dances, a pasty (meat pie) picnic, cemetery walks, tours and group sessions covering historical, cultural and genealogical topics.

Judy Locy, a member of the *Cornish World* team, shared this information with me. She invites questions and letters from any "Cornish cousin." Write her at 18 Indian Trial, Lake in the Hills, IL 60102, or call her at (708) 658-6737. Her fax number is (708) 967-3100.

One last Cornish item: The Cornish America Heritage Society offers a Cornish Heritage Certificate to anyone whose ancestor was born in Cornwall and subsequently settled in North America. The parchment certificate will be sent upon receipt of $5.00 and a completed application sent with documentation. If you'd like a the application and instructions, contact Jean Jolliffe at the address given above.

TODAY'S LAUGH: Remember, a halo only has to fall 11 inches to become a noose.

NEW DATABASE HELPS TRACE BRITISH ROOTS

In 1993, I wrote about the "British Isles Genealogical Register," a project of the Federation of Family History Societies in Great Britain. This project was to register surnames being researched in England, Ireland, Scotland, Wales and the Channel Islands — and in this way make your interests known to thousands of other family historians worldwide. Here is an update on the register, as found in the May 1991 *Family Tree Magazine* (published in England).

The advertising stated the Register would be published by county sections, meaning the Yorkshire section will contain only Yorkshire surnames, thus helping family historians to concentrate their interests within one county.

The Federation of Family History Societies will coordinate the entire project. This national society will publish those sections that are not published by the respective region.

The database contains 250,000-plus entries from more than 17,000-contributors. All entries received by Feb. 1, 1994, have been included. The only way to access this database of surnames is to contact the county history society in your county of interest: for instance, if you wish to inquire about a surname in Cornwall, contact the Cornwall Family History Society.

On other subjects

♦The Victoria County Historical Commission has begun to compile a computer database of immigrants who arrived in the U.S. through the Port of Indianola, Texas. From the landing of Prince Solm's German settlers in December 1844 until the destructive hurricane in 1886, Indianola was second only to Galveston as the major port of entry on the Texas coast. Thousands of German, Polish, Czech, English, Irish, French and other settlers stepped ashore in Indianola to begin a new life.

If your ancestor came to America through that port, the commission would like to include him or her in its database. Information will be accepted from diaries, deeds, Bibles, church records, family accounts, obituaries, news articles and official immigration records.

To obtain the form needed to register your ancestor, send a stamped, self-addressed envelope to Project Coordinator, Victoria County Historical Commission, 417, Cottonwood St., Victoria, TX 77904, or call (512) 575-0049.

♦Jackie Smith Arnold has written *Kinship, It's All Relative*, a delightful little book that explains all the simple and/or complex relationships of kinship.

For instance, do you know the degree of blood relationship, or consanguinity, between yourself and your first cousins? Do you understand the "removes?" Have any questions about adoption, extended or blended families?

And what about terms — are you aware of the variety of marriages? According to Arnold, there are five main types of marriages.

•The ceremonial marriage is performed in accordance with the law of the state in which it takes place.

•The common-law marriage is a private arrangement without a ceremony or observance of legal requirements.

•The consensual marriage requires spoken vows confirming a couple's intent, but after the vows are spoken the couple doesn't have to live together.

•A proxy marriage requires special permission because it is allowed only when unusual circumstances keep the couple apart. Marriage by proxy allows substitutes to take the vows for the couple who may be hundreds of miles apart.

•The last is a secret marriage, which is a legal marriage but kept quiet. It is a misdemeanor to publicize a secret marriage.

Each section in Arnold's book includes a beautifully appropriate quote, as witnessed by this one from the "Code of Hammurabi" in the adoption section: "If a man has taken a young child to sonship, and has reared him up, no one (else) has a claim against that nursling."

If you would like this fun and informative 120-page book for $9.95, call Genealogical Publishing Co. at 800-296-6687, or write them at 1001 N. Calvert, Baltimore, MD 21202.

TODAY'S TIP: The Swiss National Tourist Office, 608 Fifth Ave., New York, NY 10020, offers a free brochure, *A Genealogical How-To for Americans of Swiss Descent*. One of the society's functions is to collect names and addresses of individuals researching Swiss families. Write today!

INFORMATION IS AVAILABLE ON VOLUNTEER STATE

The Volunteer State entered the Union on June 1, 1796, as the 16th state. This state has 95 counties and is 34th in size.

Nashville is its capital.

Early settlers of Tennessee generally came from Virginia and the Carolinas by way of the Cumberland Gap and other land routes. Some settlers from New England and Pennsylvania poled keelboats from the Ohio River up the Cumberland and Tennessee Rivers; others came up the Mississippi River.

Most early settlers were of English or Ulster Scottish origin, although some were of German, Irish or French ancestry.

The Family History Centers can help you order a wide variety of Tennessee data from the main library in Salt Lake City: Bible records, biographies and cemetery, census, church, court, military, naturalization, newspaper, probate and vital records.

The original service and pension records of Tennessee veterans of the Revolutionary War are available on film, as are lists of soldiers who served in the War of 1812 and the Mexican War. Indexes to the service rewards of Tennessee Civil War veterans also are available.

Of special interest are the published results of a series of questionnaires sent to all Union and Confederate veterans concerning their war experiences.

Many Cherokee records from Tennessee also are available through the center, including the 1851 Cherokee Nation census and the Guion Miller enrollment records of Eastern Cherokee applications, 1906-1909. The applications were made to receive compensation for their land that the government usurped in the 1830s. The applications document Cherokee ancestry; more than 45,000 applications are indexed and available on 348 rolls of microfilm. Detailed abstracts of these applications as well as numerous verbatim transcriptions of affidavits are available in a series titled *Cherokee By Blood,* by Jerry Wright Jordan. The volumes are sold separately. Call Heritage Books at 800-398-7709 for more information and for a free catalog.

But many Tennessee resources are not microfilmed; access to these records must be made either in person or by mail. These include a collection of 100,000 alphabetized surname folders in the Williamson County Public Library, W. 611 Main, Franklin, TN 37064. The library does not do research, but if you send it a self-addressed, stamped envelope, it will advise you if a surname is in its collection and send you a list of area researchers.

The Research Outline for Tennessee, published by the Family History Library, is a nine-page guide describing everything one must know about starting a search for Tennessee ancestors. The guide may be accessed from the library at Lake City or at any local Family History Center.

Another extremely useful resource is *Tennessee Genealogical Research* by Dr. George K. Schweitzer. This 110-page book covers in great detail everything you'll need to know about researching in the Volunteer State. You may order a copy for $12.00 from the author at 407 Regent Court, Knoxville, TN 37923.

The Tennessee Genealogical Society, P.O. Box 111249, Memphis, TN 38111-1249, recently published results of its Tennessee Ancestry Certificate Program which began in 1986. This hardbound book highlights genealogical data on 568 of the state's early settlers, plus more than 4,100 of their descendants to the present. *Tennessee Settlers and Their Descendants* can be ordered for $35.00 from the society at the address above.

You also might wish to contact the society to inquire about other Tennessee resources and helpful information by mail.

Free queries may be submitted to the *Nashville Banner* newspaper for its weekly genealogy column. Send your Tennessee-related query to David R. Logsdon, c/o 1100 Broadway St., Nashville, TN 37203.

NORWEGIAN FARMS ARE FERTILE GROUND

Ever heard of "bygdeboks?" Those with Norwegian ancestry probably have.

Bygdeboks are "farm histories" — books listing all those who lived and worked on farms in Norway down through the years.

The books are arranged by farm name and are much like American county or community history books. If a bygdebok exists for the farm where your ancestral Norwegian family lived, you should be able to trace that family back for several generations.

Sources for bygdeboks are Norwegian church records, censuses, land records, probate records and tax records. Some books contain maps detailing where the farms can be found, and many contain photos. They are to be considered as secondary sources (meaning they are a source made from copying records from other sources), so, for complete accuracy, they should be compared with the actual records. And, yes, these books are written in Norwegian. But it doesn't take long to learn enough key words to get the hang of following along, especially since most farm genealogies are written in a standardized format.

Many "bygdebokers" have name indexes, both by patronymic and first names — so, even if you don't know the farm name, it's still fairly easy to find your family in the series of books.

What to do if your Norwegian ancestors moved a lot? As they moved from farm to farm with succeeding marriages, they're usually not hard to trace — because the bygdeboks most often list people who weren't born on that farm by their former farm name, or tell where they came from.

For instance, you may find your ancestor, Ole Jacobson (Ole, son of Jacob), listed as living on the farm "Sorlie," right where you expected to find him. But his name may be listed as "Ole Jacobson Gulsvik" (meaning "Ole, son of Jacob, from Gulsvik"). That means that Ole lived on the farm Gulsvik before moving to Sorlie and it's a signal for you to check the Gulsvik farm's bygdeboks to pick up his earlier history.

If you don't find that farm listed in one area's set of bygdeboks, search another area's books to find your family. And Ole, now that he's living on the Sorlie farm, would officially be called "Ole Jacobson Sorlie" instead of "Ole Jacobson Gulsvik." His "address" name changes as he changed his residence.

If Norwegian farm naming customs confuse you, don't despair. Our Norwegian ancestors always adopted the name of their farm as their third name. When they immigrated to this country, where names were required to stay the same over the generations, and where only one surname could be used, Norwegians had to choose which name they would go by — their patronymic or their farm name.

Sometimes they dropped the farm name and descendants are known by the one patronymic name. Others dropped the patronymic name because there were just too many "Ole Olsons" for example. To confuse matters, often the farm name was Anglicized to look and sound more English. For instance, Kvernum might become Vernum or even Vernon. Norwegian names containing one or more of the three Norwegian letters not found in the English alphabet were also changed to make them easier to spell and pronounce in the New World.

The Chester Fritz Library at the University of North Dakota in Grand Forks, ND, is a major repository for these books, having more than 700 in its special collections department. The library offers its "Guide to Norwegian Bygdeboker," a free guide to bygdeboks in general and the Chester Fritz collection specifically. Request your copy from Bygdeboker Guide, in care of the Chester Fritz Library, UND, Grand Forks, ND 58202.

That library does not loan its bygdeboks on interlibrary loan, but here are some libraries with a collection which do have an interlibrary loan program: Concordia College, Moorhead, MN; St. Olaf College in Northfield MN; and the University of Wisconsin in Madison, WI.

If you wish to borrow books from these libraries, work with your local interlibrary loan person at your public library. You can also check with the Family History Center. The Family History Library in Salt Lake has a large collection of bygdeboks and they might be available on film.

The key to successful interlibrary loaning these books is to know the farm where your ancestor lived. You can't expect an interlibrary loan for 100-plus books.

If you don't yet know that farm name, keep working with your family records as they are found in this country, and somewhere along the way the farm name should turn up.

Good luck using Norwegian bygdeboks!

1996

Be A Smart Consumer Of Products

Have you ever considered your responsibility as a genealogical consumer, buying and using the products or services of a genealogical business? Like consumerism in general, there are tips to alleviate needless aggravation for both buyer and the supplier.

Fran Carter listed guidelines for genealogical consumers in Issue 39 of *Heritage Quest* magazine in 1992:

◆ 1. Read the advertising carefully. Know exactly what you are ordering! Don't read more into an ad than is there, and if something is unclear, before you order, send the company or researcher a self-addressed, stamped envelope asking for clarification.

◆ 2. Do not expect suppliers to check their book or files for your surnames before filling your order. If you buy a book and your name isn't in it, consider donating it to your local genealogical library.

◆ 3. When you hire a professional, realize there is no guarantee that they will find your ancestor. You are paying for the search – the researcher earns his money by performing the search.

◆ 4. Always include an SASE – a self-addressed, stamped envelope.

◆ 5. When you order something, make sure your complete name and address are printed on the order, and not just on your check. Often your check is deposited and your envelope discarded before the order is filled. You end up waiting, frustrated and angry because your order hasn't arrived, when the company (having deposited your check) has no idea what you ordered or where to send it.

◆ 6. Never send cash! And make sure your check is signed.

◆ 7. For extra insurance, make a photocopy of your order. Write your check number on the order, the date you made the order and the date the company said your delivery would be made. This information will make a reference easier if it's needed.

♦ 8. If your order doesn't arrive within a reasonable time (usually 30 days unless otherwise stated), don't automatically expect the worst. Consult your bank statement to determine whether your check has been cashed; if not, the company might not have received your order. Write or call them again.

♦ 9. With pre-publication orders, be sure to read the fine print. Pre-publication orders are designed to give the publisher an advance on publication costs. This isn't all bad, but there should be an understood release date. If the order isn't filled by then, your money should be returned or an explanation of delay given.

♦ 10. When all else fails, write the company or researcher explaining the problem. Supply all the information from your carefully saved records. Be pleasant in your inquiry; give them a chance to correct the problem. They value you as a genealogy customer.

What about phone orders? What about giving your credit card number over the phone? I do it all the time. I figure most genealogists and genealogical businesses are honest and reputable and I've never been "burned." Nor do I know of anyone who has. But realize that when you see ads in the *Everton's Helper* or *Heritage Quest* magazines they are just that: ads. The magazines don't check them out, but you can be sure that if they receive many complaints, the ad won't run again.

And, major credit card companies are good to subtract fraudulent charges from your bill, should that occur. In this busy world, when I hear of a new genealogy resource, I want it NOW and so I'm quick and happy to make a phone call and use my card.

I might add that any genealogy resource item – book, shop or service – that I recommend in this column, has been checked out by me. If you find any problem with any of them, please let me know.

On another genealogy consumerism note, there's a new genealogy business that holds great promise. The fellows of Heritage Consulting, a professional firm based in Salt Lake, will find your ancestor's military records in the National Archives for you via their resident associate.

In my genealogy classes I teach that there are only three ways to access your ancestor's military records from the National Archives in Washington, DC: Go there and look at them in person; use NATF-80, the official government request form; or hire an agent to obtain the records for you.

Of the three, I recommend the third avenue when possible.

Soldier Search will go to the National Archives have copies made of your ancestor's records from the Union military and pension records, the Confederate military records, and from Physician's Reports during the Civil War.

They will also search records from the Mexican War, Spanish-American War, the War of 1812 and the Indian Wars.

Send your full name and address, your ancestor/soldier's name, the state in which he enlisted (if known) and his wife's name – plus your check. The fee is around $40.00. Their address is P.O. Box 4152, Salt Lake City, UT 84110. (Allow four to six weeks for delivery.)

TIPS FOR SEARCHING CIVIL WAR RECORDS:

1. Ignore family tradition and search both Union and Confederate records, especially if your family lived in a border state.

2. Don't limit your hunt to direct ancestors. It may be the records of your direct ancestor's brother that will contain your genealogical gem.

3. Learn about the battles in which your ancestors fought. For instance, the North named battles after area waters (lakes, creeks or bogs), while the South named their battles after land. Examples: Sharpsburg (a town), Antietam (a creek), Manassas (a town) and Bull Run (a creek).

NEW PUBLICATION OFFERS
SOURCES FOR CHURCH RECORDS

U.S. Catholic Sources: A Diocesan Research Guide is a new genealogical source that will be especially helpful to those with Roman Catholic ancestors.

Virginia Humling wrote the guide to make it easier to locate records "that are a precious part of our Catholic heritage."

She also hopes that "in reflecting on the faith journeys of those who came before us, we will appreciate the debt of gratitude we owe for what has been so faithfully handed down to us. Our journeys are truly connected."

Humling mailed questionnaires to every Roman Catholic diocese within the United States, and all but three responded.

She compiled the answers into a 112-page guide giving the name, address and hours of each diocese and a brief sketch of their records. She included information on Catholic newspapers in many dioceses, especially those published in the 19th and early 20th centuries.

Humling details which records are available on microfilm through various state libraries, historical societies and the Family History Library in Utah.

Since many records are maintained at the parish level, Humling suggests researchers consult *The Official Catholic Directory* to obtain correct parish addresses. The directory, published annually by P.J. Kenedy & Sons, is accessible at the main diocese office and many parish offices.

I consulted Washington state's information with its three dioceses, including Seattle's archdiocese. The guide provides the address, phone number and archivist's name for each diocese, the counties they cover, what records they hold and for which years. A suggestion of fees is included, as well as information on area Catholic newspapers.

The Rev. Theodore F.X. Bradley is archivist for the Diocese of Spokane, 1023 W. Riverside (99201); telephone, (509) 456-7100. There are 13 eastern Washington counties in the Spokane Diocese.

The guide states: "Sacramental records through 1956 are on microfilm at the Diocesan Archives, with the originals retained at the parish level. Some of the early records have been microfilmed by the Genealogical Society of Utah and are available for viewing at the LDS Family History Library and all Family History Centers.

"Early records from the Walla Walla area are included in Catholic Church Records of the Pacific Northwest, by Harriet D. Munnick, and are available from The St. Paul Mission Historical Society, P.O. Box 158, St. Paul, OR 97137-0158."

There is no set fee charged in the Spokane Diocese, but donations are appreciated.

The Inland Register is the Spokane Diocese newspaper (P.O. Box 48, Spokane, WA 99210), established in 1942. Past issues may be viewed at the newspaper office by appointment.

Do not – I repeat, DO NOT – show up at the diocese office without an appointment. The nice folks there are busy running the diocese and do not have the manpower to stop and help you dig into dusty records. Besides, Bradley lives in Moses Lake and comes to Spokane only twice a month. (This is typical of most all dioceses.)

When I visited with him a couple of years ago, he said there is no set rule in the church for parishes to turn over their records to the diocese office. Some do, some don't. He recommends researchers be prepared to check into the records at the parish level before coming to the diocese office.

U.S. Catholic Sources: A Diocesan Research Guide may be ordered from Ancestry, Inc., P.O. Box 476, Salt Lake City, UT 84110; or by calling 800-931-1790.

TODAY'S LAUGH: Oh, if it were only this easy in real life: According to an October 1994 *Newsweek* article, computer software can now "zap" a certain face from a family photograph – like a divorced spouse – and replace it with the current wife's face. Boy, won't that confuse future genealogists!

START WITH DOCUMENTS AROUND YOUR HOME AND THEN WIDEN YOUR SEARCH

Today's column is specifically written for those who want step-by-step instructions on how to begin this wonderful hobby of genealogy.

Presented here are "Seven Surefire Steps to Your Family Tree."

Step No. 1. The very first thing to do is to organize what you already know. Gather the information you have at home. You probably have many things that will yield genealogy information, like diaries, baby books, baptismal records, draft cards, family pictures and correspondence, funeral programs, life insurance papers, military awards, report cards – and especially scrapbooks.

Study these records and glean tidbits of family information and write it down on special genealogical forms – pedigree and family group charts.

The charts are available from many sources: Family History Centers, local genealogical societies and commercial companies.

You can also use a computer software program to keep track of family information. A pedigree is identification of a person's direct ancestors. Pedigree charts are begun by listing yourself as

No. 1 (I like to say that you are the most important nut on your family tree); next, write down your birthdate and birthplace thusly: 28 Jan 1996. Include the town, county and state of your birth. If you don't know the county, consult a gazetteer. It's necessary to know the county since most records are kept on the county level.

List your parents' and grandparents' full names, with their birthdates and birthplaces. Also list their marriage dates and places and their death dates and places.

Your parents become No. 2 and No. 3 on your pedigree chart, and your grandparents become Nos. 4, 5, 6 and 7.

Because there is no space on the pedigree chart to list brothers and sisters or second marriages, the companion form is the family group chart on which you list the parents and their children. You'll need a family group chart for every married couple shown on the pedigree chart. You might even need more than one if Grandpa was married more than once.

On the family group chart, list the husband's and wife's full names and identifying information. Usually, there is room for data like occupation, religion, military service. Next, list each of the couple's children with their identifying information and spouses.

Where do you get all this information?

Step No. 2. Begin to learn the facts you need from talking to your family and digging through all that accumulated family "stuff" mentioned earlier.

No public record can substitute for talking to every single family member when you're beginning this new hobby. Be sure to compare memories. Are the parents you remember different from the parents your youngest brother remembers? The grandfather I knew and the man my first cousin Karen knew must be two different men because our memories are so different. We "proved" this from reading each others' biography of Grandad.

Step No. 3. Obtain death certificates for your parents, grandparents and other close relatives. Getting the certificates is easy if you know the state in which the person died. Statewide registration of vital records began during the period of 1913-1920, and most states have vital records from about 1910 forward.

To find the address for a state's vital statistics registration office, visit a genealogy library where you can consult the government pamphlet, *Where to Write for Vital Records. Births, Deaths, Marriages and Divorces.* The pamphlet also tells the fee, which can vary from $6.00 to $25.00 per certificate, since each state has its own system of charging. For instance, Washington state charges $11.00; Idaho, $8.00.

For death certificates after 1920, it's not necessary to know the city or county of death, because you will write to the *state* office. But you must have an exact date. If you want officials to search for a span of years, you might have to pay extra.

Standard death certificates from all states include important information about the deceased, but in addition to the cause of death, they can also provide the name of the person's parents, birthdate and place, as well as the funeral director and cemetery. More recent death certificates provide the deceased's Social Security number.

Why spend money for a death certificate? Because it often provides other needed elements and clues.

And if you treat your ancestor's brothers and sisters as equals and obtain their death certificates, too, you will have a wonderful pool of potential genealogy clues.

Remember, when Grandpa died, he had very little to do with what was written on his death certificate. Who knew him well enough to fill out the form for him? It's important to know who that person was.

Step No. 4. Follow up on the clues from the death certificate. If you know the birthdate and place, it might be possible to obtain a birth certificate. That might take a bit of sleuthing, however, for you will probably need to know the county where your ancestor was born and the county's address. Again, genealogy library folks can help.

If you know the funeral director, contact the funeral home. For addresses of all funeral homes in the United States or Canada, call a funeral director and ask to use the *Yellow Book.* That's the directory of funeral homes, which provides the names, addresses and phone numbers for all funeral homes.

Be sure to follow up on cemetery clues. Wouldn't you like to know what words are chiseled on your ancestor's tombstone? And, cemetery caretakers can tell you if other family members are buried in the same graveyard.

A newspaper obituary was probably published soon after your ancestor's death, and finding these obituaries in old newspapers is well worth the effort. If you know a date and place where the obituary might have appeared, area genealogists will help locate the newspaper.

If a person died within the last 30 years or so, and if the death certificate includes the Social Security number, you're really in luck. You can write for a copy of the deceased's original application, Form SS-5. Chances of obtaining this record are very good for anyone employed since 1936.

Write to the Freedom of Information Officer, Social Security Administration, 4-H-8 Annex, 6401 Security Blvd., Baltimore MD 21235. Provide the subject's full name, date of birth and parents; you will be quoted a fee for the information.

Step No. 5. Next, begin searching U.S. federal censuses. I teach in my beginners' classes that you should attempt to find your ancestor on every census of his or her life, beginning with the last one before death and working backward in time.

Censuses have been taken every 10 years, from 1790 up to 1990, but because of privacy laws, the 1920 census is the most recent one available to researchers. The 1900, 1910 and 1920 censuses have special indexes, called Soundexes, which make searching them very easy. Most census years have printed indexes and many are available in your library's genealogy section.

Step No. 6. Search state and county records. Census records are great for pinpointing exactly where an ancestor lived, which allows you to dig into the records created about him during his lifetime. That's what state and county records are.

County courthouses keep all kinds of records: land records (who bought and sold land), tax records (who paid taxes, and how much), voter registration, court records, probate (the papers wrapping up your ancestor's life) and even things like cattle brands and dance permits.

Generally, a visit to the courthouse yields the best results because there are so many potential records to search and courthouse personnel do not have time to do it for you.

Step No. 7. Some might think the last step should have come sooner – using genealogical libraries.

Because of our country's privacy rights, not many records have been published since 1900 – and this is the time period of our parents' and grandparents' lives.

So, to achieve maximum success, consider these Seven Steps in the order presented.

Muchof this information is from a booklet by Bill Dollarhide, *Seven Steps to a Family Tree*. You can order it, $5.50, postpaid, from AGLL, P.O. Box 329, Bountiful, UT 84011-0329, or call 800-760-AGLL.

TODAY'S TIP: Shirley Penna Oakes will publish free queries about New England ancestors in her booklet series, *New England Queries & Reviews*. Each of the series' 15 booklets carries many pages of queries and book reviews, and each is indexed. The booklets are $7.00 each, plus postage. Send your query, order or questions to Oakes at P.O. Box 1179, Tum Tum, WA 99034-1179.

MANY PEOPLE HAVE ANCESTORS WHO BELONGED TO THE FREEMASONS FRATERNAL ORGANIZATION

Genealogists are always asking about Freemason ancestors. Masonry is a fraternal organization for men that has been around since at least the 17th century, with a worldwide appeal.

Many of us have ancestors who were Freemasons, and assume there ought to be some information on Masonic records, if only we could find them.

Although the primary purpose of Masonry is not to compile and supply genealogical information, there is some biographical data available on its members. Masonic records date back to the earliest days of our country and may be found in almost every city and town. These records number literally in the tens of thousands and are a vast untapped source for genealogy research.

Locating and interpreting the records is the purpose of the booklet *Researching Masonic Records,* by John S. Yates, self-published by the author in 1994.

The booklet states that the information in the applications varies widely. Applications through about 1900 asked only for the applicant's name and age along with three references. It was not until about 1930 that a more comprehensive application was introduced, and no family information was required until the 1950s.

The booklet also states that if a researcher is trying to determine the parentage of an individual, chances are very remote that a man's Masonic record will contain anything along those lines.

The primary purpose to obtain your ancestor's record of Masonic membership would be to pinpoint him in a specific place at a specific time. For instance, if you were to learn from Masonic records that your ancestor was a member of a lodge in New Hartford, CT, and faithfully attended meetings there during from 1876 to 1888, then you can assume he left his mark in other town, county and state records, too.

Yates' book lists the addresses for all the Grand Masonic Lodges in the United States, and says this should be the first place to begin looking for your ancestor's Masonic information.

When you write for the address of the local lodge your ancestor attended, include his full name, the town or county where he resided, and the dates he lived there. Do not recite his genealogy; it's unnecessary and wastes their time. These organizations receive hundreds of requests for such information and their offices are staffed by volunteers.

When you receive the address of your ancestor's local lodge, write to that group for a photocopy or transcript of his file. This request will be granted at the discretion of the lodge secretary who also volunteers his time. Be prepared for failure since many 19th-century lodge records were lost to fire.

When writing to the lodge, inquire about its history. Some lodges have written a comprehensive history and your ancestor might be mentioned. He might have played a key role in its formation, and there might be considerable information about him. Also, ask if your ancestor held the office of Master of the Lodge. If so, his photograph might be on display in the building.

Researching Masonic records includes explanations of Thirty-second Degree Masons, a Masonic-affiliated organization known as the Scottish Rite. Master Masons in good standing may join this charitable organization. The titles or degrees are not conferred by the Masonic Lodge, and they will not have any record of them. Yates' booklet gives the addresses for the Scottish Rite jurisdictions.

The booklet also provides a sample letter and copies of what the record cards might look like. Yates also included drawings of all the Masonic and Scottish Rite emblems.

You may order *Researching Masonic Records* for $7.50, postpaid, from John Yates, P.O. Box 3496, Wichita Falls, TX 76309.

For more information, there's an article by the same name, "Researching Masonic Records," published in the November-December 1992 issue of *Heritage Quest* magazine. Author Jill Rueble Hughes includes a list of state lodges and goes into the background for American Masonry.

In an old bookstore I found a copy of the *History of The Grand Lodge of A.F. & A.M. of Oregon, from 1846 to 1951 Inclusive*. Writing in 1952, John C. Wilkinson was Worshipful Grand Historian of the Grand Lodge of Oregon, and his 450-page book chronicles the history of Masonry in Oregon in great depth. The book was full of lots and lots of names!

So, I would surely agree with Yates that it's important to inquire about the written history of your ancestor's group.

Here's a book you really can use. Elizabeth Petty Bentley has put together a second edition of her *County Courthouse Book*.

This huge book lists information for 3,125 county courthouses in the U.S., and 1,577 New England towns and independent Virginia cities. It includes current addresses and phone numbers, whom to contact at the courthouse, and cost of searches and copies. There are also dates of county formation, custody, dates of coverage for vital records, probate records, land records and naturalization records.

The book also explains that in some cases, there are alternate sites for county records.

I tell my genealogy students one cannot work effectively in a given county without first learning about the county's records and repositories. The *County Courthouse Book* will help you with that homework assignment.

You may order this $39.95 book from Genealogical Publishing Co., Inc., 1001 N. Calvert St., Baltimore, MD 21202-3897, or call 800-296-6687 for phone orders.

A HUNDRED YEARS' WORTH OF COUNTY DOCUMENTS SURVIVED A TERRIBLE FIRE

"The courthouse burned!" is a phrase sure to strike terror in the heart of every genealogist.

Genealogy researchers, particularly those working with Southern records, are often frustrated to discover many of the records they need were destroyed in a courthouse fire.

Reasons for a courthouse burning in America's early history are often quite different from today's causes.

Southern courthouses, constructed mostly of wood, were vulnerable to fire with their open fireplaces and iron heating stoves. Georgia particularly suffered during Gen. William Sherman's notorious "March to the Sea," when he burned every courthouse in his path.

The Lincoln County Courthouse in Davenport, a small farming community in eastern Washington, was burned in December 1995 by an arsonist.

Whatever the cause, or whenever it occurs, fire is a tragedy. But, county business didn't cease when a courthouse burned in 1896, nor is it in Lincoln County in 1996. The courthouse staff struggled, but did persevere in doing their daily duties.

This awful sort of thing has happened before. An arsonist set fire to Ohio's Brown County courthouse in 1977. While some records were lost, the resulting new courthouse has much better storage facilities. Pre-fire records had been stored under the counters where clerks conducted daily business, in old-fashioned tall cupboards with their doors painted shut, in the damp basement, the leaky attic. Some were even in the bell tower! Luckily, most of the water-logged records were salvaged.

Now this "phoenix phenomenon" has happened in Lincoln County.

The stylish 1897 stone building that was the Grand Old Lady of Lincoln County, sat high on a hill overlooking Davenport, the county seat. Inside was the paperwork generated from nearly 100 years of county business.

Fortunately, sturdy turn-of-the-century vaults kept most of the county records safe. Surely, some departments lost everything, but old, heavy metal desks and cabinets, once the butt of office jokes, saved the day in many cases. Backed-up computer records helped, too.

Genealogists understand the disaster courthouse fires can cause. We understand the destroyed papers concerned our ancestors, our forebears — and even ourselves.

One of my genealogy students summed it up when she said, "My first thought, when I heard about the fire, was that I was so glad I'd gotten copies of my divorce papers from there."

Within a day, some semblance of business-as-usual could be seen in Lincoln County. Temporary offices were set up everywhere, papers were handwritten and justice was served in an auditorium at the county fairgrounds.

Spokane County donated a truck load of office furniture.

This same thing happened when courthouses in other places burned in years gone by. Folks pitched in, temporary offices were fashioned, records were salvaged or reconstructed and life went on.

Today we have computer backup tapes. Yesterday, folks visited sources all around the community to reconstruct their records.

As a working genealogist, be aware that, yes, county courthouses did burn down regularly in decades past, but don't let the phrase "The courthouse burned!" be a major roadblock in your research. With a little deeper digging, you'll find that all was not lost, after all. All was definitely not lost in Washington's Lincoln County.

TODAY'S TRIVIA: The bond is strong between one whose life is all tomorrows and one whose life is all yesterdays—have dinner with your parents or grandparents.

A WEALTH OF DATA IS ACCESSIBLE BY COMPUTER AT THE FAMILY HISTORY CENTER

About this time of year (winter), Inland Northwest genealogists find their thoughts turning to taking a research trip to Salt Lake City and to the wonderful Family History Library.

Airlines know of this thought process and offer special fares as an inducement. If you don't like to fly, the 700-mile drive, while admittedly long, is scenic and uncongested.

So what's new in Salt Lake?

The biggest change in recent years at the Family History Library is the opening of the Joseph Smith Memorial Building. Formerly the Hotel Utah, this stately old building now houses a visitor's theater, a church meetinghouse, church offices and two genealogy centers.

A short walk through Temple Square from the library, The FamilySearch Center on the main floor has some 200 computer stations where folks from all over the world quickly see how fun and easy it is to find ancestral information.

These computers have tutorial "programs" that actually speak to you in the form of a red-haired lady, and a small army of volunteers stands ready to sit with you and assist in your learning and searching.

In the fourth floor's West Wing is a place of peace for "serious" computing. Computers – set at individual spacious desks with comfy chairs – are loaded with Ancestral File, the International Genealogical Index, the Family History Library Catalog and other databases.

The Personal Ancestral File program is also available to each computer workstation. This is where you can thoroughly search the IGI or Ancestral File for your newly acquired names, or generate printouts from the Family History Library catalog to use in searching books and microfilms at the library. The main library's computer stations, many of which are stand-up stations, are for quick searching. Even many well-seasoned genealogists don't realize that the fourth-floor FamilySearch Center offers a quiet haven for unlimited hours of computer work.

The East Wing of that floor offers more than 15,000 binders containing family group sheets submitted between 1942 and 1978. This collection represents more than 8 million family records.

The 1920 U.S. federal census can also be searched in the East Wing, and both county and Soundex films are there along with copy machines for both paper and microfilm.

Back to the Family History Library, people are encouraged to use its collections for personal family history research and for professionals to research for clients. But LDS church policy prohibits some instances of use.

These include:

♦ Compiling a list of names and addresses of library submitters to solicit business from them or to sell them something.

♦ Searching library databases for a fee without informing clients that such information is the property of the library and is available free of charge.

♦ Advertising services that lead the public to believe certain information is available only through their firm or that it's available only to paid researchers.

WHY MICROFILM?

Ever wonder why there are more than two million microfilmed records in the Family History Library? Microfilm is, and will be for some time, the favorite way to store genealogical records. Microfilmed records are designed to last 500-plus years.

That's why the Genealogical Society of Utah uses microfilm to archive materials all over the world. Currently, teams are microfilming records in Latin America, Europe, South Africa, China, India and the U.S.

Storing and retrieving records was a hot topic at a recent convention of records managers and administrators in Nashville, TN, where one person said the problem arises because, basically, people don't speak digital.

Storing things in nonhuman, nonreadable form causes dependency on hardware and software, which can fail — which means computer storage of records is risky. So it looks like microfilming will continue to be the storage medium of choice.

The Library is open from 7:30 a.m. to 10:00 p.m. (except 6:00 on Monday and closed on Sunday). So plan a research trip for some long but fun days.

KEEP FAMILY HEIRLOOMS AND TREASURES ON DISPLAY FOR CHILDREN TO SEE

You've been busily and happily collecting all sorts of names, dates and places and (hopefully) the documentation to prove those family connections. Documentation might include photos, books and artifacts.

So, have you given a thought to what might happen to your precious collection upon your death? I'd like to share some thoughts with you on "How To Outlive Yourself."

Let me begin by asking a question. When you've visited flea markets, antique shops, garage sales and even thrift stores, where do you think all those wonderful little old items of whatever come from?

And hasn't it broken your heart to see stacks of old family photos being sold for $1.00 each to collectors? And while you're delighted to find an antique ricer, do you ever wonder who used it originally?

These wonderful treasures found at flea markets were some ancestor's household items and special treasures. Somebody fashioned them, bought them, used them, loved them — and then what? The person died and some well-meaning relative came in and cleaned everything out and gave it all to a charity or held a huge garage sale. Wouldn't it have been so much better if the owner of those treasures had identified them for his or her descendants?

There are two primary categories in genealogy gathering: paper and things.

The paper collection is obvious: pedigree charts, family group sheets, photos, birth records, military discharge papers, etc.

The "things" category includes pictures, clothing, toys, kitchen items and regular old doo-dads.

In my opinion, the tangible family heirlooms and treasures should never be packed away out of sight. How on earth will your children and grandchildren come to know and love that old doll, old ceramic pitcher or grandpa's tools if they're packed away in a trunk?

If your family never sees what these heirlooms mean to you, and if they aren't given a chance to develop their own fondness for them, then you might as well toss them out now because when the time comes, your family surely will. Why would they revere and continue to store something that they have not learned to appreciate?

Sometimes these tangible treasures will be preserved and passed down "just cuz." But most will be trashed. When you die and your kids come in to tidy up, they won't have the time, the storage space, nor the desire to keep stuff they feel is meaningless.

So what to do? How about gathering all the really special things into one place in your home. How about creating a sort of family display or a bookcase of family artifacts?

Tell the stories about these family treasures often and invite your family to become intimate with them. Why not put labels or tags on the pieces, too?

Or, take pictures of your heirlooms, make a special album of them and include a history of each item and the people who originally owned them.

I have my grandmother's doll (she received it about 1900 when she was 5) sitting in a child-sized rocker in my dining room. Heaven forbid the kids should play with it! But at least they know it is something special.

Do the same with the photos. Arrange these fabulous old photos in safe-storage albums and bring them out at every opportunity and let your descendants get to know their ancestors the only way they ever will.

So what about those paper records? How do you best safeguard them?

The safest thing to do is make copies, make copies, MAKE COPIES! See that everyone in your family has a copy. Save the information on computer floppy disks.

Who can forget our February floods and how we paled to see homes being completely devastated. Should a flood or fire destroy your home, you wouldn't have to suffer twice if your brother had a copy of your genealogy work and records.

Perhaps you've already thought of this; maybe your albums, baby books, high school yearbooks, diaries, etc. are stored in one place in your home. But is it a safe place? What if the basement flooded? Is the top of the hall closet cool enough for proper photo and slide storage? What if you had just one hour's warning to evacuate your home. What would you grab and how on earth could you grab it all?

Here's a simple solution: Visit the fabric store and buy a few yards of the strongest, cheapest, ugliest stuff they have and sew it into a huge pillowcase. Or buy an old bedsheet at the Goodwill and stitch it into a big "pillowcase." You could never carry all of your family archives in your arms, but you surely could toss them into a big bag and drag it out.

I urge you not to procrastinate doing this. You never know when disaster will strike.

I clearly remember TV coverage of a devastating fire a few summers back that began by the river and quickly spread towards a housing area on Spokane's northwest side. On the evening news, a reporter thrust his microphone in the face of a man who was evacuating, getting into his car with an armload of – guess – CLOTHES!!!

Not meaning to poke fun at the distressed fellow, but he, No. 1, obviously didn't have a game plan for such an emergency, and No. 2, couldn't have rounded up all the really important things to save even if he had thought of it or had the time.

One last thing, what about your collected genealogy stuff, things you have spent years gathering as research aids that have nothing to do with your own family history? What's to become of all that wonderful resource material? My husband assures me that he'll come in with a shovel and dump truck if I haven't specified WHO is to come in and sort out the genealogy stuff that he knows and cares nothing about.

Perhaps we should write down – somewhere where our family can find it – the name of the one person who can come into our genealogy lair/office and sort out what is important family information and what should be donated to the local genealogy society.

You'll notice that these suggestions leave not one genealogical item to be tossed out!

RESOURCES MAKE IT EASY TO BROADEN YOUR REACH

Welcome to a new century of genealogy, in which more and more genealogical resources are becoming available on CD-ROM disk. And more and more books related to genealogy are being published.

Perhaps this is because, as *American Demographics* magazine report in fall, 1995, some 19 million Americans are searching for their roots.

As you've collected names, dates and places on your genealogy charts, haven't you wondered about the historical events that shaped your ancestral family?

But, even if you did wonder, you probably haven't spent the necessary hours in the library collecting geographic and historical information and finding pictures and maps.

Now, with the advent of genealogy computer programs, you don't have to, but you can still access this material to broaden your genealogy and family history.

The Encyclopedia of American History, a new CD-ROM available through Compton's New Media, is designed like a history book. Each chapter incorporates various tables, videos, essays and slides to accompany the text that discusses the historian's viewpoint.

You can access all this material sitting at your own little desk (in your jammies, as I like to say) for a cost of $40.00.

For more information, or to place an order, call Comptons at 800-862-2206.

Weights, Money and Other Measures Used by Our Ancestors, by Colin R. Chapman, published in 1995 by Genealogical Publishing Co., is an unusual and interesting book.

Written for researchers unfamiliar with units of weights and measurements and are unsure, for example, if a particular measurement indicates a number, a coin or a capacity, this book is a great companion to keep by your side while perusing wills, inventories, accounts and old journals. This 92-page paperback costs $15.00. To order a copy, call Genealogical Publishing Co. at 800-296-6687.

Ancestry Inc., a Salt Lake City based company, also publishes wonderfully helpful genealogy resource books.

One recent title was *A Preservation Guide: Saving the Past and the Present for the Future*, by Barbara Sagraves. If you need a short, inexpensive, concise guide to preserving your genealogical documents and artifacts, then this 48-page book is for you.

Don't let your accumulated certificates, photographs and documents deteriorate in improper files or shoe boxes. Order *A Preservation Guide* for $9.45, postpaid, from Ancestry at 800-531-1790, or write the company at P.O. Box 476, Salt Lake City, UT 84110.

Another Ancestry book is *U.S. Catholic Sources, A Diocesan Research Guide*, compiled by Virginia Humling. Genealogists know that church records provide a primary resource for family history. Folks with U.S. Catholic ancestry will find this guide indispensable.

While the parish remains the most fundamental unit for research, diocesan archives often contain records from closed parishes and of diocesan newspapers. For every archdiocese and diocese in the United States this 112-page guide identifies the records available and a contact person for each location. It can be ordered from Ancestry.

Lost in Chicago? It's always been difficult to research in big cities, and disasters (like the Great Chicago Fire) compound the problems.

Author Loretto Dennis Szucs has compiled *Chicago and Cook County: A Guide to Research,* and I guarantee that this 350-page book will help you over the stumbling blocks in doing Chicago research.

Remember, too, that Chicago served as a springboard for millions of immigrants, so there is a good chance you will find that Chicago ancestor you've been seeking. This book costs $19.45, postpaid, from Ancestry.

FAMILY HISTORY LIBRARY
HAS MANY RESOURCES RELATING TO IRELAND

Are you stumbling in your search for Irish ancestors? Thinking that the only way you're ever going to find them is to go to Ireland?

Well, I have good news. Many Irish records are available on microfilm through the Family History Library in Salt Lake City.

In January, 1996, I attended a session on Irish research when professional genealogist Kyle J. Betit detailed all the research resources available in Salt Lake. There's never a reason to give up, he said.

For instance, there are census records from 1901 for all of Ireland, arranged by towns – but with no indexes. There are some pre-1901 census fragments, and religious censuses for 1740 and 1766.

A good census substitute is the Griffith's Primary Valuations, dating back to the 1840s in some cases, which include some every-name indexes.

There are many films of Catholic records, especially good for some dioceses. There are limited Protestant records which include the Church of Ireland, Presbyterian, Methodist and Quaker.

There are indexes to deeds and memorials dating back to 1708, filled with names. There are large collections of land records, papers of land owners and encumbered estates (where the courts disposed of the property of bankrupt landowners).

There are many filmed family histories, Ordnance Survey Maps dating back to the 1830s with indexes to names, and many Irish genealogical and historical periodicals.

Indexes to wills before 1858, and some films of the wills themselves pre-dating 1858, are available.

To find and use this wealth of material, visit your nearby Family History Center, where volunteers will help you order these filmed records from the big library in Salt Lake. On the computer catalog, or the microfiche catalog, look first under Ireland, and then for specific records under Ireland and county.

Betit and Dwight Radford have compiled a booklet, *Ireland: A Genealogical Guide for North Americans,* that includes extensive information on the Family History Library's holdings and many FHL film numbers. This guide is available from the authors for $18.95, postpaid, at P.O. Box 521806, Salt Lake City, UT 84152-1806.

Betit and Radford also publish *The Irish at Home and Abroad,* which furnishes background information on the whereabouts of Irish records and how to correctly interpret and use them to further genealogical searching.

Recent article titles include "Scots-Irish in Colonial America," "Irish Medieval Lineages," "Irish Research: Advice for Beginners," "All the Irish Records were Destroyed," "Irish In the British Army," and "Irish Estate Records." Subscriptions to this journal are available by sending $18.00 to the above address. Back issues are available.

Yes, there was a disastrous fire in 1922 in Ireland, and, yes, it did destroy many primary Irish records – but there are still many records left to search. Betit and Radford will help you find and use them.

TIDBITS OF INFORMATION

♦ I picked up a delightful little book at a recent genealogy white elephant sale: *The Southern Journal: The Appalachian Log,* is published monthly by the Appalachian Log Publishing Co., P.O. Box 20297, Charleston, WV 25362-1297.

The 34 pages of the September 1995 issue included articles about local Southern doings, an article on the notorious kudzu vine, a feature called Granny's Cookbook — that month spotlighting Kidney Bean Salad, Heavenly Carrots, Eggless Raisin Cake and Chocolate Fudge Pie.

There were selections of Southern poetry, a couple of genealogy how-to articles, a queries section plus a Southern Calendar of Events. And there were ads from The Southern Journal Bookstore offering personal and family sketches and remembrances.

Subscriptions to this folksy little journal are available by sending $18.00 to the address above.

♦ Are you a Ross? The Clan Ross Association was organized in 1976 as a national society to foster the Scottish clan spirit. The Clan Ross Association encourages the study and preservation of the genealogy, history, folklore and traditions of Clan Ross and their Scottish heritage. The clan offers a $1,000 scholarship towards Scottish studies. For more informationl contact Clan Ross, 5430 Fifth St. S, Arlington, VA 22204-1203.

♦ Need a particular city directory from an Idaho town to help in your research? The American Genealogical Lending Library has microfilmed many city directories for these Idaho towns: Blackfoot, Boise, Burley, Caldwell, Payette, Ontario, Weiser, Idaho Falls, Lewiston (and Clarkston, WA), Nampa, Pocatello, Rupert, and Twin Falls.

Contact AGLL at P.O. Box 329, Bountiful, UT 84011-0329, or call 800-760-AGLL for more information on obtaining these Idaho city directories.

TODAY'S TRIVIA: While we're on the subject of Ireland and Idaho, here's some trivia about an item basic to the survival of both places: the potato.

A potato is 80 percent water; people can live on potatoes and milk alone; one acre of potatoes can feed 12 people (an acre of wheat can barely feed one person); the potato produces more protein per acre than any other plant, besides soybean; the Incas had more than 1,000 words for potato; when the potato was first introduced to England in the 1590s, many thought it was poisonous because it came from the same family as deadly nightshade. The word "spud" is believed to have come from the acronym for London's anti-potato Society for the Prevention of Unhealthful Diet.

And, as most know, it was the failure of the potato crop in the mid-1800s that precipitated a mass emigration of the Irish to America.

Censuses, Tombstones, Churches, Schools And Other Sources Can Help Fill In Gaps In Records

Genealogists know that vital records are considered the most basic of all records and the place to begin family history searching. Vital records, for the uninitiated, are records maintained by civil authorities and are the primary source for birth, marriage and death records.

But what to do when vital records are not available? Such records were often destroyed in a courthouse fire or flood, or, sometimes, the year you need pre-dates when the county began keeping records.

When these primary records of birth, marriage and death are unavailable, genealogists must look to substitute records for clues, estimates, or guesses as to when and where the events occurred. By checking several substitute records, the family historian can hopefully piece together enough concrete evidence to prove when great-great-great-grandmother was born, where great-great-grandfather married, or when great-uncle Harold died.

So, what are some of these substitute records?

Fran Carter has compiled a 40-page booklet alphabetically listing some suggestions for alternatives to vital records. Some of her tips include:

• Adoption records can substitute for birth records. However, these records are a most-private thing and may be difficult to obtain. Check with churches, the county and local adoption agencies.

• Announcements of significant dates can help narrow down event dates. Just like today, our ancestors announced births, marriages and deaths by special printed notice, usually in the local newspaper.

• Apprentice records can help determine ages and parents. Before our present education system evolved, vocational training was accomplished through apprenticeships with master craftsmen. It usually involved a boy under the age of 14, and a Contract of Agreement was often signed by the master or teacher, the parents or guardian and the boy himself.

• Census records help identify the approximate birth, marriage and death dates. When a genealogist finds her ancestor on every census year of an ancestor's life, a fairly clear picture emerges of the time span for a person's life.

• Church records contain much of the same information as civil vital records. In fact, many English, Scandinavian and European vital statistics can only be gleaned from church records because civil registration began so late in time — 1857 in England!

• Midwife records, often required to be kept by some counties, contain information that would be considered primary evidence.

• Name changes were recorded at the county level when a person changed his or her name; the application usually included vital statistic information.

• Photographs can be considered a substitute for vital records. How about that box of family photos lurking in your basement? Are there dated wedding pictures? Baby pictures?

• Probate records can contain ages, birthdates and information on children and other information that would substitute for vital records.

- Report cards, first issued in the early 1840s, can help approximate a year of birth.
- Telegrams, tucked away in family scrapbooks, often announce marriages, births and deaths.
- Marriage applications can be used even if marriage records don't survive; they often contain more information than a marriage certificate. Inquire at the county level for a marriage application.
- Baby books may also contain the parents' marriage information.
- Customs records are the official records of immigrants at their port of arrival. The lists contain the names of all the passengers on a particular vessel, and often includes their ages.
- Diaries were kept by our ancestors as records of their daily lives. Historical societies across the country count thousands of diaries in their collections, which can be used as vital records substitutes.
- Divorce records began in the colonies as early as 1639, and came under the jurisdiction of the court system. In earlier centuries, high-level courts had the sole authority to grant divorces.
- Employment records, or business records, can contain a variety of vital information. Many businesses maintained their own archives, and records of smaller businesses might well be found in county or state archives.
- Histories of counties and towns often contain extensive biographies of its citizens with (hopefully) marriage information and names of children.
- Missing person ads in days gone by were placed in newspapers to locate people — like a runaway wife.
- Applications for military pensions, often hold much vital information because the pensioner was claiming help for children and his wife, not just himself.
- Plantation records contain the daily operations of running a plantation, and before 1870, may include slave records of birth, marriage and death.
- Tombstones, memorials placed on the graves of loved ones, may tell the person's birth and marriage dates as well as the death date.

These highlights are from Carter's book which includes dozens of other examples, along with why they qualify as substitutes for vital records and where to locate them.

Substitutes for Vital Records may be ordered for $12.00, postpaid, from American Genealogical Lending Library, 800-760-AGLL.

GOOD RECORDS USUALLY ARE AVAILABLE FROM NORWAY, SWEDEN, FINLAND AND DENMARK

If your ancestors came from Norway, Sweden, Finland or Denmark, then you are a lucky genealogist. Good records have been kept in Scandinavian countries from very early times, and many records are available on microfilm. So don't be afraid to begin searching for your Scandinavian ancestors.

Putting first things first, I recommend that you do some homework by reading about your country as you begin to research. Boundaries and jurisdictions have changed over the last couple of hundred years, and you need to know what country was in charge to know where to look for the records. Any basic history book of the country should furnish this information.

Another valuable tip is to become familiar with the patronymic system of naming. This will help you to trace the family when the name seems to change. You need to know, for instance, that Olaf Ellingson was the son of Elling Person, who was the son of Pers Landerson, etc.

Major sources of family history information in Scandinavian countries are parish registers, probate records and census records. The law required ministers to keep written church or parish registers, and these become the vital records. You should be able to find parish registers for Norway dating back to 1688. Swedish parish registers date from 1686, and many are available on microfilm. Danish parish registers can date back to 1573, but most date from around 1645. Finnish records exist generally from 1648, but remember that up until 1809 you will find many areas included in the Swedish records.

Probates are records of death and distribution of the property of a deceased person. The majority of these records in Norway date from the 1687 law which required the death of a person to be reported immediately to proper officials so that the estate be properly handled. Probate records in Norway are often card indexed and kept by civil jurisdictions. Earliest Danish probate records date from the 1500s. In Sweden, the probate record is really an inventory of the deceased; few Swedish probate records exist before 1750. In Finland, probates are available from 1650 to 1860.

Census records are enumerations of the inhabitants, and although the years census records were taken vary from country to country, their content and format are similar. In Norway, the valuable censuses were taken in 1801, 1865, 1875 and 1900. In Sweden, no regular census was taken, but a tax list was recorded. In Denmark, censuses were taken 16 times between 1787 and 1920, and every five years since then. These records are arranged by parish, district and county. In Finland, the censuses were taken every year from 1635 to the present, but are not considered a good source until the later time period.

In addition to those sources which are similar in all the Scandinavian countries, each country has some unique sources.

For Norway, there are bygdeboker — local area histories that frequently list the owners and even workers on the farms. The farm name is very important in Norwegian research, as it is a very important identifier.

In Sweden, there are clerical surveys which are census-type records kept in five-year spans beginning about 1686. They usually indicate names, birthdates, ages, marriage, death dates and places where each individual moved to or from, and thus you can follow an individual through his entire life.

Denmark has military levying rolls which are conscriptions or draft lists of all males born in the rural areas of Denmark from approximately 1789 to the present. These records contain the name of men 15 to 63 years old, age, birthplace and residence and name of parent.

Finland has communion records which are similar in content to the Swedish clerical survey records.

The best tip I can give you as you begin your Scandinavian genealogy would be to get yourself a copy of the Research Outline for your particular country. These multi-page guides are published by the Family History Library, and should be available for copying at the Family History Center nearest you. They can be ordered directly from the Family History Library, 35 North West Temple, Salt Lake City, UT 84150. Enclose $2.00 for each country's guide.

WORLD WAR II VETERANS CAN HELP PRESERVE
THE HISTORY OF THEIR INCOMPARABLE EXPERIENCE

The U.S. Army Military History Institute in Carlisle Barracks, PA, is conducting a major survey to acquire source material on World War II, and invites all World War II veterans to contribute.

The Institute, the Army's official central repository for historical source material, has nearly 237,000 books, more than 50,000 periodicals, 5 million-plus pieces of personal papers and nearly 740,000 photographs. It is America's finest military library.

To strengthen its holdings further, the Institute is asking WWII veterans to donate pertinent historical records: books, camp and unit newspapers, letters home, V-Mail, diaries, memoirs, correspondence and official reports, photographs, illustrations, films, audio tapes, insignia and unit patches.

The Institute also wants veterans to complete an 18-page questionnaire about general military, overseas and combat service, occupation and demobilization, and postwar experiences. Postage will be free to veterans requesting and returning these questionnaires.

To help, write to: Army Services Experiences Questionnaire, Dept. of the Army, U.S. Army Military History Institute, Carlisle Barracks, Carlisle, PA 17013-5008.

Now, for miscellaneous bits and pieces:

• Janie Cattoor-Ryland shares Native American research aids: Cherokee Cousins provides books on Cherokee genealogy, language; and culture. Its October 1995 flyer lists 26 related genealogical items, beginning with a must-have book, *Exploring Your Cherokee Ancestry,* by Tom Mooney ($10.00), and ending with a T-shirt showing Sequoyah using a pointed stick to write the Cherokee syllabary on the ground ($12.00). Request a flyer by writing to 4530 Bobs Court, Stone Mountain, GA 30083, or call (404) 294-7443.

• The Gov. William Bradford Compact, a national organization for descendants of Gov. Bradford of Plymouth Colony, was founded in 1946 to honor his memory and establish a record of his descendants' accomplishments. The group meets annually, sponsors tours to relevant places in England and Holland, and publishes an annual newsletter. Descendants who want to know more about the organization should contact Mary Ellen Pogue, Secretary, 5204 Kenwood Ave., Chevy Chase, MD 20815-6604.

• Many American families trace their ancestry back to England, but fewer know they have collateral relatives who went to Australia (about 80,000 people were transported to New South Wales before 1849). So, if you're having trouble locating a great uncle, perhaps you're looking in the wrong country. Request the brochure "Research Services" from the Archives Office of New South Wales, 2 Globe St., Sydney, NSW 2000. It lists a variety of services and the fee for each.

PCs CAN BE FAITHFUL DATA KEEPING AND TRACKING SERVANTS

Personal Ancestral File? The Master Genealogist? Roots IV? Family Tree Maker? My Family Record? Visual Roots? Reunion? Family Roots? Everyone's Family Tree?

Which genealogy computer program is right for you?

At most genealogy gatherings, folks ask which genealogy computer software program is best, which is easiest, which should they get — and which is compatible with other databases?

In my opinion, all genealogy computer programs are 80 percent alike. It's the other 20 percent, the whistles and bells, that make them different. All record family data and print it out in a variety of ways.

But how to choose the one you'll like best? That's a better question. To help you choose a genealogical program, ask what you want that program to do:

- Record family names, dates and places?
- Produce group sheets and charts?
- Track the sources you have searched and what you found in that process?
- Lay out your data in book format?
- Keep track of thousands of references?

These questions will force you to look at how you now organize your information. Determine what you like and dislike about how it appears on paper and what you want to do with the information you've gathered.

Several books explain the various genealogy software programs, but it's hard for a book to be right up-to-date. And no book can answer your every question.

Talk to your friends about which program they use and what features they like best and least. Attend your local genealogy society's computer seminars.

Make sure the program you choose has flexibility to add data, so you can enter information (like cause of death) at a later date. Another good feature is easy access to the documentation area. I've found if the "Want to Enter Notes?" message pops up after I've entered a date and place, that I'm more apt to do it right then.

Next, do you like the way the program prints out information? Do you like the looks of the pedigree and group charts? Does your name and address automatically appear on every printed chart?

Try samples of output options and make sure they will all be usable.

Lastly, a program must have GEDCOM capabilities, which allows you to transfer your information from one database into another — from your Program X into your aunt's Program Y, for instance. GEDCOM also allows you to quickly enter Cousin Jim's batch of new information. And it allows you to share information with the Family History Library's Ancestral File program, which is a dandy thing to do.

When all is said and done, you can gather the data, ask the questions — but somewhere along the line you'll need to decide what genealogy computer software seems best for your needs.

It is far better to go ahead with most any program and get your family data organized than to leave the myriad charts and pieces of paper in boxes and drawers for your descendants to work with.

If it turns out you don't like the program you pick, give it to Cousin Jim for Christmas, data and all.

FAMILY HISTORY RESEARCHERS CAN USE ALL THE AVENUES TO INFORMATION THEY CAN GET

Genealogists are familiar with U.S. federal censuses, but how many know about AIS indexes? And how many are aware of the conditions to access post 1920 censuses?

Accelerated Indexing Systems (AIS) is a commercial company that has indexed many U.S. federal census records and published them in individual books.

In 1984, AIS produced a combined census index on microfiche which is distributed by the Family History Library for use in all Family History Centers.

These microfiche indexes can help researchers simplify family history research, provide information about individuals and can lead to new ideas of where to search for further information. Indexes can also save hours that might otherwise be spent reading hundreds of pages of census films.

Before using AIS indexes (also called searches), be aware of their strengths and weaknesses.

The strengths include knowing any index can help you locate census information quicker, and each AIS index covers a fairly broad time period and large geographical area. The index's weaknesses are a known error rate ranging between 3 percent and 20 percent for some areas. Some names appear more than once in any given search index. Also, many post-1850 censuses were finally indexed long after the AIS indexes were compiled so they are not included. Lastly, it's hard to remember you're NOT looking at the entire or complete census index when using an AIS index search, but sadly, such is the case.

There are four steps to follow when using the AIS census indexes.

1. Select the right search. AIS microfiche indexes are divided into nine groups or searches for people living in the U.S. between 1607 and 1906, although the majority of the records cover the federal censuses from 1790 to 1850. The searches are divided by locality and date. Here is a summary of the nine searches:

- Search 1, 1607-1819: entire U.S.
- Search 2, 1820-1829: entire U.S.
- Search 3, 1830-1839: entire U.S.
- Search 4, 1840-1840: entire U.S.
- Search 5, 1850-1860: Southern states (not all states were completed in 1984 when this index was compiled.)
- Search 6, 1850: New England and Northern states
- Search 7, 1850-1906: Midwestern and Western states.
- Search 7a, 1850-1906: entire U.S. (Searches 5, 6, and 7 compiled together)

• Search 8, 1850-1885: U.S. Mortality schedules only

2. Look for ancestral names, listed alphabetically. There may be many listings for the same surname, so it's helpful to know a first name or a specific area where your ancestor lived.

3. Interpret the index information. If you can't find your ancestor's name, it might be because he or she was not the head of the household, the indexer or enumerator might have missed the person, your ancestor might not have lived where or when you thought he did, and the name may have been spelled differently. Or, that particular locality or census might NOT have been included in the AIS census index.

4. Go to the original record for further searching, the real census record. All available census microfilms can be ordered for a small postage fee through Family History Centers.

The AIS microfiche indexes for U.S. federal censuses can be a wonderful tool for working genealogists, so make use of them. But do use them wisely. Most all Family History Centers will have a set of the AIS microfiche; you may make copies of the fiche, too.

The NSDAR Can Be Of Help To Family Historians

The NSDAR, National Society Daughters of the American Revolution, has been around since 1890, when one October afternoon 18 women met in Washington, DC, and signed their names as founders of what would become one of the most prominent women's patriotic, educational and historical organizations in the world. Its history and growth have been a constant success story, one which need not be retold here.

What is pertinent is that, in harmony with the group's goal as a lineage society, it has maintained at its Washington, DC, headquarters one of the nation's best genealogical libraries.

Thousands of membership records submitted by nearly 200,000 women are stored there. The records and data extracted from them can be of immense benefit to family historians.

Because the library is not within easy visiting reach from many places, check out the DAR records in the genealogy section of your local public library.

Armed with your pedigree chart and family group sheets listing your Revolutionary War ancestor's information, look up

DAR in the card catalog. (DAR records are filed according to the Dewey Decimal system.)

Look up your ancestor's name in the DAR Patriot Index, a multi-volume reference listing the names of patriots' women ancestors.

If you find your ancestor's name included, next send for a copy of the original application to see what references or documentation were listed.

Next, look up your ancestor's name in the Lineage Books of the National Society of the DAR, Index. There are 166-plus volumes in this series, so do use the index. Included with the patriots' names are two numbers: the first is the volume number. The second is the page number. In the specified volume is a listing submitted by a DAR member showing her descent from the patriot. The entry will also give mention of the patriot's war service. Check for these books in the larger genealogical libraries.

Remember the principle of cluster research and look up all entries for men bearing the same surname in the same geographic area as your ancestor.

Also, look up your surname in the NSDAR Library Catalog. The library has actively collected family histories since its beginning, so you might very well find a family history on your surname written by a distant cousin.

Also, consider checking the *DAR Magazine* index and then the magazine. This periodical is mostly devoted to current activities of the various national DAR chapters, but it does have a query and genealogy section. The index covers the first 104 issues.

For more information on the NSDAR, their records or their library, contact them at 1776 "D" St. NW, Washington, DC 20006.

OBITUARIES CAN BE TREASURE TROVES OF HELPFUL INFORMATION ABOUT ANCESTORS

Most family historians and genealogists realize the importance of obtaining death certificates for each ancestor. But many fail to look for printed obituaries of their ancestors.

Obituaries can be a valuable source of family information, especially those written in the late 19th and early 20th centuries, when they were often mini-biographies. Typically, they contained a death date and place, the cause of death, where services were held, the cemetery, where the person previously lived or had emigrated from, and a large amount of collateral family information.

If the deceased had been a veteran, his military service was detailed; if he or she owned a business, that was highlighted. Fraternal memberships were explained and often the obituaries included pictures.

Newspapers often printed extensive obituaries before official vital records were kept.

Besides newspaper obituaries, ethnic groups, churches and fraternal organizations also published obits of their members. Be aware of one pitfall, however: ethnic newspapers were often written in the organization's language — Swedish or German, for instance.

So where do you look for an obituary for your ancestor?

First, look in your own family archives. Saving newspaper clippings about important family events has always been a common habit, and it's a rare family that cannot come up with a few obituaries. They might be tucked into family Bibles, boxes and trunks in the attic, or long-forgotten boxes and desk drawers.

Contact every relative you can think of about long-forgotten boxed archives they might have.

The next places to look are libraries in the geographical area of your research which might have microfilm of yesterday's newspapers or an obituary file. These might be public libraries, or historical and genealogical society libraries.

Next, look to the newspaper itself: Not the current newspaper — they're busy with publication of today's news with little or no time for genealogy requests — but a local repository with copies of the paper, usually on microfilm. They will be happy to assist you.

At the main reference counter in most libraries are three pertinent special reference books to help you locate a newspaper that might have carried an obituary for your ancestor.

The Gale Directory of Publications is a book of names and addresses of newspapers in publication today.

The American Newspapers, 1821-1936, A Union List of Files Available in the U.S. and Canada, lists by state, county and town all newspapers published between 1821 and 1936, and which repositories hold copies.

Newspapers in Microform in the U.S., 1948-1972, published by the Library of Congress, is similar to the *Union List.*

In recent years, some genealogical and historical societies have created indexes for their area newspapers and which may be available through your local Family History Center — or you could inquire of the society in question.

One last thing family historians should be aware of is that obituaries and all death records were created at a sorrowful, stressful time in a family's life. Do not be annoyed if the information you find seems to be garbled. Treat obituaries like the good source they are, but as just that — a source.

THE QUEST FOR INFORMATION ON HER GRANDFATHER-IN-LAW LED HER ON A MERRY CHASE

For 10 years, I searched for the forebears of my husband's family without success, exhausting every research avenue I could think of. We decided the only way we'd ever find the old coot (as I fondly call his grandfather) would be by a stroke of pure luck. And that's exactly what happened!

But, this "luck" came about only because of hard work.

My husband's father, known to be a gold-plated teller of falsehoods, buried his father in Seattle in 1938, telling lots of interesting stories about the man. Charles Robert Phillips was said to be born in Georgia, son of Siebert Phillips. After years of searching, however, I wondered at the truth found on the death certificate.

I could find no Siebert Phillips on any Southern record, including census records. Because I did not have a specific place, I could only check large databases.

Eventually I filled two binders with bits and pieces of gathered evidence, but nothing leading to Charles Robert's origins.

I plastered all of the South with queries: genealogy and historical societies, workshops, seminars and periodicals — especially those in Georgia. I offered a $50.00 reward. No luck.

Then last February there came a call from Ken Thomas, a genealogy columnist in Atlanta, GA. He'd seen my query numerous times and wanted to help. I thanked him, encouraged him to do whatever he wished to solve the riddle — but in my heart of hearts I didn't dare get too excited.

He called back a week later: "I've found your guy!" I nearly dropped the phone. He started rattling off names and dates, where he looked, what he found. I was dumbfounded. He had indeed, found our Phillips family's origins in Georgia. We had a start on our Phillips family history!

In short, Charles Robert was the son of Seaborn and Elizabeth Phillips. Seaborn enlisted in the Georgia Infantry in 1861 and was present at Lee's surrender at Appomattox. He suffered a gunshot wound through his left lung, and later developed a chronic ulcer on his leg and severe rheumatism contracted during the war, all of which rendered him unable to work when he was 55.

He married Elizabeth Hunton in 1866 in Troup County, GA, and later moved to Hill County, TX, settling in Hillsboro, where he was a carpenter. He received a Confederate Pension from the State of Texas in 1901. He died there in 1907.

We knew Thomas found the correct families because his information could be confirmed with what I'd collected through the years.

The moral of this story is, do your homework, be on the lookout for new research opportunities, and, send those queries anywhere and everywhere!

Here's a follow-up tip: I have written to the Confederate Research Center in Hillsboro, TX, with its collection of more than 5,000 books and a vertical file of more than 2,500 newspaper and magazine clippings. The center is a true Confederate research gold mine and works with the Texas State Archives.

If you think the center could help you find a Confederate ancestor, write to: Peggy Fox, Assistant Director, Confederate Research Center, P.O. Box 619, Hill College; Hillsboro, TX 76645.

HERE ARE SOME POINTERS FOR THOSE WHOSE ANCESTORS WORKED ON THE RAILROAD

"From the Midwest to the Northwest: The Records of the Great Northern and Northern Pacific Railroads" was the subject of Paula Stuart Warren's top-notch presentation during the 1995 Federation of Genealogical Societies annual conference in Seattle.

Our ancestors migrated west as the railroad tracks extended west, Warren said, so tracking folks back often involves using railroad records.

Records for those working on the railroads vary by time period, railroad and record type but could include payroll, personneland accident records, employee newsletters, land records, drawings of railroad stations and photos of locomotives.

Railroad material is scattered in libraries large and small all across America's railroad routes, Warren added.

The Minnesota Historical Society in St. Paul has many records for the Northern Pacific and the Great Northern railroads as well as their smaller subsidiaries. There are about 12,000 boxes of Northern Pacific records and 6,000 boxes for the Great Northern.

That's the good news.

That bad news is that few have indexes and most have not even been microfilmed.

The Northern Pacific was chartered in 1864 to run from Lake Superior to Puget Sound. Financial backers received free land along the route from the federal government. Backers expected to build the railroad and make a profit through the sale of these land parcels.

On August 23, 1883, the line was completed from St. Paul and Duluth, MN, to Seattle — a mostly straight line across the northern tier of the United States.

The Great Northern Railroad began in 1856 as the St. Paul and Pacific Railroad. Purchased in 1859 by James J. Hill, it was renamed Great Northern and extended along a more southerly route across the continent.

For more railroad history, consult Thomas Tabers' *The "Railroad History" Index, 1921-1984.* This is an index to a periodical that carried articles on railroads, equipment, records and history.

To find employment records for your ancestor, Warren said you must know the exact railroad your ancestor worked for. Railroad names changed frequently, small lines merged with larger lines. The line great-grandpa worked for in 1909 might be called a totally different name today. And, there are not just two or three railroad names, but pages and pages of branch line names.

There is no substitute for personally visiting the Minnesota Historical Society if you are serious in your search. Because most of the material is unindexed (and apparently still in boxes), and because its staff is limited, it cannot do much research by mail. However, St. Paul and the Minnesota Historical Society are wonderful places to spend a day or a week, Warren said. There are 38 binders of information for the Great Northern Railroad and 47 for the Northern Pacific — inventory guides to the large room of boxes — that can be used only at the Minnesota Historical Society.

To listen to Warren's 50-minute recorded talk, order the $9.50 tape, postpaid, from Repeat Performance, 2911 Crabapple Lane, Hobart, IN 46342; or call (219) 465-1234. Ask for Tape F-92, with the title given above.

THE NATIONAL ARCHIVES IS WORKING TO MAKE MORE INFORMATION READILY AVAILABLE

The National Archives in Washington, DC, is undergoing repairs and alterations to accommodate increased demand for its holdings. John W. Carlin, Archivist of the United States, recently discussed the changes.

A comprehensive on-line catalog of archival holdings will be developed to provide better access through the information highway. Milestone documents of American history and the federal government will be digitized, as will a collection Civil War and Vietnam War service records.

The National Archives and Records Administration (NARA) is facing an ever-increasing demand for its services without a corresponding increase in resources. Space is its biggest problem. Recently a beautiful new facility, known as Archives II, was built in College Park, MD. It contains administrative offices, archival materials, and state-of-the-art storage and research facilities.

Carlin believes NARA has a truly noble purpose and to continue fostering public trust in the government, its records must remain not only open, but accessible.

According to *The Record,* the National Archives newsletter, NARA has more than 4 billion textual documents, 7 million still pictures, 118,000 reels of motion picture film and 200,000 sound and video recordings. It's a national resource with several presidential libraries, regional archives and records centers. The main National Archives building is located at 700 Pennsylvania

Ave. NW, Washington, DC 20408-0001. (202) 501-5400. The email address is: inquire@nara.gov.

My neighbor, Floyd Miller, recently requested a photograph from the National Archives to include in the family history he's compiling. However, he was advised that as part of the government downsizing, the Archives' Still Picture Branch (and other similar branches) is now operated by private companies.

They sent Miller a list of eight companies that maintain reproduction work stations in the archives at College Park, MD, which stores still photographs, maps and drawings.

Prices quoted from these private vendors varied greatly, ranging from $7.50 to $20.00 for an 8x10 black-and-white photo. If you desire this service, write for a list of vendors at 8601 Adelphi Road, College Park MD, 20740-6001, or call (301) 713-6625, ext. 234.

For genealogy beginners, or those not on the Internet, information from the National Archives can still be had via the good, old-fashioned U.S. mail. Genealogy beginners will especially benefit from several free how-to-get-started brochures. Write to National Archives, Trust Fund Board, Washington, DC 20408, and ask for their genealogy brochures.

KNOWLEDGE OF EARLY SETTLERS' ARRIVAL AND MOVEMENTS IN THE NEW WORLD CAN BE HELPFUL TO FAMILY HISTORIANS

Tracking ancestors back through time and place is easier if you know the migration and settlement patterns that affected our ancestors.

From a very old syllabus compiled by national author and speaker Norman Wright, I abstracted for you a migrational history of America.

Our country's earliest settlement was in Virginia, along the Tidewater region — a wet, soggy, marshy area good only for certain crops. Soon, the settlers moved northwest into the Piedmont, where the climate was drier, healthier and better for crops.

As immigrants continued to arrive they settled farther and farther inland, migrating through gaps in the Appalachian Mountains into the river valleys — first the Shenandoah, then the Ohio.

Further migration pushed into the great plains of the old Northwest (the present states of Ohio, Indiana, Illinois, Michigan, Wisconsin, Minnesota) and then the Midwest.

While the Appalachians seem tame today, 17th- and 18th-century immigrants thought them a formidable barrier.

In 1607, Jamestown, VA, became America's first permanent settlement. The colonists suffered numerous setbacks and deaths, and stayed only at the convincing of Lord De La Ware. Despite the 1622 massacre, by 1634 they had organized eight shires (counties) along the four major waterways: the James, York, Rappahannock and Potomac Rivers.

For the first 100 years colonists spread into the Piedmont's higher ground, an easier migration with no mountain barriers. As they bumped into the mountains, they tended to turn north or south.

By 1630, Lord Calvert was granted the present state of Maryland. Because it was a Catholic colony, and Virginians tended not to be Catholics, they spread north into the Chesapeake Bay area, around Maryland.

In 1609, Henry Hudson sailed north (up the river later named for him) to near what is now Albany, NY, beginning a Dutch settlement; by 1624 they bought Manhattan from the Indians. The Dutch were more interested in such commercial ventures as looking for furs than in colonizing and farming. Their government granted large estates up and down the Hudson to patroons, men who would encourage settlements.

Finns and Swedes sailed into the Delaware River Valley by 1638, even though it was controlled by the Dutch.

The Dutch lost control of their land to the Duke of York by 1662. The English king's brother received the area as a land grant. New Amsterdam became New York. No vital records exist from the New Amsterdam years, 1606-1662, but microfilmed records of the Dutch Reformed Church are available through the Family History Library.

By 1701, the English system was in place in English colonies and records as we know them began to be kept.

The Pilgrims came in 1620, separating themselves from the Church of England, and slowly spread geographically into Plymouth, Bristol and Barnstable counties in Massachusetts. By 1630, the Puritans arrived. They and the Separatists did not meld, and, having the much larger colony, the Puritans soon outnumbered and outsettled the Pilgrim descendants.

By 1660, the New England coast was settled and colonists began spreading up the rivers. Hartford, Wethersfield and Springfield in Connecticut were founded in this period. The northernmost settlement was York, in present-day Maine.

By 1640, New England's best settlement areas were crowded and migration spread inland, following designated trails.

The Upper Post Road connected Boston and the New Haven colony. The Middle Post Road allowed Rev. Hooker to flee from Boston to Hartford and Windsor. The Lower Post Road helped Roger Williams escape to Providence Plantation, a refuge on Rogues Island, eventually known as Rhode Island.

Settlement continued along the northern coast: York, ME, was founded in 1638, and Portsmouth, NH, in 1635. For years, Native Americans hampered migration into inland New Hampshire and what would become Vermont; and New Hampshire and New York wrangled for years over territory that became Vermont. By 1670, the Connecticut and New Haven colonies combined into one; 20 years later the Massachusetts Bay Colony (Puritans) had gobbled up the Plymouth Colony (Pilgrims).

Immigrants moved from New England along the post roads, up the rivers, west toward New York, where new lands opened up and land speculators did (ahem) a land-office business. Migration into central or western Pennsylvania, however, was hampered by Native Americans until the American Revolution.

At that time, the French presence in America consisted of fur trappers; hardy men who had lived in the Canadian wilderness for nearly 200 years. In upstate New York they incited Native Americans to fight the British, escalating into the French and Indian Wars, fought on American soil from about 1752-1763.

In New York, the Great Genessee Road became the Erie Canal, which opened in 1825 after eight years of digging. The canal afforded a quick and cheap way to middle America and the cost of immigrants' passage to America often included a trip up the Hudson River, across New York on the Erie Canal and down into what became Illinois, Indiana, Ohio, etc.

Countryside that became Pennsylvania was first settled by fleeing Palatines, and then by William Penn and his friends.

By 1680, Europe's Thirty-Years' War ended, with many villagers along Germany's Rhine River becoming Protestant. Winds of religious change, coupled with years of bad weather and the threat of the Kaiser's troops, caused many to flee to the

New World, settling in Herkimer, New Hampshire, North Carolina and Pennsylvania.

Also at this time, Quakers were persecuted in England, but William Penn was sympathetic and welcomed them to Pennsylvania. By 1730, thousands of Palatines and Quakers and others settled in Philadelphia, Burlington, Chester, Germantown and up the Schuylkill River.

In Northern Ireland, the Ulster Scots had taken over. They had been brought in for settlement by the British, when, in the 1500s, they cleared the Irish off their land. These Scotch-Irish, as they were also known, lived for several generations in Ireland. By the early 1700s, many native Irish had been pushed out and the potato famine of the mid-1800s set their destiny.

Thousands fled to the New World. Scotch-Irish, who disdained settled towns, wanting nothing to do with authority in any guise, cheerfully settled on the frontier, becoming an unofficial buffer between settled areas and the unhappy Native Americans.

Immigrants arrived in ports of Texas, Maine and California. But by 1850, New York was the primary port of call. Ellis Island operated from 1892 to 1957; the peak year of immigration through this island station was 1910.

It's unfortunate that a single source cannot be recommended for further research, but there's not just one book that covers all the internal migration routes that developed as immigrants settled America. In point of fact, there are dozens of such books!

Historical atlases and books on specific subjects — canals, early post roads, spread of civilization — will help. American history textbooks will furnish background, and specific area histories will supply fuller information.

To help determine into which port your ancestor's ship arrived, consult the *Guide to Genealogical Research in the National Archives,* in the genealogy section of most public libraries.

As you puzzle your ancestral family's migrations, keep logic and common sense in mind. They might not have traveled from Point A to Point B over the seemingly shortest way if that route led over the mountains. It was easier to travel a longer way around if it were by boat.

Today, the eastern mountains do not appear to be a barrier, but to our ancestors they surely were. Picture a dense, brushy forest and imagine how you would get a wagon through — going uphill, to boot.

Many routes followed Indian trails, which in turn followed earlier game trails. Many paralleled water courses: migrating animals and people need water.

Knowing how your ancestor traveled from place to place adds so much to your family history. You might know the family came through the port of New York, but how did they get to Wisconsin? My German family ended up in the Midwest — which port would they have come through?

Historical fiction can help: James Michener devotes an entire chapter in *Texas* to tell the story of a German family coming to early day Texas. In *The Immigrant,* John Jakes tells why a young boy left Germany, how he traveled, and how he walked from New York to Chicago! Wilhelm Moberg's classic stories of Swedish immigrants to the Midwest help us see and understand.

I'm glad I kept my notes from that long-ago seminar by Norman Wright so I could share this information with you today.

COMPILING FAMILY HISTORY
INVOLVES GATHERING ALL SORTS OF INFORMATION

Today's column is a potpourri of miscellaneous genealogical information.

Ancestry, Inc., has two new books to help you research and compile your personal history:

Chicago and Cook County Sources: A Guide to Research, by Loretto Dennis Szucs, is an expansion and update of her 1986 book. This is far and away the best guide to consider if your ancestral research takes you into Chicago or Cook County. The book covers history, libraries, censuses, cemeteries, ethnic organizations and churches, newspapers, fraternal organizations and the Newberry Library. It can be ordered for $16.95, plus $3.50 shipping, from Ancestry, 800-531-1790.

Dear Diary: The Art and Craft of Writing a Creative Journal, by Joan R. Neubauer, is the book for you if you want to tell the history of you and your times but are nervous for fear future grandchildren will laugh. In 50 pages, Neubauer takes readers through the steps of journal writing, gives tips for success and a great pep talk on the joys that come from journal keeping. Included with the book is *From Memories to Manuscripts,* by the same author. The two, designed to help you write a quality autobiography, can be ordered for $15.50, plus $3.50 shipping, at the above telephone number.

Are you looking for information on an ancestor who made his living on water, such as in the U.S. Navy, or on a canal or riverboat? The addresses below might be of help. These places could possibly furnish a biographical sketch of your ancestor, details on his service, and perhaps a photo or drawing of his boat, barge or ship:

Inland Rivers Library, Cincinnati Public Library, Eighth and Vine, Cincinnati, OH 45202

Mariners Museum, Newport News, VA 23606

National Maritime Museum, Foot of Polk Street, San Francisco, CA 94109

Peabody Essex Museum, East India Square, Salem, MA 01970

Philadelphia Maritime Museum, 321 Chestnut St., Philadelphia, PA 19106

Steamship Historical Society of America, University of Baltimore Library, SSHSA Collection, 1420 Maryland Ave., Baltimore, MD 21201-5779

Naval Historical Center, Washington Navy Yard, Washington, DC 20374

Naval Photographic Center, Commanding Officer, Washington, DC 20374

Center of Military History, Dept. of the Army, 20 Massachusetts Ave. NW, Washington, DC 20314.

Be sure to remember a self-addressed, stamped envelope.

The Swedish Emigrant Institute and the House of Emigrants, both in Vaxjo, Sweden, are well worth putting on your Wish-Trip List if you are of Swedish descent.

The Swedish Emigrant Institute documents with records and memorabilia the period of Swedish emigration from 1846 to 1930 when 1.3 million people left Sweden.

This national institution, founded in 1965, has a library of 25,000 titles, and its comprehensive database and church record inventories contains millions of names, dates and places.

It is open weekdays for research; the flyer said nothing about a research-by-mail policy. Contact the Swedish Emigrant Institute at Museum Park, Box 201, S-351-04, Vaxjo, Sweden.

Don't forget to include two IRCs (International Reply Coupons), available at the post office, for return postage.

TODAY'S LAUGH: Ann shares this bit of tombstone humor from Kent, England:

> "Grim death took me without any warning.
> I was well at night and dead in the morning."

AT LEAST TWO GROUPS ARE CONCERNED WITH TRACKING THE HISTORY OF GERMANS FROM RUSSIA

Dale Lee Wahl of Bremerton is involved in a wonderfully historic group with an exciting project. He is a member of the Germans from Russia Heritage Society, which is assigning individual researchers to tackle and keep track of various records from area villages.

Wahl said there are two basic organizations of German Russians in this country: the American Historical Society of Germans from Russia, out of Lincoln, Neb., and the Germans from Russia Heritage Society, out of Bismarck, ND, also known as the Black Sea or South Russia organization.

The first emigration of Germans to Russia occurred during the reign of Ivan the Terrible, 1533-1584, with German military officers, technicians, craftsman, merchants and scholars invited to help build Moscow.

The second major movement was during the reign of Peter the Great, 1672-1725, who welcomed Germans to strengthen his policy of developing a window to the West.

The third and most significant migration resulted from the manifestos of Czarina Catherine the Great, who ruled Russia from 1762-1796. Her reasons were political: to bring in Western immigrants capable of cultivating vast stretches of untilled land on the steppes, and to provide a protective wall of colonists against Asiatic tribes that posed an invasion threat from the East.

In response to her manifestos, large numbers of Germans came into the Volga and Black Sea regions. By 1867, there were nearly 2 million Germans in Russia.

Germans felt secure in their new homeland only as long as the Russian government allowed them to speak their own language, attend their own churches and maintain their own identity. This was the policy until the late 1800s when the Russian government tried to assimilate them in a transparent cover-up to take the accumulated German wealth and lands for themselves.

Jealousy was a factor. German farmers were far more successful than their Russian counterparts. Both their churches and schools operated in a unified German language, and both thrived. This in contrast to poor and fragmented Russian schools. Their language was key in keeping them together, and when the Russian tongue was mandated in 1880, the Germans grew concerned.

Fortunately for those who migrated to America, the Great Plains were being opened up to agriculture and settlement. Once here, railroads easily reached this geographic area which was very much like the steppes they left in Russia.

Some 200,000 Germans from Russia emigrated to the United States between 1870 and 1920.

Wahl does not do research for those with German Russian ancestry. His focus is coordinating the GRHS Village Project in which volunteers, often descendants from a particular village in Russia, gather information to re-assemble the history of a village, its parishes and people. This information is being entered into a computer database and will be available to all future descendants. If you want to assist in this project, contact Dale Lee Wahl at 7370 Grevena Ave., NE, Bremerton WA, 98311-4046, or call (360) 692-8052. His Internet address is dwahl@ linknet.kitsap.lib.wa.us.

HEADING INTO THE DOG DAYS OF SUMMER, LIGHTEN UP WITH TIPS AND MISCELLANY

August is best spent with genealogical miscellany, not heavy duty lessons. So this month, we'll feature tips on various resources for your family history search.

The Military Index is a part of the Family Search computer program available at Family History Centers, including those found in area Churches of Latter-day Saints.

This index lists service members who died or were declared dead in Korea or Vietnam from 1950 to 1975. Using it, you can find birth and death dates, identify residences and the person's military service information. Use the Military Index to find missing uncles, cousins or friends.

Bruce Vails shared an article from *Shift Colors, The Newsletter for Navy Retirees,* that gave tips for locating former shipmates and crew members. Write to the Bureau of Naval Personnel, Washington, DC 20370 and request a copy of p. 16 from the Fall 1995 (Vol. 40, Issue 3) of *Shift Colors.*

The Oregon-California Trails Association, Office of the Census of Overland Emigrant Documents (COED), wants to survey all emigrant diaries, reminiscences and letters written by those who traveled west overland in covered wagons. Documented information is being entered into a computerized database to serve anyone interested in the subject. COED, begun in 1985, now has a database of more than 52,000 names. For more information and to request a research form, send an SASE to COED, 1019, Independence, MO 64051-0519.

The Holland Library on the Washington State University campus in Pullman, WA, has 41 rolls of Indian census records spanning the years 1885 to 1940. Areas include Fort Lapwai, Fort Hall, Colville, Coeur d'Alene, Warm Springs, Umatilla, Spokane, Nez Perce and Yakima. Anyone may use the WSU library, and during the school year, it's even open on Sundays.

Parsons Technology has released a CD-ROM version of "Webster's Biographical Dictionary," a collection of biographical info of more than 30,000 important, celebrated and notorious figures from history. The lives of many of our ancestral families have been influenced by a prominent person. If such a person affects your family tree, wouldn't it be fun to add the information to your history records? Order this CD-ROM by calling 800-223-6925.

The fifth edition of *Genealogical and Local History Books in Print, The Family History Volume,* is available for $25.00, plus $3.50 postage, from Genealogical Publishing Co., by calling 800-296 6687. Divided into two parts — family histories and compiled genealogies — this book contains nearly 5,000 entries alphabetically arranged by family name. An easier or more convenient method of locating books can hardly be imagined.

From Hamburg-Departing Émigrés
To A Deal On Massive CD-ROM Databases,
Sources Facilitate Genealogical Prospecting

Today's column continues our summer genealogy miscellany.

The Historic Emigration Office in Hamburg, Germany, offers the service of finding your ancestors' names on a passenger list if they left Europe via Hamburg between 1850 and 1934. The fee in 1996 was $60.00, U.S. funds (personal checks accepted), and the address is P.O. Box 102249, Hamburg 20015, Germany. Including all known details about your ancestor will greatly help the search. However, expect a wait of nearly a year.

(Remember, you can tackle the problem of finding an ancestor on a passenger list yourself by using microfilms available through the Family history Center.)

Shary Jackson shares a different kind of success story: Jackson located all but nine of 169 of her classmates from Walla Walla, WA, High School for a 50th reunion. She says her sources have been the usual ones — car registration, church and cemetery records, college alumni books, employment and newspaper records. To inquire about her searching details, write to her at 40 NW B St., College Place, WA 99324-1003.

Tracing Your Donegal Ancestors, by Godfrey Duffy, is the first of a new series published by Flyleaf Press. This book details church, census, civil registration records, land, probate and newspaper records from County Donegal in Ireland. Next in the series will be similar books for counties Mayo, Galway and Cork. James Ryan, noted Irish researcher, says Donegal families were an interesting mixture of native Irish and Scots-Irish who arrived from the late 17th century onward. It's one of the Irish counties to experience a high level of emigration. Order this book for $18.50 (includes airmail postage) from Flyleaf Press, 4 Spencer Villas, Glenageary, Co. Dublin, Ireland.

Big news, Arkansas researchers! Portions of the Arkansas vital records indexes are available for sale on microfiche. Death indexes span 1914-1916; marriage indexes cover 1933-1939; and divorce indexes are for 1923-1939. For more information, send an SASE to Arkansas Research, P.O. Box 303, Conway, AR 72033.

The Arkansas Historical and Genealogical Magazine carried a short article on "monsters" hiding in your family records. The article identified these monsters as common transparent tape (which turns dreadfully sticky), rubber bands (which undergo a metamorphosis into a sticky, staining, ugly worm before they die and petrify), and paper clips and other metal fasteners (which rust and stain at the first hint of moisture). Deal with this issue now, was the article's advice. Go through your records and eliminate the monster-makers!

If your ancestor has a Methodist connection, send a self-addressed, stamped envelope to the United Methodist Archives Center, c/o Drew University, P.O. Box 127, Madison, NJ 07940. An initial search of their records will be made at no cost, but expect a small photocopying charge. The archives' records apply mostly to ministers, not members.

Producing a Quality Family History, by Patricia Law Hatcher, is a new offering from Ancestry, Inc. The book spells out the necessary details to turn paper into people for an interesting and quality family genealogy book. The book is available for $15.95, plus $3.50 postage; call 800-531-1790.

♦ Need Alabama vital records? Indexes to these records are available on 18 rolls of microfilm from the Alabama State Board of Health, Center for Health Statistics, P.O. Box 5625, Montgomery, AL 36103. Death indexes span 1908 to 1959, marriages cover 1936 to 1969, and divorces include 1950 to 1959. Each roll is $40.00. (Also check with the Family History Centers for these and other filmed Alabama vital records.)

♦ *The Kishwaukee Genealogists' Newsletter* covers Boone and Winnebago counties in Illinois. Contact them at P.O. Box 5503, Rockford IL, 61125. This group recently produced an index to area Methodist records, 1854 to 1925. It also sponsors an annual ethnic potluck (doesn't that sound like fun?).

♦ *Family History Monthly* is a new magazine published in England, containing articles of interest to Americans with British roots. Recent offerings include "Are you entitled to a coat of arms?," "Spotlight on Durham records" and "Derivation of names from birds." Each issue carries a how-to article ("Using the Edinburgh New Register House") and a special monthly feature on one family surname. Subscription is £35; to subscribe contact the magazine directly at 45 St. Mary's Road, Ealing, London W5 5RQ, England. To send the fee, contact Reusch International at 800-424-2923. For about $2.00 they will send you a draft for the proper amount.

♦ Do you have West Virginia folks in your family tree? The "Mining Your History Foundation," wants to network with all those having West Virginia roots. Membership, $20.00 annually, includes free queries in the quarterly newsletter. Contact them c/o the West Virginia Archives and History Cultural Center, 1900 E. Kanawha Blvd., Charleston, WV 25305-0300.

♦ Reunion Apparel, 1007 Johnnie Dodds Blvd., Mount Pleasant, SC 29464, offers great deals on reunion shirts. Their flyer shows several styles with pre-printed designs that allow your family name to be inserted into the design. The cost is $8.95 each for 36 or more T-shirts. If it's too late for this year, get ready for next year's reunion.

♦ Gear up for resuming your genealogy this fall by subscribing to *Ancestry* magazine. Each issue of this full-color, bimonthly publication contains six or more timely and helpful articles that teach methodology and resources. This is one subscription you won't let lapse. Call Ancestry at 800-531-1790 to order the $18.00 magazine.

TODAY'S TRIVIA: The U.S. Census Bureau admits to having missed 1.6 percent — or 4 million – of the U.S. population in the 1990 census. With no modern technology available, how many people do you suppose were missed in 1840 or 1880?

CANADIAN RESEARCH COULD BE PROBLEMATIC

Folks with Canadian ancestry who are beginning their family history quest sometimes become discouraged when they learn that Canadian censuses are less available than are U.S. censuses. Canadian censuses are closed by law for 100 years.

However, there are many parallel sources, including one fantastic library of Canadian materials in Surrey, British Columbia, a Vancouver suburb.

Cloverdale Library is the genealogical branch of the Surrey Public Library. Its holdings are so extensive that there is a 200-page *Guide to the Materials Held at the Cloverdale Library.* The collection includes Canadian census and estate records, immigration, passenger list and naturalization records, border entry records, land indexes and petitions, Loyalist and military records, parish and vital records, plus a section for 20th-century Canadian research.

I suggest you order the guide before you visit or before you write to them requesting research help. Send a check for $27.50, postpaid, made out to Surrey Public Library, to: Surrey Public

Library, Cloverdale Branch, 6542-176A Street, Surrey B.C., V3S 4G9, Canada.

To further help with your Canadian research, here is a short list of general guidebooks. All three can be found on the shelves of most public libraries:

♦ *In Search of Your Canadian Roots: Tracing Your Family Tree in Canada,* by Angus Baxter.

♦ *The Canadian Genealogical Handbook: A Comprehensive Guide to Finding Your Ancestors in Canada,* by Eric Jonasson.

♦ *Tracing Your Ancestors in Canada,* by Janine Roy.

The Family History Library in Salt Lake City has published an inexpensive resource guide for Canadian research, plus a smaller pamphlet for each province. You can make copies of these or order your own copy at any Family History Center.

Regarding Canadian research, did you know:

♦ Acadia was a French colony in southeast Canada ceded to Britain in 1713. Acadians are of French descent, living in the Canadian Maritime provinces, known as Cajuns in the U.S.

♦ Lower Canada meant the area now known as Quebec.

♦ Upper Canada was the area now known as Ontario.

In other genealogy news:

♦ *Understanding and Using Baptismal Records,* by John T. Humphrey, is a new book researching American families, working with a variety of baptismal records, all of which have different meanings and carry different implications.

This book provides an in-depth study of baptismal practice and the recording of baptismal information in 17th- and 18th-century colonial America. The 166-page book can be ordered for $20.95, postpaid, from the author at P.O. Box 15190, Washington, DC 20003.

TODAY'S LAUGH: Now that I have a computer for my genealogical records, I find that my records are just as confused as before. However, now my confusion is better organized.

ANYONE RESEARCHING GERMAN ANCESTRY CAN BENEFIT FROM THE *GERMAN GENEALOGICAL DIGEST*

The *German Genealogical Digest* was featured in this column once before, but since it's getting bigger and better with each issue, I thought you should hear about it again.

The quarterly digest has been around for 12 years, teaching those with German ancestors how to do research in Germany, how to read the records, where to write for information and provide a forum for surname and information exchange.

For instance, the Spring 1996 issue featured "Cities Along the Rhine and their Records." Many German-speaking people traveled down the Rhine River to emigrate to America, and records in these cities reveal sources documenting that movement.

Departments in the magazine include "Surnames, Sources and Places," "Microfilm Update" (new German filming acquisitions in the Family History Library), "Book Reviews" (German history, resources and references), "Ancestral Search" (queries from readers), and "Ask the Experts," a section in which readers can submit tough research problems to be answered in print. My favorite section features specific geographic areas.

One of the magazine's all-time popular articles, "Writing to Germany," by Horst A. Reschke, is available as a booklet for $6.00, postpaid.

Back issues of the *GGD* can be ordered for $8.00. Some of general interest include: Volume 11, No. 1, with its 24-page article on "Church Records in Germany." Volume 9, No. 1, carried an article titled "Using the Meyers Gazetteer." Volume 5, No. 1, told about "Locating German Places of Origin in American Church Records." Volume 11, No. 2, spotlighted "German Military Records."

The fully indexed *GGD* averages 35 pages with each quarterly issue printed in a bold, easy-to-read style. Subscriptions are $24.00 per year. Send inquiries, subscriptions or periodical orders to the *GGD* at 245 North Vine, Suite 106, Salt Lake City, UT 84103.

If you have German roots — and census population figures reveal that about one-fourth of Americans do — then you will surely benefit from a study of the *German Genealogical Digest*.

TODAY'S LAUGH: Every family tree has some squirrels and some nuts — even yours.

GENEALOGISTS CAN GAIN FROM MEMBERSHIP IN A GROUP — PROVIDED THEY BEHAVE THEMSELVES

Fall. It's that time again when: genealogical societies, like most groups, plan the year's schedule and renew monthly meetings, classes and workshops.

Usually, a small group of dedicated folks does most of the work, for the benefit of all genealogists. While none of YOU would be inclined to do such things, you might be interested to know that there are . . .

13 WAYS TO KILL A GENEALOGY SOCIETY:

1. Stay away from meetings, and if you do come, find fault and talk loudly.

2. If you get to a meeting, keep quiet until it's over, then tell everyone how things should be done.

3. Decline an office or appointment to a committee — let others do it all.

4. If volunteers are asked for, don't raise your hand or sign the passed clipboard. Get sore later if you are not appointed, nominated or asked. If you do volunteer, then complain about the leadership and policies of the group.

5. If you should be elected to an office or named to a committee, don't attend board meetings or do much of anything to fulfill your obligation.

6. Avoid work whenever possible. If someone volunteers, tell them they're wasting their time or are not qualified for the position.

7. If things don't go the way you want, threaten to not cooperate or just silently quit attending.

8. Oppose all ideas of cooperation with other groups. Whatever they want is sure to be work and might cost money.

9. Oppose all extra functions — picnics, luncheon meetings or banquets — as a waste of members' money, time and effort.

10. If anyone has a new idea or a project, be sure to oppose it. Justify your opposition, saying, "We have done it this way for the last 23 years."

11. If everything is strictly business, complain that the meetings are dull and the officers are a bunch of old sticks. If the meeting has variety, then — of course — complain that they are not tending to business.

12. Give the speaker a challenge by interrupting, walking around the room or visiting with your friends. Sit as far back as possible so the guest speaker must talk louder. If they are willing to come without pay, they certainly can't expect much courtesy.

13. Don't rush to pay your dues; let the board sweat. After all, they approved the budget.

I would now like to give you the Genealogical Society Fitness Test:

Breathe on the star above.

If it turns green, you have the flu.

If it turns blue, you have a cold.

If it turns yellow, your arthritis is acting up.

If it turns red, you have tired blood.

If it turns pink, you have a hangover.

If nothing happens — you are healthy enough to volunteer at your local genealogical society!

MISSING RECORDS FROM ELLIS ISLAND WEREN'T DESTROYED BY FIRE: THEY'VE BEEN FOUND AND ARE BEING PROCESSED

Questions continually come my way asking about Ellis Island passenger records. Here is an update on computerizing these records.

Some 1.5 million people, mostly Europeans, sailed past the Statue of Liberty to the Promised Land during the first five years after Ellis Island, an immigration receiving station, opened in January, 1892. But in June, 1897, a fire destroyed the center's wooden buildings.

It's long been believed that the fire destroyed all records compiled during the island's first five years of operation, thereby losing all hope of descendants ever finding any record of an ancestor's passage through the center.

But, now comes the good news that all the records have been found, according to Phillip Lax, president of the Ellis Island Restoration Commission. Records were stored in a variety of areas, including warehouses of the Immigration and Naturalization Service, and the Balch Institute.

The restoration commission searched for more than a year before finding that record of these immigrants survive in the form of ships passenger manifests retained by the shipping company, and in ships' lists held by the naturalization service in locations other than Ellis Island.

Using similar records, and as funds permit, the commission hopes to eventually compile a computerized index of some 25 million names. Ira Glazier, director of the Balch Institute, says this database will one day be available for those who have home computers with a modem. Some 10 million names have been indexed so far and are available for searching now at Ellis Island. Also check for this wonderful database at the National Archives and its branches and the Family History Library and its branches.

A major part of the funding for this indexing project (estimated at six million dollars to complete it) comes from names enrolled on the American Immigrant Wall of Honor on Ellis Island. Some 470,000 names have already been engraved, and wall space remains for another 30,000 names.

Anyone can have an immigrant's name included on the wall for a $100 contribution to the restoration project. You need not be descended from the immigrant to honor him or her in this fashion. The address for this project is: P.O. Box Liberty, New York, NY 10117.

The ships' passenger manifests and immigration records, generated as the names were logged in, provide a wealth of valuable genealogical data. In addition to the names of immigrants, records contain the names and addresses of their relatives in America, how much money the immigrants brought with them, and the names of other family members sailing on the same ship.

All of that information is available — in addition to the date and port of European departure and American arrival.

Many New York passenger immigration lists have long been available on microfilm through the National Archives and the Family History Library. A few indexes exist, but the crucial period — 1846 to 1897 — has not been indexed. It is this group of records that the Ellis Island Restoration Commission seeks to index and make available to researchers. (This group of records is sometimes commonly referred to as the Ellis Island records.)

For further reading on this subject, I recommend *They Came In Ships: A Guide to Finding Your Immigrant Ancestor's Arrival Record,* by John P. Colletta, available from Ancestry, Inc. at 800-531-1790. A second title is *American Passenger Arrival Records,* by Michael Tepper, available from Genealogical Publishing Co. at 800-296-6687.

LIBRARY STAFF MEMBERS CAN BEST HELP A GENEALOGIST WHO UNDERSTANDS THEIR RELATIONSHIP

Do you see the person behind the desk in a genealogy library or archive as a guard or as a helper?

Pauline Parpart, a genealogist and librarian at the Missoula Public Library, shared some tips for researchers in a lecture presented at the Montana State Genealogical conference last April.

To be a good researcher, she said, a genealogist must know that librarians and archivists are there to protect the books and records and to help patrons use the collections.

They are not necessarily genealogists, may not want to be genealogists and surely do not want to be your family's genealogist.

When visiting a research facility, be brief and to the point with your requests. Do your homework before going so you know what materials and resources they do and do not have. Go prepared to ask for specific information. Have your facts and needs clearly listed; do not shuffle through a pile of papers. Help the staff member in all possible ways to help you.

Limit your storytelling; librarians and archivists have their own family stories.

If the library or archive does not have what you seek, ask about other research resources and libraries in the community: museums, churches, etc. Librarians know those answers, too.

Know the hours of the facility you visit; do not arrive in the last 30 minutes of the day. Know the rules of the facility and obey them. Do not grumble about the rules; the person behind the desk did not make those rules. If you know your time there is limited, ask about their policies regarding interlibrary loan.

If you use the interlibrary loan process, be patient and correct. Be prepared to give the exact title of the book, the author, compiler or editor. Know the book's ISBN or Library of Congress number; know whether your item is part of a series. If you are requesting a magazine, include the title, issue date, name of the article and page numbers. Do not ask for more than three or four items at a time, and be willing to pay up to $10.00 per item. Realize, too, that requesting from an out-of-state library often subjects the patron to the non-resident fee.

To demonstrate to genealogists the seriousness of being correct when requesting materials, Parpart said the Missoula Public Library receives 60 research requests each day. They have gone from needing a staff person one half-day per week to handle interlibrary loan requests to a full-time staff of six, and they have a three-week backlog!

Parpart said she has found genealogists to be the most demanding of her interlibrary loan patrons: "They expect anything and everything immediately!" She urges researchers to understand that librarians only have control over the collections in their own library, and are subject to the rules of other libraries.

Her final advice regarding interlibrary loan: "If you need it today, you should have requested it a month ago, not yesterday."

While this lecture was given by a librarian from Missoula, I would bet that any librarian would echo these sentiments. Let's all strive to be better library patrons, and to consider librarians as our friends.

THOSE WHOSE FAMILY RESEARCH LEADS THEM TO MONTANA CAN GET LOTS OF HELP

In our Big Sky neighbor to the east, the Montana State Genealogical Society (MSGS) is a confederation of nine districts and 31 societies. Helena's Montana Historical Society also stands ready to help Big Sky researchers. This means if you need research assistance in any Montana county or area, the help is there.

The Montana State Society "queries person" is Kay Beck, 651 Greenhouse Rd., Deer Lodge, MT 59722, phone (406) 846-2452. If you contact her with a specific query, she will direct it to the appropriate area of the state. Do not forget your stamped, self-addressed envelope when you write.

"About Montana" is a new project of the society. Members hope to identify all literary works concerning Montana: books, pamphlets, theses, microforms, paperbacks, newspapers, manuscripts or handwritten papers. They want to know if the items can be purchased or borrowed. Coby Johnson of the University of Montana, and Paulette Parpart of the Missoula Public Library, are the project coordinators.

Another society project is to catalog the location, size and number of burials for every Montana cemetery. If you have information that would help, send it to Pauline Parpart, Missoula Public Library, 301 E. Main St., Missoula, MT 59802.

The Montana State Historical Society was founded by the Montana Territorial legislature in 1865. Located near the state capitol, it features the Mackay Gallery of Charles M. Russell art, a large exhibit on "The Montana Homeland," and an extensive archive.

This archive library is the repository for all old marriage and naturalization records, all newspapers ever published in Montana, local histories, city directories, biographies, photographs, oral histories and federal and Indian censuses.

The society does not do research by mail, but will send a list of in-house private researchers for your SASE.

Membership in the historical society brings you subscriptions to *Montana, the Magazine of Western History,* and their newsletter, *Montana Post.* Members also receive discounts from the group's large catalog of Montana and Western books, plus special invitations to their annual Montana History Conference.

Send your $20.00 membership check to Montana Historical Society, Box B, 225 N. Roberts, Helena, MT 59620.

Nothing beats traveling to Montana to use these resources yourself, and if you plan such a trip, contact the societies first to schedule their guidance and help.

According to the book, *State Census Records,* by Ann Lainhart, Montana has no state censuses, but it does have two items useful for locating early people in the state:

In 1876, the Montana Society published a list of early settlers (except Indians) who were in Montana during the winter of 1862-1863. The names on this list are arranged alphabetically by geographic area. In 1864, the territorial secretary produced a poll list of registered voters for the October election. Inquire of the Montana Historical Society about both lists.

A FINE RESOURCE CAN HELP THOSE OF SCOTTISH ANCESTRY TRACE THEIR FAMILY ORIGINS

The Scottish Church Records Index is the newest database, or records collection, in the FamilySearch computer program, available at any Family History Center.

But just what is it?

The Scottish Church Records Index is a database of nearly 10 million names listed primarily in Church of Scotland (Presbyterian) parish registers and similar records. The index contains entries dating from the late 1500s through 1854, with a few later entries.

Information in the index includes given name or names, surname, names of parents or spouse, the person's gender, birth, christening or marriage date and place, and source information.

You can use the Scottish Church Records Index to search for an ancestor's birth, christening or marriage information, search for the spouse or parentage of an individual, or identify a specific parish where your ancestors lived.

The Scottish Church Records Index, however, does not include every kind of Church of Scotland record. It only includes births, christenings and marriages. Death and burial records, for example, are not included. Neither does this index include records from any non-conformist church (any non-Church of Scotland).

To use this database, you should know your ancestor's name and an approximate event date. A person may be listed in two places in the index: under a birth or christening listing and under a marriage listing.

Some pitfalls you may encounter with the Scottish index include finding surnames listed under the second part of the name: Donald instead of McDonald. The given name may be listed under a nickname or middle name: Sally instead of Sarah. Your ancestor may not have belonged to the Church of Scotland, or somehow missed being included in the index. To double check for this last error, investigate the original parish registers.

This index, the newest and best source available for identifying pre-1850 Scottish ancestors, can be accessed at any area Family History Center.

While we're on the subject of Scottish research, two excellent guidebooks are *Tracing Your Scottish Ancestry,* by Kathleen B. Cory ($16.95); and *Scottish Roots: A Step-by-Step Guide for Ancestor Hunters,* by Alwyn James ($13.95). Either will get you off to a good start hunting your Scottish ancestors, whether or not your kin are listed in the Scottish Church Records Index. The books can be ordered from AGLL, P.O. Box 329, Bountiful, UT 84011-0329, or by calling (801) 298-5446.

TODAY'S LAUGH: Be thankful for today's FDA food standards. Back East in the 1880s, butter production was done by imagination with an eye single to profits. So-called butter was often rancid, a mixture of casein and water; or of calcium, gypsum, gelatin fat and mashed potatoes. A margarine factory employee in 1889 told New York state food investigators that his work made his hands so sore that his nails dropped off. Customers bought the stuff because artful grocers relettered the packages as Best Creamery Butter.

STUDYING YOUR ANCESTORS' BIRTH, WHEREABOUTS, RELOCATIONS AND DEATH IS ONLY PART OF THE FUN

Most experienced genealogists want more than just the names, dates and places penciled on to charts. The serious family historian wants to know about the life and times of his ancestors; she wants to get to know these ancestors as real people.

Few genealogists are lucky enough to have a diary or other written record from our 18th- or 19th-century ancestors. But we can feel lucky because others wrote books about the places and times where our ancestors lived.

Many of my Maine ancestors lived in that state for 100 years before migrating west in 1840. How excited I was to find a history describing the little towns of Topsham and Bowdoin in the late 1700s and early 1800s, just when my family lived there.

Ye Galleon Press, a small book publishing business in the farming community of Fairfield, 30 miles south of Spokane, has been publishing books of local history for nearly 50 years.

Publisher Glen Adams proudly proclaims that he's nearing the 600-book mark for his published works, and offers a 22-page catalog to prove the point.

These books concern Western Americana: the Oregon Trail, the California Trail, Indians, maritime, whaling, church-related Western history, Northwest history, Northwest Coast voyages and the North American fur trade.

Adams' offerings include insightful, specialized books such as John C. Fremont's memoirs, *Pioneer Life in Deep Creek, Stevens County, Washington; Warrior of the Mist*, a biography of Chief Qualchan; *Autobiography of Calamity Jane; Diary of a Cattle Drive; Prosser in 1910;* and many books concerning Chief Joseph and the Nez Perce.

Such books provide background to flesh out the names, dates and places on your charts. To know how any family came on the Oregon Trail in 1884 is to know about your Oregon Trail family. To read a 1910 history of Prosser is to know what it was like for your family living there, then. If your ancestor was an early settler near Spokane, he no doubt knew of Chief Qualchan. To read *Warrior of the Mist* will bring real meaning to that knowledge.

Ye Galleon Press' free catalog is available by calling (509) 283-2422, or writing to Box 287, Fairfield, WA 99012.

To locate books concerning the times and places where your ancestors lived, check the ads in genealogical publications. Drop a postcard to these book sellers to request their lists:

Clearfield Co., 200 E. Eager St., Baltimore, MD
County Heritage Books, PO Box 34, Waynesville, NC 28786

Genealogical Publishing Co., 1001 N. Calvert St., Baltimore, MD 21202-3897

Picton Press, PO Box 1111, Camden, ME 04843

Family Line Publications, Rear 63 E. Main St., Westminster, MD 21157

New England Historic Genealogical Society, 160 N. Washington St., Boston, MA 02114-2120

Family Tree House, PO BOX 7262-G, Granite Bay, CA 95746

Heritage Books, Inc., 1540-E Pointer Ridge Pl., Bowie, MD 20716

Southern Historical Press, P.O. Box 1267, Greenville, SC 29602-1267

JOINING THE DAR
CAN BE MEANINGFUL IN SEVERAL WAYS

Arlene Eakle, nationally known genealogist and author, and her associate, Linda Brinkerhoff, were in the Pacific Northwest last summer. Coeur d'Alene, ID, was one of their destinations.

Brinkerhoff presented a terrific discussion, "Finding Proof to Join the DAR."

She first asked, "Why join the Daughters of the American Revolution?"

Her reasons: 1, support a patriotic organization in its altruistic aims and endeavors; 2, honor our Revolutionary ancestors; 3, register our genealogical descent from that patriot; and, 4, be eligible for scholarships.

To learn if your ancestor served in any capacity in the Revolutionary War, first ascertain his age; if, in 1775, he was between 15 and 55, it's likely he served. Next, check the many compiled histories for the Revolution in the library. And, check with other lineage societies: Daughters of the Cincinnati, Daughters of 1776, and Sons of the Revolution.

Investigate county histories where this ancestor lived. If he was a patriot, it will likely be mentioned. Look into colony, town and state records where he lived; many early colonial, town and state records have been published, making this search easier.

From 1774 to 1783, several colonies and towns conducted military censuses; check for these.

Check the pension lists for your Revolutionary War ancestors, and Virgil White's books of pension and service abstracts, available in most larger genealogical libraries. The National Genealogical Society has published a list of such pensioners in book form.

Other military-related records that might contain mention of your ancestor would be lists of deserters, those rejected to join (too old, too small, humpbacked, unfit in every way, etc.). Orderly books and muster rolls are worth checking, as are records of military hospitals, prisons, and prisoners of war.

Some areas had specialized name registers, such as the salt lists of the South. Salt was issued by the government to Southern families devastated by the war.

Brinkerhoff's closing advice was to always be alert for newly published compilations and lists that might contain the name of your Revolutionary War ancestor. And when you do find his name, proving he aided the cause of American independence, consider joining with the other women who are Daughters of the American Revolution.

Besides her many books, Eakle has also produced two instructional videos, "Do Your Family Tree," parts I and II.

Part I covers basic tasks, such as filling out charts, how to interview relatives, cemetery searching and using different sources. Part II explains using U.S. census records, and "Expanding Search Dimensions" (locality, relationships, surnames, evidence, documentation and strategies).

Each video costs $29.95, plus $5.50 postage, but both may be ordered for $53.00, plus $7.50 postage. Call toll free, 800-377-6058, to order yourself an early Christmas gift. Also request her publications list.

RESOURCES ARE VITAL
TO THOSE RESEARCHING THEIR FAMILY HISTORY.
HERE IS A DISCUSSION OF ONE OF THE BEST

If you are struggling to locate information on a city-dwelling ancestor, don't overlook the wonderful resource of city directories.

A city directory can help locate people in place and time; it's often a true genealogical gold mine in itself and can lead to other records.

A city directory might well furnish these gems of information: given name and surname, date of birth, race or color, occupation, marital status, the names of spouses, children, father and mother, as well as date of death, residence and age.

City directories were a tool created by businessmen to advertise their services and products in a vehicle that would pay for itself. These businessmen wanted residents to pay to be in the city directory and then to buy a copy of the directory.

Over the years, city directories have included such things as lists of returning soldiers, lists of colleges and universities and their graduates, midwives, a map of the businesses and a list of who moved where. Often, a city directory was like an unofficial census, as was the 1840 Cincinnati, OH, City Directory, which included all free blacks.

The best reason to use city directories in your search for urban ancestors is to pinpoint where they lived so you can then find them on the federal censuses.

In 1870, for example, there were 150 places in the U.S. with a population of more than 10,000. These cities were divided into wards or subdistricts. New York City, for example, with an 1870 population of nearly a million, had 22 wards. Yankton, Dakota Territory, with a population of 737 that year, had three wards.

Maybe the best use of city directories to locate an address for your ancestor is to save your eyes hours of looking at microfilms.

City directories are very available. Go first to the public library nearest the city you are researching. If you cannot travel there, phone or write the library's Reference Desk and ask them to please photocopy the city directory's pages with your surname; enclose $1.00 and a stamped, self-addressed envelope.

Most libraries, historical societies and archives on the state level have a fairly extensive collection of in-state directories. Addresses for these places can be obtained with Elizabeth Petty's *Genealogists Address Book,* available at your genealogy library or by purchase from Genealogical Publishing Co. at 800-296-6687.

On the national level, the Library of Congress in Washington, DC, and the American Antiquarian Society in Worcester, MA, contain major collections of city directories. The Family History Library in Salt Lake City has a very nearly complete collection on microfilm which can be accessed via your nearby Family

History Center. (Using the FamilySearch computer program, request state-county-town-city directories.)

The following story illustrates why you should use city directories in your research: A man thought his ancestor had lived in Buffalo, Rochester or Detroit, but wasn't sure which city. He checked the city directories, but since his ancestor had a common name, he just couldn't be sure of finding the correct person. He had an old, undated letter of his ancestor, telling of a Trinity Lutheran Church just down the block. Comparing addresses in the age-appropriate city directories he found that Buffalo was indeed the town where his ancestor lived.

On your next visit to the pubic library, have a look at its city directories and then visit your Family History Center and order a film for the one you need. Good luck!

ARE EARLY NEVADANS AMONG YOUR ANCESTORS?

Nevada is known as the Silver State for its lure of mineral riches that first drew our ancestors to the mostly hot, dry and barren state.

Before the Civil War, thousands of overland travelers trekked through Nevada Territory on their way to California. But in 1859, many stopped and stayed a while when silver was discovered in Virginia City. By 1862, enough people lived in Nevada to begin talking statehood.

Was your ancestor one of the riches-seeking thousands?

There are partial territorial censuses for 1862 and 1863, and a complete, published and indexed census for 1875, listing all household members. Both the 1862 and 1875 census microfilms can be ordered at any Family History Center.

While some counties have birth and death records dating back to 1887, mandatory state reporting didn't begin until 1911. Prior to 1969, marriages were recorded in the county.

By Nevada state law, only abbreviated birth or death certificates may be provided by the county — and the applicant must have a real and tangible interest in the matter. The state vital records office can issue certified record copies.

The best bet for birth records before 1887 are the newspapers.

From early times, Nevada law required county coroners to issue burial certificates based on either death certificates or circumstances of death. It was the coroner's duty to maintain these files, which can date back to 1879. A master compilation of these names is available at the Nevada State Library (Capitol Complex, 401 N. Carson Ave., Carson City, NV 89710).

Nevada was among the states to receive federal land grants, and after 1863, miners often became homesteaders. Nevada has large holdings of land records, what with mining claims and homestead records. *The Red Book,* available at any genealogical library, has a good section explaining Nevada land records.

Beginning in 1858, newspapers were published in the state, and can be ordered on microfilm through interlibrary loan from the Nevada State Library to your library. Check *The Red Book* for the list of available newspapers.

Because of its mining history, Nevada had a large foreign-born population. Yugoslavians and the Basques were two important ethnic groups in Nevada's history.

If you have a Nevada ancestor, there are many background books to provide you with a better understanding of his life and times. Check with your local public library to locate these books.

A Research Outline for Nevada can be copied at any Family History Center, or, for $1.00, ordered from the Family History Library, 35 N. West Temple, Salt Lake City, UT 84150.

By 1880, the town of Austin in Lander County, dead center in the middle of Nevada, had a population of more than 10,000. It was a super-rich silver mine that drew the folks who stayed to develop a substantial town. Now, a near ghost town, it woud be a fascinating place to visit, especially if you have Nevada ancestors.

TODAY'S LAUGH: Carl Sandburg said people are what they are because they have come out of what was.

NO GHOST OF CHRISTMAS PAST: AMERICANS' CHRISTMAS HERITAGE

Early Americans — Puritans, Cavaliers and Knickerbockers — not only helped shape our country's destiny, but our Christmas traditions, as well.

Some, however, did not even observe the day, as difficult to believe as that may be.

Staunch Puritans, as had the Pilgrim Fathers before them, outlawed the observation of *all* holidays, including Christmas.

The law of the General Court of Massachusetts stated that anyone found observing Christmas by not showing up at work, enjoying a special meal or making the day special in any way, was fined five shillings for each offense. Five shillings in colonial America was a lot of money.

On the other side of the Atlantic, members of the Church of England (the church of New Englanders' motherland) observed Christmas by attending church and indulging in mince pie and plum pudding. But in the New World, founders vowed things would be different.

Cavaliers in Virginia, however, along with the rest of the South, celebrated the holiday — even the very first Christmas Days in this country. The second year at Jamestown, when Capt. John Smith was leading a band of colonists against powerful Chief Powhatan, he and his soldiers kept the traditional yuletide customs of Merrie England as best they could.

"The extreme cold, rain, frost and snow," recorded their chronicler, "caused us to keep Christmas among the savages, where we were never more merry nor had more good oysters, fish, flesh, wild fowl, and good bread, nor ever had better fires in England."

Once Virginia evolved into a colony of planters, the religious and social forms of English Christmas were introduced: halls decked with evergreens, tables shining with silver, houses crowded with guests — and a few American touches were added, including a big roasted turkey gracing the head of the table.

Christmas celebrations in Dutch Manhattan were prolonged as much as possible. Sometimes, all business was suspended for the rest of the waning year. Families and friends spent as much time as possible together by their firesides, exchanging good wishes and drinking to the coming year.

Citizens of New Amsterdam held a sturdy resentment against the anti-Christmas notions of their neighbors to the northeast, which did little to foster the feeling of "goodwill to all men."

On Christmas Day 1805, at Fort Clatsop at the mouth of the Columbia River, William Clark recorded this journal entry: "At daylight this morning, we were awoke by the discharge of the firearms of all our party and a salute, shouts and a song which the whole party joined in under our windows. After breakfast we divided our tobacco to the men who used tobacco, and to those who do not use it we made a present of a handkerchief. I received a present of Capt. Lewis of a fleece hosiery, shirt, drawers; and of (Pvt. Joseph) Whitehouse a pair of mockersons, and two dozen white weasel tails from the Indian woman.

"We would have spent this day, the nativity of Christ, in feasting, had we anything either to raise our spirits or even gratify our appetites." Their Christmas meal was spoiled elk and fish, eaten out of necessity, along with a few roots. "The day proved showery, wet and disagreeable."

Why not spend part of your Dec. 25 recording how your family marks the day. Won't it make fun reading in 100 years?

Did you know? When the French were tracing their ancestry, they used the standard family tree to map family lines. A three-pronged symbol imitating the tree came to represent genealogy. Because it looked somewhat like the track of a crane's foot, the symbol was called *pied de grue*, meaning foot of the crane. That phrase has come into our language as pedigree.

INDEX

Teachers, p. 146